AN ADAMS BUSINESS ADVISOR

Managing People

Other titles in
THE ADAMS BUSINESS ADVISORS

Accounting for the New Business, by Christopher R. Malburg
The All-In-One Business Planning Guide, by Christopher R. Malburg
Do-It-Yourself Advertising, Direct Mail, and Publicity, by Sarah White & John Woods
Entrepreneurial Growth Strategies, by Lawrence W. Tuller
Exporting, Importing, and Beyond, by Lawrence W. Tuller
Marketing Magic, by Don Debelak
The Personnel Policy Handbook for Growing Companies, by Darien McWhirter
Service, Service, Service: The Growing Business' Secret Weapon, by Steven Albrecht
The Small Business Legal Kit, by J. W. Dicks
The Small Business Valuation Book, by Lawrence W. Tuller
Winning the Entrepreneur's Game, by David E. Rye

AN ADAMS BUSINESS ADVISOR

Managing People

Creating the Team-Based Organization

TOTAL GROUP PARTICIPATION
EMPLOYEE EMPOWERMENT, and
ORGANIZATION DEVELOPMENT

DARIEN McWHIRTER, Ph.D., J.D.

ADAMS PUBLISHING
Holbrook, Massachusetts

Published by Adams Media Corporation
260 Center Street, Holbrook, MA 02343

ISBN: 1-55850-485-0

Printed in the United States of America.

J I H G F E D C B A

Library of Congress Cataloging-in-Publication Data
McWhirter, Darien A. (Darien Auburn)
Managing people : creating the team-based organization : guidelines for total group participation, employee empowerment, and organizational development / by Darien A. McWhirter.
p. cm. — (An Adams business advisor)
Includes index.
ISBN 1-55850-485-0
1. Work groups. 2. Employee motivation. I. Title. II. Series.
HD66.M396 1995
658.4'02—dc20 95-7928
CIP

This publication is designed to provide accurate and authoritative information with regard to the subject matter covered. It is sold with the understanding that the publisher is not engaged in rendering legal, accounting, or other professional advice. If legal advice or other expert assistance is required, the services of a competent professional person should be sought.

— From a *Declaration of Principles* jointly adopted by a Committee of the American Bar Association and a Committee of Publishers and Associations

Cover design: Marshall Henrichs

Table of Contents

PART II
PRACTICE

Preface

This book grew out of a lifetime of searching for real participatorily managed, team-based organizations. All too often, I found that people could not even agree on what a participatorily managed organization would look like, much less on how to achieve such an organization. I hope that this book makes identifying and creating such organizations easier.

This book is divided into two parts. Part I, "Principles," sets out what I believe are the major characteristics of a participatorily managed, team-based organization. "You can't get there if you don't know where you're going" is as true in organizational development as in everyday life. Part I spells out what I believe to be the major characteristics such an organization must have.

Many people who believe strongly in employee empowerment have tried to teach its principles through the use of fiction. Often this means telling stories that involve dragons and magic arrows. While this is useful, I believe that fictional case studies involving modern people dealing with modern organizational problems are more interesting and more educational. Part II, "Practice," contains eight fictional case studies. I have tried to make these stories as entertaining as possible. I hope they will both stimulate thought and, in a group setting, stimulate discussion.

The stories in Part II of this book are *fiction*. They are intended to serve as an educational device, not to relate truthful information about any person or organization. All names of people and organizations have been invented by me, the author. There may be similarities to real people and organizations (every name we can think of has probably been taken by some person or organization), but these are a coincidence. No one should draw any factual conclusions about real people or organizations from the stories in Part II.

It is my hope that an organization that wishes to create a team-based organization and empower its people can provide this book to everyone in the organization, from the top to the bottom, and that everyone will find something useful in it. I believe that participatory management is the wave of the future, and that the faster we get there, the better off we will all be.

— DARIEN A. MCWHIRTER
Austin, Texas
January 1995

Part I
Principles

Chapter 1

Trust and Empowerment

During the 1990s, there has been a lot of discussion concerning what participatory management is. Reading the many books on the subject, one might conclude that it is different things to different people. In Part I we will try to pin down the major characteristics of an organization that is using participatory management. An organization may not have every one of the characteristics we will be discussing, but if it does not have a majority of them, it is not making use of participatory management.

During the 1990s, everyone seems to be trying to achieve a "team-based" organization. This is a very worthwhile goal. In general, participatory management is not going to work without some kind of team approach to organizational design. In most cases, real participation is not going to work without teams, and real teams are not going to work without participatory management.

The term *employee empowerment* has also been used a great deal in management literature in the early 1990s, often in conjunction with the word *zapp*. The use of words like *zapp* suggests that empowerment is easy. It is anything but easy. Empowerment means giving front-line employees the power to make major decisions about how they will run their own worklife and workspace. Most of all, it means trusting employees to do the right thing most of the time and helping them to learn from their mistakes and the mistakes of their coworkers in a way that is not threatening or intimidating.

Hiring Trustworthy Employees

How do organizations hire people they can trust? That is, of course, the first order of business. In an organization that is run on participatory principles, the first job is to hire managers who are capable of managing people in this way and employees who are capable of being trusted. While the need for mid-level managers may be reduced in such an organization, the need for a human resources department is increased. People are worthy of trust because of their background and experience. Therefore, it is necessary to take the time, before hiring, to find out about that background and experience. This means checking references, credit, educational credentials, and all the rest. It means putting employees through simulated work sessions to see how they react. It means letting current employees meet and interview candidates to see how they will fit into the organization. It may even mean hiring some employees on a part-time basis for a while to see how they perform.

Hiring Team Members

You might be surprised, but our selection and hiring process is an exhaustive, painstaking system designed not to fill positions quickly, but to find the right people for those positions. What are we looking for? First, these people must be able to think for themselves...be problem solvers...and second, work in a team atmosphere. Simply put, we need strong minds, not strong backs. ...We consider the selection of a team member as a long-term investment decision. Why go to the trouble of hiring a questionable employee only to have to fire him later?

Fujio Cho, president of Toyota Manufacturing USA
Speech to the City Club, November 15, 1991, Cleveland, Ohio

Trust sounds easy. All you have to do is "trust" your employees. Actually, creating an organization in which all employees are trusted (and those who cannot be trusted are either fired or not hired in the first place) is the most difficult part of creating employee empowerment.

Take the case of a bank—we will call it the Redundant Bank—that had an extensive trust department. A dozen trust department secretaries had been given the power to use the check-writing machine. When it became clear that one of the dozen highly trained and experienced secretaries, and only one, could not be trusted to use the machine, the bank developed an elaborate procedure. Two new employees were hired to operate the check-writing machine. A check request form was created, and the dozen secretaries were required to fill out the form and submit it in triplicate to the two new employees, who were supposed to get the check back to them by the end of the day (but seldom did). This was the Redundant Bank's response to one untrustworthy employee.

The response of many organizations is similar. Because they cannot bring themselves to discharge or transfer one untrustworthy or incompetent employee, they create elaborate procedures and hire additional employees—and as a result, more mistakes are made because of all the new possibilities for miscommunication and mishandling. In fact, this new system works so inefficiently that far more money is "lost" after the new procedure is put into place than before.

Trust as a Company Value

Trust is easy in a trusting society. However, the more people live, or feel they live, in an untrustworthy society, the more difficult it is to create an organization in which trust abounds. It is not impossible; it just means that a firm in America, where people are surrounded by media telling them how untrustworthy their fellow citizens are, has to work at it more than a firm in Japan might have to.

> ***Trust as a Company Value***
>
> Trust and respect for the individual:
>
> We have nothing of greater value than our people. We believe that demonstrating respect for the uniqueness of every individual builds a team of confident, creative members possessing a high degree of initiative, self-respect, and self-discipline.

One way in which many manufacturing companies try to show that they trust their employees, and prove their commitment to quality at the same time, is to institute a policy of allowing every worker on the assembly line to stop the whole line if the worker sees a quality control problem that he or she feels warrants such an action. Some that institute such a policy have had to ask managers to encourage employees to stop the line once or twice before the employees actually begin to believe that they have that power. It is quite a sight to see a large assembly line come to a stop not because the boss pulled the plug but because an assembly-line worker saw a problem that warranted that action.

Although Americans tend to focus on the negatives of American society, one of the many positives is the fact that American society encourages people to make their own decisions in life and to enjoy the individual freedom that past generations fought so hard to guarantee. One of the problems many people face when they get their first job is that they are often expected to give up many of the habits that society has spend two decades trying to develop and replace them with absolute obedience to the boss. People who have been encouraged to ask questions as students are now expected to keep quiet and do as they are told. People who control their own lives sixteen hours a day are expected to become unthinking robots for the other eight.

Training for Participation and Teamwork

Training is the other side of the trust coin. If people are going to be trusted to write checks or stop the assembly line, then they need training on how to use the check-writing machine or on what kinds of problems warrant stopping the assembly line. That seems like an obvious statement, but many organizations have tried to institute the "new trust" without proper training and then declared trust to be overrated and inappropriate for their organization. In an organization dedicated to employee participation, training must include extensive discussions concerning what participatory management is and how it works. People who say that they encourage employee participation and cannot then point to the training that all new employees, including managers, get concerning what participatory management is and how it works are not telling the truth. They are pretending to institute participatory management, and that is probably the worst thing they could ever do.

Employees who are told that they have the freedom to control their own worklife but are not given the training to really exercise that freedom are not going to be productive. They are going to be filled with insecurities and frustrated by uncertainty. Imagine that you were suddenly placed in the control room of a nuclear power plant and told to take charge. That is the same feeling many employees have when they begin a new job without the necessary training. While the harm they might do is not as great, the insecurity is just as great.

One of the advantages of having empowered employees is that employers get access to all their employees' ideas. Every employee really does come complete with a brain, and with different educational and life experiences. Take the company that decided to go after the Hispanic market. It hired several advertising firms to create potential advertising campaigns and then hired consultants to help pick the right advertising campaign. It never asked the hundreds of Hispanic workers in the company if they had an opinion. Given the culture of that company, it probably would not have done any good to ask. The workers would have labored mightily to tell the gringo bosses what they thought the gringo bosses wanted to hear.

What would training at a participatory organization look like? First of all, the program would have been created with a great deal of input from the current employees. It is disheartening to have a company explain that it has created a basic training program on how to get along in a participatory company without asking the employees who work in the company for their ideas concerning what that training program should entail. We can imagine just how participatory that company really is. We would also expect to see an ongoing program of interviews after an employee had been with the company for a few months to find out how the training program had met the employee's needs and how it could have been improved.

This does not mean that employees would not be expected to take courses at the local community college or that specialized training experts would not be brought in to provide specialized training programs. It does mean that the organization's human resource department would be responsible for conducting training that was general to the entire company, or that arose on a regular basis.

Once employees have been trained to do their particular jobs and have been given special training on how to function in a team-based organization, they should be trusted to do their jobs and participate in the company. If they do things such as stop the assembly line for what turns out to be a silly reason, they should be allowed to provide input into that part of the training program. Every mistake should be seen as a chance to learn and go forward, not as a chance to lay blame and go backward, as is the case in too many organizations. Success teaches us very little compared to failure. Humans as a species have become dominant on the planet because of the ability of both individuals and groups to learn from their mistakes and change as needed. In the past, societies that did not allow change have existed. They are no longer around. That should tell us something about how organizations must function in the twenty-first century.

While we are on the subject of training and trust, some people need training on how to trust people. Others need to be convinced that they can trust the training. You get the idea. Too many people do not live in an environment of trust and find it a new experience to both trust and be trusted. Other people need parameters concerning what they can be allowed to trust people to do and when and where they will be trusted.

An empowered organization trains people on when to ask for training. Employees who can take the initiative and say they need training and explain what kind of training they need are going to save a lot of money and time in the long run. The human resources department should become a resource for all employees, helping them to identify their training needs and supplying necessary training. The human resources department should become a service organization that makes sure everyone has the training he or she needs. The human resources department should also gather information about what employees think and feel about basic policies that affect everyone. There are many personnel policies that the employees will accept more easily if they have been allowed to provide input into these policies. Of course, asking employees for their opinions requires more time and effort, but it is what empowered organizations do with trusted employees.

How Do You Treat Trusted Employees?

How are trusted employees treated? We know how "trustees" in a prison are treated compared to the other inmates. Regular inmates have to follow every rule to the letter or face punishment; they may not talk except when allowed, and they may not go to many parts of the prison. Trustees are allowed almost to range freely over the facility; they may come and go from one building to another as they wish, and they may even have authority over some of the other inmates when it comes to some activities. Trustees may even have keys to some buildings. Of course, even trustees are not allowed outside of the prison. Many employees would find it a refreshing change if they had the freedom and authority enjoyed by the trustees in a prison.

Trusted employees are assumed innocent until proven guilty. Many employees have found that they are guilty until proven innocent. There is a big difference between the two. People who are presumed innocent feel some level of security in their job and are willing to give a little extra when that is called for. People who are presumed guilty often feel that they might as well see what they can get away with, since they are going to be blamed anyway. People who are presumed innocent will go out of their way to help find out what really happened or who really made the mistake. People who are presumed guilty are concerned only with proving their own innocence. People who are presumed innocent make the same presumption when they deal with others, helping to bring about a general feeling of trust. People who are presumed guilty assume that everyone else is guilty and act accordingly.

People who are trusted are told why they are expected to fill out forms, and their input is sought out and appreciated when it comes time to revise the forms to make sure that they actually do what they are supposed to do with the least amount of wasted work. People who are not trusted very quickly learn how to fill out forms in such a way that they are seen in the very best light, regardless of reality. People who are trusted can be trusted to tell the whole story. People who are not trusted never do.

Trust is much more than assuming that people are honest. It also involves believing that people want to work, want to do their best, and want to make a contribution to the company they work for and the society they live in. While some people will certainly disappoint anyone with these assumptions, many more will live up to them. People may not live up to the expectations we have of them, but they seldom surpass them. The lower the expectations of management, the worse the employees will be, by definition.

GIVING EMPLOYEES POWER

Empowered employees have power. That seems like an obvious statement, but some people don't seem to have made the connection. Power means control over circumstances and the ability to make decisions. That means that if only one employee is involved with a situation, that employee will make the decision. If many employees are involved, then many employees will make the decision.

Having a Great Place to Work

Robert Levering found that places that people consider to be great places to work have some things in common.

1. There is a friendly atmosphere without a strict social hierarchy.
2. There is not a lot of office politics.
3. People are free to speak their minds without fear of reprisal.
4. People are treated fairly when it comes to discipline.
5. People are given a lot of responsibility and control over their own work.
6. There is a belief that both the employees and the employer have made a long-term commitment to each other.

Robert Levering's definition of a great place to work is one in which the employees trust the people they work for, have pride in what they do, and enjoy the people they work with.

Further reading: Robert Levering, *A Great Place to Work* (New York: Random House, 1988).

Since power means the ability and freedom to make decisions, a company with empowered employees will provide training for them on the best ways to make decisions. If most decisions are made by groups, then guidance in the best approach to group decision making is in order. Of course, regardless of how many people participate in the making of a decision, the qualities of good decision making are well known. Good decisions come from gathering the necessary, relevant information and then weighing the alternatives in light of that information.

Most people can tell the difference between an organization that trusts its employees and one that does not. Organizations with trust usually have more communication going on because people trust what they are hearing and know that communication will help further the goals of the organization. Organizations without trust are very quiet places. Organizations with trust have employees who are quick to take responsibility for their actions and decisions, good and bad. They know that they are trusted and that if a mistake has been made, it will be treated as a learning experience. In organizations without trust, employees can be seen pointing the finger at other employees when something goes wrong. That is a real morale buster.

Just because an organization is trusting does not mean it does not have a security system, audits, and all the other things any large organization is expected to have to protect its money, property, and trade secrets. In a trusting organization, this system is explained to the new employees, and employees are allowed to provide input into what security measures make sense and what seem to them to be just a waste of time and money. A trusting organization would probably not have a general drug testing program for employees, for example. At the same time, employees in jobs where a small mistake could result in great damage or loss of life might be expected to live with drug testing. Or, these employees might be asked to examine alternative ways in which their ability to function could be tested and pick one for the group that would meet the safety needs of the organization and minimize the invasion of employees' privacy.

Participatory management means *asking* rather than *telling*. It means giving employees the goal to be achieved and the authority to gather information and make a decision that meets that goal.

BUILDING TRUST

Trust is a fragile thing. Take the No-trust Insurance Company. This company had to send a dozen people from company headquarters to a regional office to help with a sudden overload of work. The home office employees were given money for the trip without any training concerning how to account for the travel expense money or how much they were expected to spend for living expenses. The home office employees did a great job, and the regional office was quickly able to absorb the extra work and send them home. When they got home, their boss wanted to see their expense forms. They had not been given any expense forms when they left, so they did not have expense forms to show. The boss then gave them expense forms, and the employees tried to reconstruct what they had spent their expense money on over a two-week period. Their success at having done a good job was turned into failure because they had not been given the right forms, something that was not their fault. The dozen highly competent employees were eventually fired for insubordination because they found the boss's request that they reconstruct their expenses to be silly and a waste of time. The boss had expected that each employee would bring back one or two hundred dollars out of the two thousand dollars he or she had been given. For the want of a few hundred dollars, a dozen good employees were lost, and a great deal more money was spent to replace them. Of course, we know who should have been fired in this case, but wasn't.

TRUSTING NEW EMPLOYEES

The greatest opportunity for a fresh perspective comes when new employees are hired. Every new employee comes with expectations about how things will be done. If new employees have received basic training and then have been sent into the organization, they will probably have a lot of ideas about how things can be changed to increase efficiency and effectiveness. This is a resource that most organizations ignore. Imagine an organization that gave every new employee a small notebook in which to write down his or her ideas, impressions, and thoughts and then set up an appointment for thirty or sixty days later to go over the notebook. We can only imagine the ideas that might flow as these fresh minds looked at what to everyone else has become routine. If something feels unnatural or wrong to them, then there just might be a better way of doing that task. If every new employee were treated like an outside consultant brought in to bring a fresh perspective, who knows where that might lead? It would certainly teach the new employees to begin to think about everything in terms of how it might be done better.

Every company has some kind of advertising program. What if the employees were allowed to form teams and submit ideas, with winning ideas resulting in bonuses for the team members or prizes such as a trip to Europe? Could average employees actually come up with advertising ideas that would be accepted over the ideas of high-priced advertising firms? What is there to lose? After all, the average employee is exposed to advertising all day, every day, and the employees certainly know about the product or service. We could go further. What if a randomly selected group of employees were put in charge of picking the winning advertising campaign, with the advice of the marketing department, of course? Given the sorry state of most advertising, it is hard to imagine that they could do a worse job.

Expanding Employee Focus

What if employees sent on a business trip were trained to do more than simply accomplish their goal? What if they were trained to gather information about the location as a potential market or a potential location for the company? What if they were expected to report on anything they observed that might suggest a new product or service, or a better way to market the current products or services? What if they were given laptop computers so that they could write down their ideas on the flight back and use electronic mail to dispatch observations and ideas to the relevant departments the moment they returned? What if they were given feedback on any ideas that actually led somewhere and credit in the form of recognition and even a bonus for a good idea? We can only imagine the possibilities.

As a general rule, governments spend a great deal of time and money making sure they are hiring trustworthy people and then treat them as if they were untrustworthy. It is assumed that these carefully selected people will steal money or take a bribe from a supplier at the first opportunity. It is also assumed that they will be unable to make any decision without the guidance of elaborate regulations and procedures. Of course, the few really corrupt public employees are almost never actually fired or prosecuted, which makes the whole process seem ridiculous when viewed from the moon. We have gotten so used to the idea that this is the way government is supposed to function that it becomes difficult to imagine how things might be done differently.

A funny thing happens when people work in an environment that lacks trust: They begin to act accordingly. For example, in some government agencies, the game becomes trying to see how little work can be done before anyone notices. In other agencies, where the emphasis is on trying to prevent theft, the game becomes trying to take something without getting caught.

Every worker is constantly learning. In most organizations this learning is not planned or recognized. In a participatory organization, one of the goals of the organization is the development of every worker in every way possible. Tuition is paid for courses taken, and employees are paid more as their skill level improves and their knowledge increases. Trained and trusted workers are paid because of who they are and what they know, not because of what they do in a particular day or week. At the same time, goals must be established and met.

When people think of bureaucracy, they often think of the military. They have not looked at the military lately. The military at the end of the twentieth century is a far cry from the military of a century ago. The average soldier is hired only if he or she meets rigorous requirements. The soldiers are put through an extensive training program that gives them the skills and knowledge to do complex jobs. Then, in many circumstances, they are expected to use their own initiative to get the job done, without orders from above. The military is formed into teams, and even though the team leader is provided by the organization rather than being chosen by the team members, there is a real team spirit. People are trained to observe and report back relevant information, and no one has to ask in the field what is relevant.

Of course, the modern military has not made as good use of its modern, highly motivated, highly competent, highly trained soldiers as it could if it realized that empowerment could be used in many military situations. These soldiers could be put into task forces and asked to redesign everything from uniforms to equipment, including tanks, planes, and ships. Their input would be invaluable. The concern in any military organization is insubordination. When an order is given in the heat of battle, everything depends on instant obedience. But people know this. The story of Desert Storm is the story of thousands of highly trained and well-equipped soldiers using their individual initiative to win a very lopsided victory over the army of Iraq. While the news media focused on the high-tech equipment, the soldiers facing each other were also very different.

Building Empowerment

Empowerment means letting people, either as individuals or as groups, discover the best way and follow it. It means spending the time and resources that are necessary to allow front-line workers to be involved in or make major decisions. This should pay dividends when it comes time to implement the decision. It means really listening to employees, instead of just pretending to listen to them. It means allowing people to make a mistake and then using that mistake as a learning device for the entire organization.

We can only imagine how an organization that really took participation and empowerment to heart might deal with a major mistake. The person making the mistake would be treated as a hero, first of all, because he or she would have saved others in the organization from having to make that mistake themselves. By making the mistake and then coming forward, the person can potentially save the organization a great deal of time and money. The mistake should be integrated into the training program if appropriate. The mistake should be communicated to everyone. The employee should be rewarded—not for making the mistake, but for coming forward to help others avoid the same mistake in the future. Only people with power who are trusted can afford to come forward with mistakes and help others avoid what they did wrong.

Trust is a two-way street. If an organization trusts its employees, the employees may, over time, learn to trust the organization. It is amazing what can happen when employees trust the organization they work for. Communication really does flow uphill. Ideas really are forthcoming. People really do announce their mistakes so that everyone can avoid doing the same thing in the future. People really do work together to make things that are not working work better.

Training is also essential. People who have been well trained know that they know what they are doing and can be confident that other people in the organization also know what they are doing. Employees know that they can trust their coworkers because those coworkers have also been well trained. If people are well trained, they can trust the organization.

Trust is a fragile commodity. Many leaders who have tried telling just one or two untruths have found that their credibility was completely gone. If someone has told one important lie, we can never know when or if they will tell another one. The advice to new presidents is to say "no comment," but never tell an outright lie.

Firing Employees

Some people assume that a team-based organization never fires people. That is certainly not true. What it fires people for should be very different, however. People should not be fired for making a mistake, but they may have to be fired for not sharing the mistake with everyone else and doing what they can to help others avoid that mistake. People should be assumed to be innocent until proven guilty, but once they are proven guilty, they should be fired. If such a person is not fired, then other people in the organization are put in a position where they can't trust that person and begin to doubt if they should trust anyone. People should not be fired for communicating bad news, but they may have to be fired if they fail to communicate bad news. People should not be fired for trying to be team players, but they may have to be fired if they are unable to be team players. Someone who cannot master the training should not be allowed to go out into the organization. It is as simple as that.

The key is to have empowered employees. Trust and training are the key to developing empowered employees. While they are not the only factors, it is clear that without trust and training, there can be no empowerment. And without empowerment there can be no participatory management.

Trust in a Very Small Business

Most of what has been discussed in this chapter can be easily applied to even the smallest business. The key is taking the extra care and time to hire trustworthy employees. Training is the most difficult part for a very small business. It is what usually gets neglected. This is where courses at the local community college or a short course taught by a local consultant can make up for the lack of a human resources department. Owners of very small businesses need to be creative in solving the training problem. What they cannot do is expect employees to operate in a trusting environment without some training.

It is usually easy for small-business owners to give employees power because they have no other choice. What is usually more difficult is allowing employees to have real input into policies that the owner created and has a personal stake in. The only answer is that a small business must allow employees to have meaningful input into policy if teams and empowerment are ever going to be a reality.

Characteristics of Participatory Organizations

1. They trust their employees.
2. They have extensive training programs that also train people how to function in a team-based organization.
3. They spend more money on training and less money on direct supervision.
4. They presume that employees are innocent until they are proven guilty.
5. They view mistakes as opportunities to learn rather than as opportunities to place blame.
6. They ask employees to make decisions and meet goals rather than to perform specific tasks.
7. They hire trustworthy people and discharge untrustworthy people.
8. They trust their employees, and so they provide these employees with the authority they need to fulfill their responsibilities because employees are trusted.
9. They do not fire people because they make a mistake, communicate an idea, challenge routine, or question authority.
10. They do fire people who fail to report mistakes, prove to be untrustworthy, fail to function in a team environment, or are unable to participate when participation is called for.

Chapter 2

Communication and Information

If participatory management depends on empowered employees making decisions as individuals, groups, and an entire organization, and if the quality of all decision making is directly dependent upon the quality of the information available, then it stands to reason that empowered employees need to be provided with the most and highest-quality information possible. Of course, the average employee has very little information about either his or her function or the organization in general. In some cases the employees are not making decisions; in other cases they are. Regardless, in most organizations they do not have the information they need.

Giving Employees Information

What kind of information do employees need? Imagine that you had to live your life, but you never knew how much money you made in a month, what was in your bank account, how much you paid in taxes, or whether any of your actions had positive or negative results. Imagine that you lived in a giant black box and that you engaged in activity all day, every day without ever knowing if what you were doing was having any effect on the real world. That is what work is like for many employees throughout America and the world. They know they are participating in a giant enterprise, but they have no idea how what they do affects that enterprise. Many Americans know more about the workings of the federal government than about the company or agency they work for.

Information comes in all shapes and sizes. There is general background information that might be provided in basic training or in a course at a community college. There is information about the organization that helps employees to better understand why things are done the way they are in that particular organization. There is information that is specific to a particular employee, such as the level of quality of the products the particular employee has produced.

Specific information is often the most useful and the most difficult to provide. Science teaches that systems can "improve" only to the extent that they receive feedback. Young humans learn not to touch hot things by touching a few hot things. If a child's nervous system does not function correctly, then the child will not receive this feedback, and eventually we would expect the child to be burned to death. Many employees in government agencies work for years with little or no feedback concerning how they are doing. They know they are doing things, but those "things" may or may not be making life better for the citizens of the country. They may, in fact, be making things worse. Without direct and accurate feedback, we cannot begin to talk about empowerment. People who do not know, in detail, how they are doing cannot begin to have an impact on the quality or quantity of their performance.

For too many people, their job involves taking something from the in box, doing something to it, and placing it in the out box. Was the process ever completed? Did it have any impact on the world? Did that impact do any good or cause any harm? How can people improve the quality of their performance if they have no feedback on what the quality of their output currently is? We can imagine the kind of food a chef might cook if he or she could not see or taste the food and never received any comments from those who ate it. What are the odds that the food would be of high quality? Yet people are constantly astounded to discover that employees who have no way of knowing what the final result of their labor is are not very interested in improving the quality of what they do. We would consider it the height of cruelty if we saw a scientist experimenting with rats who were rewarded and punished at random, regardless of how well they performed the task they had been given. Scientists have in fact done experiments in which this was done and the rats, to put it scientifically, went nuts! How many employees operate in a similar environment?

PROVIDING FEEDBACK

It is often difficult to find objective criteria to use in providing feedback to some employees. That does not mean that the effort is not worthmaking. People respond more to tasks that provide some kind of accomplishment feedback. If feedback is provided for only certain aspects of the job, people will tend to concentrate on those aspects. For example, the average citizen is often shocked to learn how little time college professors at state universities spend preparing and improving their courses. That is because there is very little positive feedback for them when the content of a course is improved. When an article is published, university teachers receive promotions. When they complete a consulting contact or are awarded a grant, they receive money and recognition. When students learn more than the students in the same class the year before, no one knows it except, perhaps, the professor. Student evaluations passed out at the end of the semester provide feedback on issues such as how friendly the professor was, which encourages professors to be friendly. That is not necessarily a bad thing, but it is not what most citizens thought they were paying for. Would it be impossible to provide faculty with feedback concerning how much people learned and retained from attending their course? No, but in many situations it would be expensive and difficult to provide that kind of feedback. Most universities operate like the man who was seen searching for something under a streetlight. When asked what he was looking for, he answered that he had lost his pen fifty feet away from the streetlight and that he was looking for it. Why wasn't he looking for it in the area where he lost it? Because the light was better under the streetlight!

Much of what we might call the quality revolution in the United States during the 1980s would have been impossible without sophisticated feedback for workers concerning the quality of their individual output. While much that is silly has been done and written in the name of "total quality," the major change in many organizations has been to provide as much objective feedback as possible to the people who can actually make a difference. If one of the goals of participatory management is to improve the quality of performance, then that process cannot really begin without objective feedback about the quality of performance. People cannot improve unless they have some idea of how they are currently doing.

BEYOND THE BASICS

Empowered employees need a great deal of information beyond specific feedback concerning the quality and quantity of their own personal performance or the performance of their team. That is really just the first step. Once we know we are doing a good job at this particular task, the next set of questions is:

1. Is this the task we should be performing, given the desire to meet customer needs and improve profitability?
2. How can we change the current process in order to improve quality, quantity, and product mix?
3. How can we reduce expenditures without sacrificing quality?
4. What other products and services should we consider providing?
5. How can I change what I am currently doing in order to help someone else in the organization do his or her job better?
6. What trend in society should we be paying attention to in order to maintain and expand the organization?
7. How can marketing, production, and design be better coordinated and improved?
8. How does what I do affect the bottom line, and what can I do to improve the bottom line?
9. What new ideas can I make use of to improve my performance?

The list is, of course, endless. The point is that if employees are really going to get involved in helping an organization improve, they are going to need a lot of information that in the past was given only to top executives. A truly empowered and involved employee needs information that only the CEO might have gotten in the past.

One of the advantages of a capitalist society is that many organizations have a "bottom line." Either they make a profit or they don't. If they don't, then they cease to exist, which is not good for the employees, the stockholders, or the managers. Capitalism is a game. Investors win when they pick companies that make ever-expanding profits, causing dividends and stock prices to go up. Employees win when they pick a company that stays in business or expands so that they can keep their jobs and maybe even make more money or receive a promotion. Managers win when they pick a company that is able to provide them with promotions and bonuses, which means picking a company that makes an ever-expanding profit. Everyone has a direct interest in the bottom line. If that is the case, then why keep the bottom line a secret from the people who can have the greatest impact on it—the employees?

Speak Up at IBM

At IBM an employee may ask a question or make a comment and receive a personal reply without ever revealing his or her identity except to the "Speak Up" administrator, who is sworn to keep it a secret. An employee fills out a form, typing the question or comment so that the handwriting cannot be identified. When the form arrives, the Speak Up administrator removes the section of the form with the employee's name and address and places that in a special file. The question or comment is given a file number so that the response can be sent to the employee when it arrives from upper management. IBM has eighty Speak Up administrators around the world.

While direct information on the quality and quantity of production helps employees improve their individual performance, information about the financial picture can help everyone see why some things are being done and may even encourage employees to make changes themselves. More and more, large organizations are breaking themselves up into "profit centers." This simply means that if financial information about different products or services can be broken out, it becomes easier to see which activities are profitable and which are not. Employees who can see that what they are engaged in is not profitable will understand why changes need to be made in order to increase revenues and reduce costs and may even come up with suggestions concerning how those changes can be made.

Many companies are afraid to release financial information to employees for fear their competitors will find out something they do not already know. In the real world, that is very unlikely. In most cases, the only people who are being kept in the dark are the employees. Everyone else who has any interest already knows everything he or she needs or wants to know.

Besides encouraging employees to make changes, another reason to share profit and loss information is to allow employees to feel that they are part of a giant team and to actually enjoy the game of capitalism. If capitalism is a game, and profit is how you win, then why not get all the players involved by letting them know what the score is? How enthusiastic would you be if you were forced to spend eight hours a day playing a game without ever knowing the score, or even whether you were winning or losing? How long would you be enthusiastic about the game? Of course, employees have been playing this game for over two centuries without knowing the score, which might be all right if they were not being asked to make anything more than a minimal contribution to the game. If they are going to be expected to "get in the game," then it seems only fair that they should be told the score once in a while.

The first way we keep score is by looking at the price of shares in the company. If an employee works for a public company whose shares are listed on a stock exchange, this is easy. If an employee works for a small company whose stock is not freely traded, this is more difficult, but not impossible. Many smaller companies find it useful to have a professional valuation firm do a valuation of the company every year or two. If that is the case, then why not tell the employees how the company is doing?

Financial Statements

Every company of any size also keeps score with three accounting statements: the cash flow statement, the income statement, and the balance sheet. The cash flow statement is often overlooked when people discuss providing basic financial information to employees, but it should not be. First of all, it is fairly easy for people to understand if it is presented as nothing more than a summary of a giant checking account. Deposits are made from revenues instead of from a paycheck, but the principle is the same. Money made from the sale of assets such as land or surplus equipment and money borrowed from banks or bondholders would also show up as deposits into the account. On the outflow side, we see money going out for wages, supplies, dividends, taxes, interest on debt, and rent for buildings and machines (or the purchase price of the buildings and machines). Everyone knows that a positive cash flow is a good thing and a negative cash flow is not a good thing. You do not have to be an accountant to figure that out. Everyone knows that when you spend more than you take in, you will have to pay the piper in the long run.

An income statement uses some of this information in order to show how the basic operation of the business is doing. Is the business making a profit? On one side we see revenues from the sale of goods or services. While the company may also acquire cash from other sources, such as selling a building or borrowing money, that does not count when we want to know how the basic business is doing. On the outflow side, we would put the cost of supplies, wages, interest, rent (or depreciation if buildings and machines are owned). This lets us know whether the business is making a profit. If it is, then taxes will have to be paid out of that profit, and the company can pay dividends if the profit is sufficient.

The balance sheet tells us how much the company is worth based on the value of its assets. On one side we put the value of cash, inventory, accounts receivable (money owed to the company), land, buildings, and equipment. On the other side we put liabilities, such as money owed by the company and debt. If the assets are greater than the liabilities, then we would say that the company is worth something. Of course, in the real world, the value of assets is only one aspect of valuing a company. The value of the assets and the amount of profit the company can generate in an average year can be used to make a reasonable estimate concerning the value of a company. Of course, companies, like everything else, are worth only what someone is willing to pay for them.

Why should we bother the average employee with this kind of information? For many reasons. First of all, many employees think that they are not making much money and someone, presumably the owner, is making a lot. That is usually not the case. Once employees see where the money comes from and where it goes they may be more willing to help cut costs. If employees are to become more and more involved in suggesting ways to cut costs and generate more revenue, they have to realize that there are more costs than just wages and benefits for employees. In most companies the "other costs" are going to be significantly larger than the money spent on wages and benefits. For a product or service to make a profit, it has to pay both wage costs and its fair share of the other costs, such as supplies, and the cost of buildings and interest. Employees can see the advantage of not having to borrow money when they realize the drag interest payments put on the cost side of the income statement.

Most companies try to increase revenues and decrease costs. They would like the employees to help in that process. The employees are probably not going to be very enthusiastic about that idea unless they are showed simple accounting statements that tell them how the score is kept and what the score is. They also can see that if the stockholders are going to get a dividend and if they would like to see the wage part of these statements go up, they are going to have to help either increase revenues or decrease costs. Companies that want to practice empowerment need to include in their basic training for new employees a short course in how to read and understand these basic accounting statements. It is not really that difficult. The average baseball fan has to deal with far more complex numbers than those contained in the average cash flow statement, income statement, and balance sheet.

If a company is broken up into profit centers, then the employees should also be shown what the cash flow statement, income statement, and balance sheet would look like if the profit center were a stand-alone company. This may cause problems, as employees in profit centers that make a high profit may expect more money, but these problems can be dealt with. If everyone understands where the money and profit come from they can begin to work to help increase profit and reduce costs.

In the United States we hear a lot of negative comments from some people about the high cost of American labor. In a few cases this is justified, but in many cases it is the high cost of overhead that is killing the bottom line. Companies that break out overhead from direct costs can begin to get a handle on this problem. There is an old saying in economics that it is time to sell the stock of any company that feels justified in building a giant, and very expensive, headquarters for the executives. This giant, and very expensive, headquarters will simply be overhead and will be difficult to carry when times get tough, as they always will. Teaching employees to understand the drag overhead can have on a company helps everyone to focus on what is important.

Jack Stack, CEO of Springfield Remanufacturing Corporation and author of *The Great Game of Business*, tells the story of his company's efforts to cut costs and improve cash flow. In one case, everyone was assigned a particular overhead cost to examine and try to minimize. The costs were assigned by putting cost items on slips of paper and pulling the slips of paper out of a hat. The employee put in charge of toilet paper costs did a study and found that when the company was busy, toilet paper use went down. When the company did not have enough work, toilet paper use went up. Other employees took their assignments just as seriously. Jack Stack reports that the overhead charge on work done went from $39 an hour to $26.32 an hour as a result of this process, and since all of that reduced overhead cost went right to the bottom line, the company went from just better than breakeven to really profitable. And, of course, everyone in the organization gained a new appreciation of the impact of otherwise nondescript overhead costs on profits.

GETTING INFORMATION FROM EMPLOYEES

Once employees have been taught how the score is kept and know what the score is, they then have to be allowed to play the game. That means they have to be allowed to do much more than simply their own individual job. Of course, the first thing that they have to do is their own job the very best they can; just as on the football field, the first job of every player is to play his position. If the players don't, we know our team is going to lose. However, just because they play their positions doesn't mean we are going to win. For that we need something extra. Generally, that something extra is information that the players have and the coach does not have. In professional football, the players are taught to look for things that they might see and that no one else might know. Perhaps one player on the other team is favoring an injured leg. Perhaps there is a soft spot on the field. Whatever it is, this information is not going to do the team any good until the coach knows what the players know. On a football field, telling the coach is a fairly easy process. In many companies and government agencies, it is almost impossible. If you knew before a football game that the players on one team would not be able to provide information to their coach during the game, whereas the players on the other team had been trained to do just that, which team would you bet on to win? Coaches on the football field get information by constantly asking for it. Leaders of businesses or government organizations have to do the same thing.

Everyone has heard the story of the new manager brought in to save a dying small manufacturing company. The first thing he does is have a group talk with the workers, during which he explains that the company is in trouble and that if changes are not made, it may have to close. He then asks for suggestions. For a long minute there is silence. Then one hand goes up, and a worker points out that the machines in the plant were laid out decades ago and have not been moved since. If the machines were actually rearranged to coincide with the way the current products are being produced, a great deal of time could be saved. The new manager tells the workers to rearrange the machines to fit what they actually do, and production time is cut in half. When the manager asks the worker who spoke up at the meeting why he had never told anyone about this before, the worker responds, "No one ever asked before."

Active Listening

Psychological research suggests that most of the time people do not really listen to other people. They are instead planning what they will say in response, often in an effort to defend themselves from what they believe is some kind of attack. This kind of listening is destructive to communication. Active listening means:

1. Having and expressing a willingness to listen to the entire message before drawing any conclusions
2. Restating the message to make sure it has been received accurately
3. Asking questions to make sure the message is understood
4. Reflecting on the message before providing a response

Further reading: Carl Rogers and R. E. Farson, "Active Listening," in A. R. Cohen, S. L. Fink, H. Gadon, and R. D. Willits, *Effective Behavior in Organizations* (Homewood, Ill: Richard D. Irwin, 1976); T. F. Mader and D. C. Mader, *Understanding One Another: Communicating Interpersonally* (Dubuque, Iowa: Wm. C. Brown, 1990).

There are a lot of ways to ask, but the main thing is to ask. We all know about executives with "open door" policies. When we ask them how many workers have actually walked through that open door in the last year, the answer all too often is none. Anyone who thinks that workers are simply going to volunteer their ideas or even their special knowledge about what is right and wrong with the organization is dreaming. Even in companies that are really trying to use participatory management, there need to be as many avenues for information to flow up to the top of the organization as possible.

Suggestion Programs

One way to encourage the exchange of information is to have a real suggestion program. These programs come in all shapes and sizes. When we compare many American companies with their Japanese counterparts operating in the United States, one of the amazing differences is the number of employee suggestions many Japanese companies receive in a year. These suggestions range from cost reduction ideas, to safety improvement ideas, to design suggestions. This difference is due, in part, to the lengths to which some Japanese companies are willing to go in their effort to encourage suggestions. Some of these companies have targets for the number of suggestions they expect to receive in a year at a particular facility. A numerical goal can work wonders in itself. Also, when we compare companies that receive a lot of employee suggestions with companies that do not, we usually see immediately that at the high-suggestion companies, employee suggestions are taken very seriously, even if they never lead anywhere. No idea is rejected out of hand, and even if an idea does not result in immediate changes, the discussion of an unused idea may lead later to a useful idea.

American companies that wish to begin to develop a culture of free communication and employee suggestions have found it useful to institute contests complete with prizes in different categories, such as most revenue creation, greatest safety improvement, greatest cost reduction, best idea for a new product or service, and so on. These contests may encourage or even require employees to work in groups that cut across organizational lines in order to provide a wide diversity of information and viewpoints.

Of course, if prizes are promised, they should be awarded. Only in the United States do we find employees suing their employers because the promise of rewards for suggestions has not been kept. You only have to read the complex, legal language of some company suggestion plans to know that the company is not really serious about encouraging suggestions. You only have to look at what front-line managers do to encourage ideas and suggestions to see that no one really wants to know what the workers think.

Take a company we will call the WILD company. At WILD, every even-numbered year the company puts on a suggestion contest. It is voluntary, but employees are encouraged to participate, and 90 percent do. They must form into seven-member teams, and the members of each team must be from at least three different departments. Managers dress up in costumes for the kickoff meetings, a series of large meetings during which everyone is told the rules of the game and the prizes. There are prizes for the winning teams and additional prizes for the facilities where the winning teams work. In other words, everyone at a facility wins if that facility comes up with a winning idea. There is a game kit that is given to everyone. The kit contains the rules, in easy-to-understand language, and pictures of some of the major prizes. In this contest, the teams must come up with realistic numbers. If their idea is a cost cutter, they must project the cost saving based on real numbers. The accounting department is involved with every team to help write the suggestions. If the idea is a safety suggestion or a service improvement suggestion, realistic data must be gathered. That means interviews with employees about whether or not the safety suggestion is a good one or interviews with customers concerning their reaction to a service improvement idea. Ideas for possible new sources of revenue receive the largest prizes. Everyone learns that cutting costs is great, but the company cannot really grow unless it can bring in more money. The WILD company has noticed a great many extra dividends from this form of suggestion game. With suggestion teams formed from different departments, cross-departmental communication continues long after the game is over. Also, people throughout the facility gain a real appreciation of what people in other departments actually do. As part of the game, the employees learn a great deal about the organization and what has to be done to improve profits. Another result of the suggestion game is that everyone begins to see work as more fun.

Fun is a word most people do not associate with their work. Work is not fun, by definition. Most of us know that whether or not something is fun has very little to do with the actual activity. It has much more to do with the attitude people have when they engage in the activity. People who are playing a game are much more likely to see what they are doing as fun. It is fun to know the score and try to improve it. It is not fun to never know the score. It is fun to play a suggestion game with team members every year or two. It is not fun to put a suggestion in a suggestion box and never hear about it again. It is fun to get feedback concerning how you are doing. It is not fun to never know if what you are doing is making a contribution.

USING TECHNOLOGY

Modern technology can be used to increase the flow of communication. For example, at one major university, every professor has a computer on the desk and there is a series of university computer bulletin boards. Instead of finding a dozen pieces of paper in the mailbox every day announcing everything from the new grade deadline to the state of the president's health, professors are expected to check the bulletin boards for information every day or two. There are official computer bulletin boards for the university, each school, and each department. Then there are bulletin boards at these three levels for comments by faculty. There is a special bulletin board for ideas and suggestions. While the expense of providing every faculty member with a computer and training was high, it paid for itself by cutting the cost of paper and internal mail service.

Once CEOs realize that much of what only they know will have to be communicated to everyone before participatory management can really be established, they can actually come up with ideas (there's a twist, a CEO with an idea) that are quite ingenious. Take Bill the CEO. The consultant told him to imagine that he was half of a two-CEO team (much as the ancient Greek city-states had double kings). Bill started keeping a journal of everything he knew that he thought his imaginary double needed to know. Bill soon realized that he knew a lot of things that were never communicated to anyone, or to very few people, and that might be of interest to employees who were really playing the game. Bill began writing a very interesting column entitled "To My Twin" in the monthly employee newsletter. The employees agreed that it was the best part of the newsletter and began writing the CEO with comments, feedback, and ideas inspired by his column. Suddenly, these employees in a very large organization had a coach that they could identify with and sympathize with.

The same can be applied to every employee at every level of the organization. Everyone knows things that only he or she knows. Every effort has to be made to get people to share these things with everyone else. Again, prizes for the funniest item, the most significant item, the most heart-warming item, and so on, submitted to the employee newsletter in a year can encourage people to share information in a way that is fun for everyone. Imagine a Communication Awards Dinner each year during which many employees, including the CEO, receive some kind of award. That would be a real communication company. Of course, the highest award would have to be given to the person who brought the worst news. That is what most organizations never receive until it is too late. We have only to look at history to see that kings who punished the bearers of bad news did not last as long as kings who rewarded them. That is still a very tough lesson for any leader and any organization.

New employees are a resource that most organizations waste. What is obviously silly to the new employee is accepted by everyone else as just the way we do business. If it seems silly to the new employee, perhaps we should reexamine what we are doing and why. New employees want to make a good impression and take their rightful place in the organization. Before they become enmeshed in a web of networks, they can provide a fresh look at almost everything. For organizations that market to the mass, these new employees are typical potential customers, ready and willing to explain in detail what they like and don't like about particular products and services. A great way to both get new employees' ideas and help to train them is to have them go around and be customers for a few days, or even longer.

Using Informal Channels of Communication

Much useful information flows through informal channels. Any organization that wants to make the best use of opportunities for communication must make use of informal channels of communication. How much information will flow from front-line workers to upper managers if both groups eat lunch only with their own kind? How do you get such different groups to eat lunch together? How about pairing them up and making an upper-level manager eat with a particular front-line worker at least once a week? Of course, the upper-level manager has to be seen as a friend and not a spy. In other words, everyone has to accept the idea that we are all working together to achieve a common goal.

Company activities such as a company softball team with members from every level and department can do wonders for communication. Every time a company activity has to be planned, that is an opportunity to bring people together from many parts of the organization. One rule for such planning groups might be that no one can serve with anyone he or she works directly with or knows very well. Every special task force is a chance to increase the number of lines of informal communication between departments.

People often think of good ideas at strange times of the day or night. The difference between people who make a difference and people who don't is often that people who make a difference actually write down their ideas and try to do something about them. Imagine an organization that did everything possible to encourage this, including giving everyone a small "ideas notebook" to carry around.

A participatory organization has a human resources department that does a thousand and one things to help information flow up, down, and throughout the organization. Computers, newsletters, meetings, journals, suggestion plans, contests, award dinners, and all the rest are used to encourage everyone to help the flow of information. People who communicate usually do a better job of working together. People who know what the score is are better able to respond to bad news in a way that results in productive ideas and quality work.

Communication in a Very Small Business

Small-business owners often assume that their employees know a lot more about what is going on in the business than they actually do. While employee newsletters may not make sense in a very small business, an owner could imagine that he or she had a partner, write that partner every week saying how things are going, and then distribute the letter to employees. A small business can set up a system whereby employees can ask anonymous questions and receive answers posted on the bulletin board. Even the smallest business can set up some kind of suggestion program.

Even the smallest company can make use of advanced technology with today's small computers. In other words, with some creative effort on the part of the owner or manager, a small business can do many of the things large companies do.

Characteristics of Empowered Organizations

1. They encourage everyone, from the CEO down, to provide everyone else in the organization with information.
2. They have institutionalized ways of communicating, such as electronic bulletin boards and newsletters.
3. They have suggestion plans that provide prizes and encourage everyone to have fun.
4. They provide every employee with meaningful feedback concerning the goals that employee is trying to achieve.
5. They train new employees in how to communicate and how to understand the communications they will receive, such as how to read accounting statements.
6. They reward the bearer of bad news.
7. They provide meaningful financial information to every employee.
8. They encourage the development of informal channels of communication.
9. They ask employees for their ideas concerning how everything, including communication, can be improved.

Chapter 3

The Lost Art of Constructive Criticism

One of the major reasons Americans have trouble, as both employers and employees, with the idea of participatory management is the way criticism is given and received in the United States. In some countries, someone receiving criticism assumes that the person giving it has the best interests of the recipient at heart. In other countries, including the United States, the approach to getting and giving criticism is very different.

The average American learns about criticism at home and in school. At home we might hear the following:

"Hey, get your hair cut, you look like a shaggy dog."

"You really are too dumb to live, aren't you?"

"This room looks like a pigsty. I don't want to have to tell you again—clean up your room."

"Don't talk back to me. When you have something worthwhile to say, I'll let you know."

"What did you think you were doing, anyway? Have you lost your mind?"

At home, criticism is too often of the harmful, name-calling variety. The intention is not really to communicate, just to put someone down or shame him or her into doing something.

At school, particularly in the United States, students are taught that teachers give out grades, and that if you argue with the teacher, you might get your grade raised. Teachers never lower grades as part of this process, so it is worth a try. Also, if you challenge the teacher's grading often enough, the teacher might just give you a higher grade to avoid the hassle. Criticism in school becomes the first step in a special kind of argument process in which the student tries to defend what he or she put on the test. It is not really a part of the constructive learning process.

Ten Steps to Constructive Criticism

By watching people take lessons that they have paid for in order to master a skill that they really want to master, we can begin to see the potential for constructive criticism. The professional master—let's say a master of archery—does not call the student names or try to belittle or shame the student. A bad shot does not bring shame. And when, outside of the realm of grades and report cards, the master provides the student with some of the master's knowledge and wisdom, the student does not respond to every criticism or suggestion with an argument. Rather, we have a student who is motivated to listen and a teacher whose only concern is helping the student to improve. We see the student take the bow and make a shot. The arrow is far from the center of the target. The master's criticism has several stages.

Social Changes that Affect Management Processes

1. Increased global competition mandates a new concern with quality of products and services.
2. Emerging technologies from computers to robotics mandate that workers be given the chance to make use of new technologies.
3. The presence of highly educated workers (relative to a century ago) mandates greater freedom for worker initiative.
4. The changing nature of the workforce (more women and minorities) mandates greater concern with interpersonal relations at work.

Further reading: Daniel Bell, *The Coming of Post-Industrial Society: A Venture in Social Forecasting* (New York: Basic Books, 1973); R. B. Reich, *The Work of Nations: Preparing Ourselves for 21st Century Capitalism* (New York: Alfred A. Knopf, 1991); Judith B. Kamm, *An Integrative Approach to Managing Innovation* (Lexington, Mass.: Lexington Books, 1987); D. L. Kanter and P. K. Mirvis, *The Cynical Americans: Living and Working in an Age of Discontent and Disillusion* (San Francisco: Jossey-Bass, 1989); Katharine Esty, Richard Griffin, and Marcie Schorr Hirsch, *Workplace Diversity* (Holbrook, Mass.: Adams Media Corp., 1995).

First, the master asks questions: Why did you do that? Have you had lessons before? Does this feel better when you do it this way? Tell me what you were trying to do when you did this and that. The student responds with honest answers because he or she knows that anything other than honest answers will hamper them in their joint goal of improving the student's skill.

Second, both the student and the master have a joint goal that they are working toward: improving the student's skill level. This is a goal that they both accept as worthwhile and important. The student will get as much out of the lesson as he or she is willing to put in. The master and the student are involved in a joint exercise, moving toward a mutual goal, that will benefit the student in tangible and easily recognizable ways. The master makes a suggestion, and the student shoots another arrow. The master does not "grade" the student; the target does that, and there is no arguing with the target. The arrow is still very far from the center. The master and the student can both see that immediately. With evaluation separated from teaching, the master can concentrate on teaching. The target will provide the evaluation. The master is a kind of special team member with the student rather than being the source of grades and bad feelings.

Third, the master and the student have a mutual respect for each other. The student would not have sought out the master if the student did not believe the master could help. The master would not have taken on the student if the master did not think the student could improve with instruction and practice. The goal of the relationship is to improve the skill level of the student. If the student improves, the student will be rewarded, and so will the master. Calling someone names or making personal comments that are unrelated to the task at hand would be all but unthinkable.

Fourth, the master makes constructive suggestions designed to improve the student's skill. "If you do it this way, you might find that the bow feels better in your hand." "If you hold your head this way, you might be able to see the target better." The student has received concrete suggestions that can be tried out immediately, not a grade or a personal attack. The student holds the bow differently and moves the head a little.

The arrow strikes closer to the center of the target. The pupil and the master have both received satisfaction from that result.

Fifth, the student is not worried about things that have nothing to do with the task at hand. The student is not worried about flunking out or being fired or saving face or being liked or avoiding punishment. The student and the master are focused on getting the arrow closer to the center of the target.

Sixth, the master is willing to experiment with the student and allow the student to learn anew all the things that everyone must learn if he or she is to become a master. The student should try out every idea, every grip, every strange position that he or she can think up. The student and the master will both laugh together as the student finds out that most of the old ways are best, but perhaps not all. The master is also willing to be the student. The master knows that different things work with different people and that everything in the universe is changing.

Seventh, the master respects the art that he or she teaches and conveys that respect to the student. The student is allowed to do and say many things, but not to question the art of archery itself. That is the basis of the relationship between master and student, and to question that is to end the relationship. It is their mutual respect for the art and the student's desire to know more that have brought them together. If the student cannot respect the art, then the student must go.

Eighth, the student does everything the master directs to the best of his or her ability and reports the results honestly. The master's advice is wasted if the student does not make an honest effort to do what the master directs. The master needs honest feedback from the student just as much as the student needs honest feedback from the target.

Ninth, the master encourages the student to ask questions and offer ideas. The master is not a mind reader. The only way he or she can find out what the student is thinking is for the student to ask questions. The master also must ask questions constantly of the student in order to see how the lesson is being learned.

Tenth, the master and student are both rewarded when the student improves. That was their mutual goal, and without progress toward that goal, both the master and the student will become discouraged.

We can take these lessons learned from the master/student relationship to provide us with guides to constructive criticism. The person giving the criticism should

1. Ask questions to discover what the person thinks he or she is doing and why.
2. Avoid any personal or irrelevant criticism.
3. Provide only specific and constructive suggestions.
4. Avoid suggesting that a failure will result in punishment.
5. Clearly identify how success will be measured.

The person receiving the criticism should

1. Listen to the suggestions and try to implement them, rather than arguing that they are incorrect.
2. Provide feedback concerning the result of trying to implement the suggestions.
3. Try to experiment in order to improve on the results that flow from the criticism.
4. Not argue with a suggestion before it has been tried, or at least thought about.
5. Recognize that the person making the suggestion is doing so to help the receiver of the criticism, not to do harm.

It is not easy to bring the average American around to this way of giving and receiving criticism. By the age of eighteen, most Americans have learned so many wrong things about giving and receiving criticism that we cannot expect them to change in a day. At the same time, old habits can be broken and replaced with new ones. The first step is training for both employees and managers in the lost art of constructive criticism. This training can be combined with a short course on how to write better. Using the rules of constructive criticism to help people improve their writing skills allows everyone to give criticism to their fellow students and receive it as well. When people are placed in a situation in which they are both giving criticism to and receiving it from other members of the same small group, they have to begin to rethink their approach to criticism. In a participatory organization we expect managers to both give criticism to their workers and receive it from them, and vice versa, so that this is a good beginning.

Putting Teacher and Pupil on the Same Team

Using the art of constructive criticism is much better than the usual way criticism is provided in the United States, but it is not the only way to approach teaching. The master is the teacher because the master knows much. In some cases, someone who knows little can be the best teacher. Let's explore the story of David. David was not very interested in school; but then, in his junior year, his home room teacher turned out to be the speech teacher, Ms. Curtis. After observing David for a couple of days, she decided that he should be on the debate team. David signed up for the seventh-period debate team. On the debate team, there was not the usual grade and no usual student-teacher relationship. Ms. Curtis was a great master of drama, but she did not claim to be a master of debate. Her teaching method was simple: David and other new members of the team were brought along to the first two debate tournaments to observe. Ms. Curtis knew which teams were probably going to win, and she sent the new debate students to watch the best and report back to her and their fellow students. After each tournament, the new students demonstrated and discussed what they had seen while watching the best. The techniques were broken down and explored. The methods of good debate were discovered by both the teacher and the students. Ms. Curtis mainly asked questions and explored options. She did not judge anyone or direct anyone. Soon the new debate team members were put into teams to begin to compete themselves. Some won, and some lost. Those that won received positive feedback. Those that lost watched the winning teams as they went to the final rounds of the competitions. Discussion back at school revolved around what the winners were doing right, not what the losers were doing wrong. By the end of the year, Ms. Curtis had a winning group of debaters, and David and his partner were winning debate tournaments. David enjoyed learning how to debate in a way that he had never experienced before.

Organizational Culture

Organizations have cultures, which helps us to explain why they behave the way they do. Factors that determine an organization's culture include the following:

1. *Values*: Organizations value some things more than others.
2. *Heroes*: Organizations have heroes that define the culture.
3. *Myths*: Organizations have myths that explain the organization.
4. *Rituals*: Organizations have rituals that control behavior.
5. *Symbols*: Organizations have symbols that express the culture.

Further reading: A. A. Kennedy, *Corporate Cultures: The Rites and Rituals of Corporate Life* (Reading, Mass.: Addison-Wesley, 1982); H. M. Trice and J. M. Beyer, *The Cultures of Work Organizations* (Englewood Cliffs, N.J.: Prentice-Hall, 1993); V. J. Sathe, *Culture and Related Corporate Realities* (Homewood, Ill.: Irwin, 1985); E. Schein, *Organizational Culture and Leadership: A Dynamic View* (San Francisco: Jossey-Bass, 1985).

The story of David can be applied to many situations in government and business. Company X wanted to make the best use of a new technology. Instead of hiring expensive consultants, the president of the company sent a team of workers to visit other companies that were already trying to use the new technology. These workers could talk to the workers in the other companies in a way that no manager ever could. The team of workers then consulted some experts, knowing at that point what they had seen and heard. Finally, the team of workers made a series of recommendations concerning how to implement the new technology. The implementation was a big success, in part because the workers who served on this team were part of the group that had to make the new technology work. Equally important, the president never understood the new technology and therefore never tried to second-guess the workers who were given this task, but did understand faster production times and lower levels of waste, which were the result of the new technology. Everyone understood the increased level of profit that resulted from the new technology. Other workers began to explore how they could use the new technology in their departments.

USING OUTSIDE EXPERTS

The way consultants are used can tell us a lot about an organization. Most people who have studied management are familiar with the Fredrick Taylor approach. Fredrick Taylor would come in and observe the work task. He would then devise what he felt was a better method and teach it to the workers. People who followed in Fredrick Taylor's footsteps came to be known as time and motion experts, and time and motion experts came to be the most hated people in American industry. Workers soon learned that time and motion experts were there to find ways to fire people. There were usually firings when the time and motion experts finished their work. Time and motion experts observed people the same way psychologists observe rats. Psychologists do not ask the rats questions (that would be foolish) and neither do time and motion experts. Psychologists reorganize the maze to see how the rats react, and so do time and motion experts.

Imagine how a team-based organization might make use of time and motion experts. What if time and motion experts were brought in to work with a team of workers who were trying to improve a process or work task? First, the workers might sit down with the expert to tell him or her what they thought about the process. Then the expert might observe in the usual fashion, asking questions to gain more information in a shorter period of time. Imagine a relationship between the time and motion expert and the workers that mirrored the relationship between the master and the student. What if they were both rewarded if unnecessary motion and time were eliminated? What if the expert asked questions and worked to help the workers meet concrete goals? What if a team of workers viewed experts such as this as a resource they could call on to help them achieve their goals?

Of course, these experts would have to be trained in the lost art of constructive criticism, something that is not true of most experts. Most consultants come in and tell people what they are doing wrong, often laughing at them for being so stupid, and then lay down the law. Their model seems to be the stern mother putting an intentionally bad child in his place. Consultants who act like this often get a response, but lasting changes, particularly at the level of the front-line worker, are often not achieved.

Constructive criticism works only if both sides are willing to play by the rules. Someone who constantly gives constructive suggestions, only to see that no one ever tries to implement them, eventually goes back to giving orders and getting some kind of results. People should be reprimanded not for doing a bad job, but for not being willing to try suggestions and provide feedback on the results. In other words, the main use of negative rewards should be for people who are not willing to play the game in the first place. In fact, in most sports, someone who is not willing to play the game is soon kicked off the team. What good is a player who won't play? That goes for managers, too. If they won't play the game of constructive criticism, they are not much use to the organization.

A significant part of any master/student relationship is a lot of encouragement from the master. Every time the student makes an improvement, however slight, the master says, "Good shot." Every failure is met with "Try again." An entire school of management was built in the 1980s with one goal: to catch employees doing something right and then tell them they were doing something right. The idea was to balance negative comments with positive ones. Actually, it would be nice if negative comments were very few and far between. An employee who receives mainly negative comments from a manager learns to avoid contact and communication with that manager. Negative comments should come from someone else whenever possible and should be unnecessary if objective standards of performance are being used. The employee can see that the targets were not hit as easily as the archery student. No one has to yell at the archery student or say, "Bad shot." The master would never do that. Instead, the student sees the less than hoped for result and asks the master for help in improving. That is an ideal to shoot for in any organization.

Imagine a school in which the teachers were viewed not as the enemy, giving grades and report cards, but as friends. How could that be accomplished? First, objective goals for performance would have to be set, and the person or organization providing feedback on learning would have to be different from the teacher the student worked with every day. Oh, the teacher might give the student an ungraded quiz now and then to see how much progress was being made, but real tests would be given and graded by someone else. The teacher and the student would then be on the same team working for the same goal, higher grades for the student. Both the student and the teacher would have been trained in the use of constructive criticism. The student would be told in advance what the goal was and given a chance to suggest how that goal might be met. If the goal is making a high score on a standard test, the student would first take a look at a sample test to see what the process was all about. Teachers, librarians, and fellow students would all be seen as resources to be used in achieving the goal, a high grade on the test. Students might work in small groups on some learning exercises and consult the teacher when the group could not figure something out.

Separating the person giving feedback on whether or not the goal is being met from the teacher-student or boss-employee relationship allows the teacher and student or boss and employee to be on the same team. In a very real sense, they both do well only if the student performs well or the employee meets the goal. The feedback to the student/employee is also feedback for the teacher/boss.

Constructive Criticism Is a Two-Way Street

Constructive criticism should work both ways. Executives and managers should expect to receive constructive criticism from the employees on a regular and formal basis. Nothing makes people more resentful than to be receiving criticism from people who can dish it out but can't take it. If the rules of constructive criticism are good enough for the workers, they should be good enough for the executives. If the accounting department is putting out a lot of numbers that are of no use to anyone, the people who are trying to use these numbers should be able to point that out. If the chief executive officer is making too many decisions without using randomly selected groups of workers to provide input, that should be pointed out. If the chief financial officer is unable to control overhead costs, he or she should receive feedback on that, with suggestions on how to improve.

Constructive criticism does not just happen. An organization filled with people who give and receive criticism in a constructive way must be developed over time. People should be reprimanded for failure to follow the basic principles of constructive criticism, not for doing something wrong. People who do something wrong should be given constructive criticism that includes suggestions on how they can avoid the mistake in the future.

In the master-student relationship, the master tries to encourage the student whenever possible. In team-based organizations, most communication should be either factual or positive. Negative comments should be few and constructive. An employee who sees an executive coming toward him or her should not shrink away because he or she knows that something bad is about to happen. Just the opposite; the employee should be glad to see the executive because the executive will be bringing either praise or useful information that will help the employee do a better job.

Exploring ways to use constructive criticism in any organization can be an eye-opener. There is a marketing department, and everyone in the organization sees the kind of advertising the marketing department puts out. Imagine if everyone felt free to make constructive comments and the marketing department responded with enthusiasm. Imagine a CEO who expected, and got, constructive criticism from everyone in the organization, and who asked people who did not supply constructive criticism why they weren't getting into the spirit of the organization. Imagine hundreds or thousands of workers who knew the difference between useful, relevant, constructive comments and everything else. Would we need experts in how to deal with race and sex if everyone were trained to give only constructive criticism? Would we need to talk about sexual harassment if everyone were trained in how to respect everyone else equally?

Criticism is difficult for some people to deal with because of the way it has been dished out to them over their lifetime. A short training course can only begin to break old habits. At the same time, if everyone in the organization has come to accept the basic principles of constructive criticism, the new person will be receiving constructive criticism when he or she does not engage in constructive criticism but slips back into a name-calling routine. If everyone, from the CEO on down, has accepted the principles of constructive criticism, then it will be easy for everyone to criticize people who do not follow those principles.

Stress is one of the great enemies of any organization. There are external stresses that can be minimized but not eliminated. However, much of the stress people in modern organizations feel can be eliminated because it is internally generated. Some of that stress is caused by the use of nonconstructive criticism. People who know that at any moment some kind of personal, unfair criticism is going to be leveled at them are not relaxed people. People who have been taught the art of constructive criticism find receiving and giving criticism to be much less stressful. While not all stress can be eliminated, the reduction of stress should be a goal for everyone.

People who live in a world of nonconstructive criticism outside the organization will have more trouble using constructive criticism at work. Perhaps a training session for spouses and significant others would be in order to help them use constructive criticism at home instead of what we might call destructive criticism. Destructive criticism is truly destructive because it destroys relationships. Any organization is simply a network of relationships. To the extent those relationships are destroyed, there is really no way to repair them.

Attribution Theory

Attribution theory suggests that in general, people tend to attribute their own behavior to forces outside of themselves and beyond their control, whereas they tend to attribute the behavior of others to personality factors internal to those individuals. If we saw someone kicking a dog, we would tend to say, "What a terrible person." However, the person doing the kicking would attribute his or her behavior to the fact that the dog had attacked him or her and there was no other choice. Getting people to focus on the external factors when they consider the behavior of others has been the major contribution of attribution theory to human management.

Further reading: H. H. Kelly, *Attribution Theory in Social Interaction* (Morristown, N.J.: General Learning Press, 1971); H. Kelly, R. Nisbett, S. Valins, and B. Weiner, eds., *Attribution: Perceiving the Causes of Behavior* (Morristown, N.J.: General Learning Press, 1972).

What if someone is not capable, after much effort, of giving constructive criticism? The person simply cannot think in terms of providing concrete suggestions and focusing on tasks rather than personalities. He or she has learned ways of giving criticism over the course of a lifetime and is not about to change them. There is really only one answer: This person cannot be a part of this organization. There may still be organizations that will value this approach to criticism, but a participatory organization cannot afford the luxury of keeping such people.

Of course, if the training program is on target in this area, anyone who cannot function in an environment of constructive criticism should find that out and quit long before becoming part of the organization. This demonstrates how a good training program can be part of the hiring and evaluation process. It also demonstrates the kind of materials that should be given to potential employees. The preemployment handbook should explain to potential employees the organization's commitment to the philosophy of constructive criticism.

People who receive constructive criticism and see positive results in their work soon can be seen seeking out constructive criticism. Imagine employees who seek out advice and suggestions from other employees and managers as to how they could help them do their jobs better. Imagine a set of objective goals that can provide everyone in the organization with feedback on performance. Imagine an organization in which everyone gets and receives constructive criticism. Would you want to buy stock in that company?

Using constructive criticism is often the most difficult part of creating a team-based organization. It requires both training and a change in corporate culture. But it can also have many positive side effects, from lower turnover to better health and safety. People who think in terms of making concrete suggestions to improve performance begin to think differently. Most of us would consider it an improvement.

Constructive Criticism in a Very Small Business

While people assume that using constructive criticism should be easy for a small business, the opposite is often true because it means making a fundamental change in the way the owner interacts with people, not just employees, on a daily basis. Without the help of a human resources department, the transition from boss to coach can be very difficult. This is where an outside expert can help.

Characteristics of Team-Based Organizations

1. They use constructive criticism.
2. They train everyone in the organization on the use of constructive criticism.

3. They bring in consultants to help teams of workers find the best approach by answering their questions and providing ideas. They do not bring in consultants to provide the right answer.
4. They make sure that supervisors are not the ones who provide feedback on whether or not goals are being met.
5. They do not allow personal attacks by anyone on anyone.
6. They allow workers to participate in developing the right training whenever possible.
7. They use worker task forces to make major decisions whenever possible. Workers who will have to implement the new process or procedure are on the task force that chooses the new process or procedure.
8. They view every increase in the skill and knowledge level of the workers as very positive, and reward it accordingly.
9. They punish people who do not follow the principles of constructive criticism.

Chapter 4

Team Work

If we had a nickel for every copy of every book with the word *team* in the title sold in the United States during the first half of the 1990s, we could certainly retire. The reality is that for participation and empowerment to really take hold in any organization, people have to be put into teams, even if only nominally.

Sally the swimmer may compete only as an individual swimmer against other individual swimmers from other teams, but she is still on a swimming team. She is still part of a team that trains together, plays together, gets both group and individual feedback together, and wins together. While she may win a ribbon for her event, the team wins or loses only if enough swimmers from the team win ribbons. Sally may be involved in helping to train other team members in how better to compete in what is basically an individual competition sport. She would not do that if she were not part of a team. At the same time, she has two incentives to win: the desire to win for herself, and the desire to win for her team.

Teams in Action

When Corning Inc. decided to build a new plant in Blacksburg, Virginia, it also decided to make use of multiskilled team-based production. The company sorted through 8,000 applications and selected 150 employees who demonstrated problem-solving ability and a willingness to work in a team setting. A Blacksburg team, made up of workers with interchangeable skills, can retool an assembly line to produce a different kind of filter in ten minutes, compared with the one hour it takes at other Corning plants. Corning is now converting its other twenty-seven factories to team-based production.

Some people who preach participatory management say that sometimes teams are necessary and sometimes they are not. That is simply wrong. In an organization that is really making use of participatory management, everyone should be part of at least one team, and hopefully several teams. The entire organization should be seen as a team in the same way a professional football team is a team. There is one head coach, and everyone should look to the head coach for leadership. At the same time, every player is part of other teams within teams. A defensive lineman is part of the defensive line team and the defensive team. The kicker may do most of his practicing alone, but he is still part of a special team, called the "special team." Everyone is rated both as an individual player and as a member of a team. Players have a lot of feedback during a game about how well they are doing, and, of course, they know what the score is every minute of the game. Players expect information to flow to them from the "guys upstairs," and they also expect everything they can observe to be listened to.

Creating Teams

If everyone in the organization is a member of the "big" team, where do we draw the line for smaller teams? Michael Hammer and James Champy, in their book *Reengineering the Corporation,* have argued convincingly that organizations need to focus on processes. They discuss the process of filling a customer's order, purchasing supplies, or making a particular product. They provide example after example of what teams of highly cross-trained individuals can do when given the latest computer and communication equipment and the freedom to act as a self-contained team. The teams they discuss are also able to see from concrete results, such as the reduced time to fill orders or the reduction in quality defects, that they are doing a good job. We read that Kodak created faster new product development and that Ford greatly reduced the size of its accounts payable department by combining teams with technology. In most of the examples of "reengineering" they give, a team has been given the training and resources to take on a logical chunk of work, with dramatic results in terms of quality and quantity of output. They talk about process teams, virtual teams, and casework teams. They tell us that process team workers share joint responsibility for performing the whole process, rather than working as individuals to perform a small part of a process. They tell us that teams that perform "process-oriented work are inevitably self-directing." By that they mean that once the objective criteria of performance have been established, the team can be left more and more on its own to meet those goals or hit the center of the target. They require more coaches and teachers and fewer supervisors. They tell us that in reengineered organizations, "training" becomes "education." They tell us that with today's computer and communication technology, amazing things are now possible. Of course, at all times, they are trying to see things from the customer's perspective. Focusing on the things the customers care about makes a big difference.

Why Teams?

There are a lot of reasons to focus on teams. First of all, it is usually more fun to play a game with a team than alone. People are basically social creatures. When they are forced to be isolated or behave as if they were, they are not happy. Unhappy people do not perform in a participatory way. Second, people who are part of a team can really take advantage of the strengths and knowledge of the diverse team members if they are given the right training and incentives.

We want people to have an objective goal to shoot for, but it is often not possible to provide that to an individual worker. A team can shoot for an objective goal that would not make sense for an individual worker. A team can receive feedback on its performance and make changes accordingly. A team can work toward major goals that relate to logical work processes. A team can be rewarded as a team for work well done in ways that would not make sense for individual workers.

A team can communicate with its external customers and suppliers in ways that would not be possible for individual workers. Teams can help to select and train new team members and even take part in the evaluation of team members. Teams are able to react to changes quickly because the entire group can learn about and respond to change.

Orientation for Teamwork

At Toyota Manufacturing USA, the new employee orientation takes four days.

Day One: Begins with an overview of the company's structure. An hour and a half is devoted to discussing Toyota's history and culture. Two hours are devoted to discussing employee benefits. Two hours are devoted to discussing the importance of quality and teamwork.

Day Two: Begins with a two-hour course devoted to the Toyota "way of listening." This session emphasizes mutual respect, teamwork, and open communication. The rest of the day is devoted to issues such as safety and environmental protection.

Day Three: Begins with two to three hours of communication training. The new employees are taught how Toyota employees "make requests and give feedback." The rest of the day is devoted to quality assurance and problem solving.

Day Four: Begins with teamwork. The company suggestion program is covered, along with building team skills. The afternoon is spent on fire prevention.

Potential team members need to be trained in team skills. Many people do not feel comfortable speaking up in a group. Team members need to speak up in a group. Some people do not feel comfortable in situations that might result in conflict or require negotiation. Of course, team members need training in the lost art of constructive criticism as much as managers do. If teams allow organizations to adjust to change faster than they otherwise would, then team members need to be given the training and skills they will need to recognize and adjust to change.

TURNING SUPERVISORS INTO COACHES

Teams need coaches and team captains. Who these people are and how they perform will, of course, depend on the task at hand. A professional football team has a head coach, a defensive and an offensive coach, and various special coaches. In some cases there may be a special coach for only two players, such as the kicking coach for the two kickers or a quarterback coach for the two quarterbacks. The number of coaches depends on the importance of what is being done to the success of the organization. The same should hold true in any organization. Coaches teach people to achieve performance goals. They may give orders, but more often they give advice to the team or subteam.

People may be on different teams at the same time. They may be put on special teams for special projects, such as a new product task force or a suggestion game team. A person may be the elected team captain of a suggestion team, the official secretary of the new product task force, and just a team member when it comes to performing his or her regular job. The same person might be part of a team designed to improve the training of new employees in team skills. Another team may be working to improve the way employees are hired and evaluated when they first join the organization.

The Hawthorne Effect

During the 1920s and 1930s, a group of industrial psychologists performed a series of experiments at Western Electric's Hawthorne plant. They chose a group of workers, put them into a special room, and conducted experiments on them. They wanted to measure the effect on production of changes in the work environment. What they discovered was that the workers selected for the experiment performed significantly better at their jobs, regardless of how their work environment was changed. The psychologists decided that the major change was selecting the workers and taking them out of their usual work environment. Because these workers were made to feel special, they worked harder almost regardless of how their work environment was altered. This has come to be called the Hawthorne effect and is still one of the most powerful effects ever studied by psychologists.

Further reading: Frederick J. Roethlisberger and William J. Dickson, *Management and the Worker* (Cambridge, Mass.: Harvard University Press, 1939); George Homans, *The Human Group* (New York: Harcourt, Brace, 1950).

Research suggests that groups can be very dynamic or very static; they can bring out the best in people or the worst; they can be a force for change or for retrenchment. Teams are, after all, groups by definition, and everything we have learned in the twentieth century about group behavior applies to teams. The Hawthorne effect is a good example of a recognized group effect. When researchers studied the Hawthorne plant in the 1920s and 1930s, they discovered that if they took a group of workers out of the main assembly plant and put them in a special room, they acted differently. The researchers changed a number of variables to see how these factors affected the quality and quantity of work. They turned up the lights; they turned down the lights. They turned up the heat; they turned down the heat. They moved things around. The result was that the new, special group performed better than other groups out in the "real" world, regardless of what the researchers changed. The Hawthorne effect tells us that if a group of people are made to feel that they are special, they will perform at a higher level than people who are simply doing their jobs day in and day out. There are a lot of ways to make people feel special and a lot of ways to make them feel unspecial. One of the reasons nothing succeeds like success is that once a group is successful, the members feel special, and that feeling leads to differences in attitudes and behavior. Those differences, in turn, lead to better performance, and the cycle goes on and on. This is also why nothing fails like failure.

After a century of doing social psychological research, one of the most significant findings is the existence of the Hawthorne effect. In other words, when people are put in a research environment, they act differently than they otherwise would. Social psychologists have to try to control for this effect when they do research. People out in the real world can use it to their advantage. Whatever your opinion of some of the twentieth century's dictators, one thing many of them did was to make an entire nation feel that "the whole world is watching us."

Many companies that share ownership with employees have been able to take advantage of the Hawthorne effect. They say, quite truthfully, that the whole country is watching us and expecting us to fail. Contrary to popular myth, most employee-owned companies don't fail, and many have been great successes. Of course, you can't keep the Hawthorne effect going forever. Castro used it well in Cuba for two decades, but finally the obvious lack of food and medicine overcame even his ability to inspire. Hopefully, companies that use the Hawthorne effect will create an organization that is strong enough to withstand the withdrawal pains when it no longer makes sense to think that everyone is watching.

For some people, being on a team is a new experience. For many people, being on a team where everyone is treated with respect and consideration will certainly be a new experience. That means spending time helping people to break old habits and old ways of looking at teams. How many people have been on teams where the coach thought the way to get the best out of people was to humiliate them at every opportunity or to yell and push and hit? Training in the fine art of constructive criticism should help to break them of that idea. For some people, a team is a group with an absolute leader who rules absolutely. They will have to get rid of that idea as well. If there is an internal team leader, it will probably be someone chosen by the team. If a leader is imposed by the organization, he or she will be trying to act more as a facilitator and coach than as a leader in the traditional sense. That will take some getting used to for many people.

Building Effective Teams

On a real team, every player does what he or she does best. Linemen usually do not try to run with the ball most of the time. Running backs do not try to be linemen. In the real world, however, we often find linemen who are trying to be running backs, and vice versa. On an effective team, people who have strengths need to play to those strengths. People who have weaknesses do not impose those weaknesses on the team. Also, on a participatory team, if there is a dirty task that no one likes to do, it gets rotated. Even the most experienced player gets to clean the toilets when the time comes.

Toyota Advertisement

Built with Incredibly Sophisticated Technology and Surprisingly Old-Fashioned Ideas.

At Toyota's five American manufacturing plants, we employ robotics, computers, and advanced technology. We also employ people who share the belief that quality is a team effort. In fact, last year alone more than 60,000 team-member suggestions were introduced into our U.S. production lines. It's this combination of technology and teamwork that is helping us bring world-renowned Toyota quality to everything we build here in America.

The *New York Times Magazine*, March 26, 1995

One of the many differences between effective teams and ineffective teams is team spirit. Some teams have spirit, and some teams don't. Spirit is very intangible and easily destroyed. However, it is something every team should try to build because there simply is no substitute for it. Teams with spirit never give up, never take no for an answer, and manage to pull the rabbit out of the hat when necessary. Teams without spirit do not. Again, many of the basic principles of participatory management should be used to help build team spirit. First of all, nothing builds spirit like winning. A winning team has spirit because it wins. A team with spirit wins. It becomes a circle of success. Some organizations have tried to begin participatory management by setting unrealistic targets. That is a mistake. If people have no chance of hitting the target they usually don't even make the effort. Nothing destroys team spirit like having targets that are impossible to meet. Imagine being handed a rifle for the first time and being told to hit a target two hundred yards away.

Successful teams have symbols that help to make everyone think of himself or herself as a member of the team. In World War II, many of the Allied bombers had a name and a picture painted on the side. The men who flew over China at the beginning of World War II were the Flying Tigers. (It is difficult to imagine the Flying Muskrats winning any battles.) Some organizations seem to think that this kind of thing is silly or unnecessary. It is not. No matter how adult or sophisticated people are, they can still respond to this kind of spirit building if it is not done in a silly way.

Teams use a vocabulary of teamwork. While that seems obvious, many organizations seem to think that they can get the advantages of teams and still use the old titles. It simply doesn't work. Team members need to be "players" or "members" or "associates." The word *employee* does not inspire anyone to reach new heights. Leaders need to be "captains" or "leaders" or "facilitators" or "coordinators." Supervisors do not play on teams. Managers need to become "coaches" or "gurus." People might win one for the Gipper, no one ever won one for the Boss!

Of course, a real team-based organization would allow the employees to decide what new vocabulary to use and what kind of mascot to have. Discussing issues of this kind can allow people to begin to see what we mean by ideas such as "teams" and "participation." The same goes for a lot of decisions that would usually be made by a small group of executives. The more decisions that can be given to a task force or decided by an employee survey, the more people are going to feel like they belong to the big team.

DEALING WITH STARS

Teams allow people to make mistakes as long as they learn from those mistakes. That is a key difference between a group of team members who consider themselves basically equal and a hierarchy. On a professional football team, even though some players make ten times as much money as other players make, they are still members of the same team. The great running back knows that he will not be a great running back for long if the linemen do not block the other team. It is just that simple. The stars may make a lot more money, but they are still members of the team.

Most organizations simply don't know how to deal with stars. In some organizations, people who stand out too much are fired. That plan would not work long in professional sports. Stars are a great resource to any organization, but they have to be turned into team players. That means that they cannot be rewarded totally outside the team structure. Of course they are going to make more, but they should also have to rely on their teammates for some part of their reward. Also, stars should not be given a significantly different contract from everyone else's. It is one thing to pay someone who really does produce more a lot more money. It is another thing to give that person a long list of special privileges and contract rights that everyone else does not enjoy. At that point, the person becomes the object of envy and is no longer seen as first among equals.

It can be difficult to tell the difference between a star who is the first among equals and a prima donna who costs the organization more than he or she is worth because of the negative feelings that are generated in everyone else. Nevertheless, the distinction is an important one. In some cases, stars can also be coaches part of the time, and everyone can see that they are sharing some of their special knowledge. In other cases, stars can be brought in for a short time to provide a special skill and then sent on their way. The television show "Saturday Night Live" has managed to be a team of almost equals with a lot of team spirit for many years, in part, because it has a guest host every week. The stars come and go; the team goes on. Of course, over time, some of the "Saturday Night Live" players have become stars and left. That is great. Everyone has something to shoot for, while the potentially disruptive force of a star on the team is kept to a minimum.

In the world of business, private consultants can in some cases take the place of the guest star. Someone can be brought in at a higher salary for a short period to provide a special expertise. If we were going to use teams in a movie studio, we would sign on hundreds of actors, writers, technicians, and musicians. A stable of directors might work in the organization, but stars would be hired only to do particular movies. They would get their big salary, but they would not participate in the studio profit-sharing plan or the stock bonus plan. That would be for the regular "team players." The stars would be treated differently from everyone else, but at the same time they would not have the privilege of being on the team. Being on the team can be very special and a reward of its own if things are handled correctly.

Making Everything a Team Effort

Many activities that people usually think of as individual efforts can be made into team efforts, with very positive results. The movie *Casablanca* began life as a play. A team of two writers was then charged with turning it into a screenplay. Other writers were brought in to work on specific problems. One added more comic dialogue. Another worked on the flashbacks. Some of the writing took place while the movie was being filmed and two different endings were written and filmed. Although the director was, of course, in charge, there was a producer who was very much involved. The production team of technicians and minor actors had worked together on many other pictures. They knew what to do and what to expect from one another. Thus, a series of teams produced the greatest movie ever made.

An organization that wants to emphasize teamwork has to promote and reward team players, rather than the lone eagles who might be promoted and rewarded in other organizations. That can be very difficult. The emphasis has to be on helping the team hit the target, not on hitting the target alone. Imagine an archery contest in which the best average score wins the contest. The team with one great archer and four terrible ones is not going to beat the team with five average archers. Five average players are going to beat four terrible players and a star any day. Even if the star is a great runner, where is he going to run to with no blockers?

Being an equal team member means being able to say anything without fear of reprisal. The freedom to express opinions, state facts, and present ideas allows everyone to feel like a team member. Inability to allow people to speak their minds has kept some organizations from making use of effective teams. The fear of free speech has cost many organizations potentially profitable ideas. It is difficult for an organization that has spent years or decades discouraging free speech to switch over. It requires a great deal of effort and a lot of special processes, such as suggestion plan games and communication award dinners. Most of all, it requires a CEO who is clear on the commitment to free and open discussion. Remember, free speech must still be in the context of the principles of constructive criticism. While as a citizen of the United States I am free to say that the president of the United States is a fool, that is not what we mean when we talk about free speech in a team-based organization. To call someone, even the CEO, a hurtful name does not get us anywhere, and it will not make the CEO a fan of free communication. To say that the CEO's decision to buy 200 new machine tools without talking to the people who use and maintain the machine tools was a clear violation of the principles of participatory management would be appropriate. (In a real team-based organization, such an action should get the CEO fired, or at least reprimanded by the board of directors.) Just as head football coaches get replaced when the team fails, so should CEOs who cannot produce a winning team.

Fitting the reward to the team, rather than the individual, is often very difficult for organizations. Telling someone who works hard that he or she will get no bonus because the team has not met its team targets can reduce morale for a while, particularly if people have been used to being rewarded as individuals. This is a necessary growing pain for any organization that hopes to become a group of successful teams instead of a stable with one great racehorse and a lot of nags.

Outline Team Authority

Teams need to understand what they are responsible for and where their authority ends, just as individuals do. The idea that people in an organization should have enough authority to achieve what they are trying to achieve also applies to teams. As part of the standard training, people should be told what kinds of responsibilities they may have and what kind of authority they have to meet those responsibilities. These might include

1. Setting work schedules and break schedules
2. Making equipment repairs or asking for equipment repairs
3. Making sure supplies are available for coming production
4. Keeping work records
5. Picking and training new team members
6. Checking quality
7. Contributing to budget calculations
8. Maintaining safety
9. Conducting a variety of meetings
10. Stopping production if something is wrong
11. Asking for help with problems from inside or outside the organization
12. Working directly with customers on some orders
13. Contributing people to organizational task forces
14. Helping the CEO to make major policy decisions
15. Keeping up with new technology
16. Solving small problems before they become big

The list is almost endless, depending on the organization.

Teams need to be told the limits to their individual decision-making authority. Many organizations, including the federal government, have found that they spend hundreds of dollars to purchase items that cost only a few dollars. This is because the checks and forms that make sense when thousands of dollars are being spent do not make sense when only a few dollars are being spent. Teams need to be told that when purchasing supplies, they can spend up to a set limit without authorization. This gives them clear authority. At the same time, there should be someone in the organization a team can communicate with if it needs help making a purchase or guidance as to where to get the best price. As consumers, we know the difference between a service that helps us get the best price and standard government purchasing, which requires us to fill out a dozen purchase order forms that simply get put somewhere to take up space into the next century.

Providing Support for Teams

While teams have many advantages, there are also new problems that arise when any organization tries to move toward teams. Interpersonal problems that were ignored before must now be dealt with. Resources must be provided somewhere in the organization to help teams that become bogged down in personality conflicts. There are a variety of solutions, from transfers to training, but these conflicts cannot be ignored. Many problems can be dealt with by the team itself, but there has to be somewhere in the organization that a team can go for outside help, just as a couple whose marriage is in trouble can get outside counseling. While outside counseling doesn't always work in family situations, it has certainly been more successful than no counseling at all.

Some work can be characterized as 90 percent routine, 10 percent crisis. Teams that work under these kinds of conditions need to know that there are people they can turn to in a crisis. These experts might be in-house, or they might be consultants who are on call. It is usually possible to make much better use of people with specialized knowledge if you are able to call them in to deal with a special problem. In this age of high-speed communication, there is no reason why the expert at the home office cannot be just a phone call or teleconference away.

Cross-training is often a key to a team's success. One of the advantages of a team is that it can adjust if someone is out sick or on vacation without the need to hire a temporary worker (who in many situations is simply a costly disruption). Short-term temporary workers usually provide very little bang for the buck. Rewarding people for gaining the necessary cross-training is essential. More and more, the availability of computerized expert systems and experts at the home office has made it possible for the teams that actually work with customers to be closer to the customers. A customer who can call and talk to the same person each time, or at least the same team, is much more likely to be a repeat customer. We expect government to shift us to half a dozen different people and then put us on hold for half an hour. We don't have to put up with that kind of treatment in the free market. A team or team member who can build up a relationship with a customer over time should be able to increase business, or at least customer loyalty.

Organizing for Teams

Exactly what process teams are formed around can be a key to success. Some organizations have broken up the work in strange ways and then found that teams did not bring about any increase in job satisfaction or productivity. In such a case, an outside consultant can provide help. An airline that tried to form teams that combined customer service representatives (the people who sell tickets and take bags) with baggage handlers might find that its teams were not very effective. People who work in very different environments are not going to make a good team. On the other hand, the people who work with the plane (baggage, fuel, supplies) are one logical team, and the people who work with customers in the airport are another logical team. Through cross-training and team reward systems, these teams should be able to provide better service at a lower cost in the long run.

Not only do people need to be trained in how to do their job and how to function on a team, but they should also receive training concerning how the particular team they will be on functions. An airline could use videotapes showing a team successfully dealing with a plane or an angry group of customers, for example. A manufacturer could show trainees how different teams in the factory do their job in the same way. Too many companies rely on on-the-job training to create team players. That is not good enough, particularly in an organization that has just begun using the team concept.

Teams should be used whenever possible, even if one person could do the job. While it might be cheaper in the short run to assign a particular task to one person, that is usually short-sighted. What happens when that person has mastered the task and then leaves the company? What happens when the task grows to be too big for one person? What happens when circumstances that cannot be foreseen cause a major change in the function?

There has been research done on how teams work, and teams should be told the findings of this research. For example, research suggests that women speak up less in a group made up of men and women. That deprives the team of their input unless everyone in the group understands that this is a potential problem. The team members and the team leader should be conscious of the need to ask women for their input, and women team members may need training in how to get their point across without violating what they have been taught about how women should behave in society.

Teams require a greater initial investment in terms of training and organization. They can pay that investment back many times over, given the right environment. There is little doubt that the successful organizations of the twenty-first century will be organized around teams.

Teamwork in a Very Small Business

A very small business may have to think in terms of teams made up of two or three employees. There is nothing in the laws of nature that says that a team must have five or six members to be a real team. Providing feedback to the team and keeping the team informed are often difficult for a very small business. Turning the owner into a coach may be the most difficult part of the transition to teams for a very small business. Owners who wish to make that transition must recognize that they cannot do it alone. Making use of resources that are available in the community will often mean the difference between success and failure. Also, small businesses have difficulty dealing with stars because of the perception that the star is more important than the rest of the employees put together. The question that small-business owners must focus on is not how valuable the star is today, but how valuable everyone else will be in the future as the business grows. The goal of most small businesses is to become big businesses, and if that is the case, the need to focus on teams rather than on individuals will become even more apparent.

Characteristics of Team-Based Organizations

1. They use teams whenever possible.
2. They train people to work in teams.
3. They allow the employees to help structure the teams.
4. They do a variety of things to build team spirit.
5. They provide some rewards based on team performance.

6. They use cross-training and communication to make the best use of the team concept.
7. They design teams to allow for the development of customer loyalty.
8. They plan for the future with team design in mind.
9. They use teams even when teams are not immediately as efficient as lone eagles.

Some of Saturn's Thirty Work Team Functions

Each Saturn team will

1. *Use consensus decision making:* No formal leader (will be) apparent in the process.... All members of the work unit who reach consensus must be at least 70 percent comfortable with the decision, and 100 percent committed to its implementation.
3. *Make their own job assignments:* A work unit ensures...safe, effective, efficient, and equal distribution of the work unit tasks to all its members.
5. *Plan their own work:* The work unit assigns timely resources for the accomplishment of its purpose to its customers while meeting the needs of the people within the work unit.
6. *Design their own jobs:* This should provide the optimum balance between people and technology and include the effective use of manpower, ergonomics, machine utilization, quality, cost, job task analysis, and continuous improvement.
8. *Control their own material and inventory:* Work directly in a coordinated manner with suppliers, partners, customers, and indirect/product material resource team members to develop and maintain necessary work unit inventory.
9. *Perform their own equipment maintenance:* Perform those tasks that can be defined as safe, and those that they have the expertise, ability, and knowledge to perform effectively.
13. *Make selection decisions of new members into the work unit:* A work unit operating in a steady state has responsibility for determining total manpower requirements, and selection and movement of qualified new members from a candidate pool will be in accordance with the established Saturn selection process.

14. *Constantly seek improvement in quality, cost, and the work environment:* The work unit is responsible for involving all work unit members in improving quality, cost, and the work environment in concert with Saturn's quality system.
18. *Determine their own methods:* The work unit is responsible for designing the jobs of its team members consistent with the requirements of the Saturn production system and comprehending the necessary resources and work breakdown required.
21. *Provide their own absentee replacements:* The work unit is responsible for the attendance of its members.... The work unit will be required to plan for and provide its own absentee coverage.
22. *Perform their own repairs:* The work unit will have the ultimate responsibility for producing a world-class product that meets the needs and requirements of the customer. In the event a job leaves the work unit with a known or unknown nonconformance to specification, the originating work unit will be accountable for corrective action and repair.

Chapter 5

Rewards and Compensation

It always seems to amaze people who focus on rewards that the people receiving the rewards also focus on them. If people are rewarded for putting in time, then they put in time, even overtime. If people are rewarded for production, then they produce—not necessarily quality, but they produce. If people are rewarded for quality, then they come up with quality.

The free enterprise democracy that is the United States assumes that most people are rational. However, as often as not, people are treated as if they were irrational. Take the state of California (please). In California, the state government says that one of its major goals is to try to convince as many Californians as possible to drive new cars because new cars put out less air pollution. (Heaven knows California could do with a little less air pollution.) However, a person who actually lives and drives in California soon finds that the older a car is, the lower the car insurance and the lower the car registration fee. Given that a new car may cost a thousand dollars a year extra for insurance and fees alone, it is small wonder that California has a lot of old cars on the road. This is astonishing to no one except the state government, which cannot seem to figure out why, despite all its pleas, Californians continue to drive old cars.

The same applies to any organization. Someone who is paid the same amount whether or not he or she is nice to the customers may be nice to the customers or may not be. The person certainly has no incentive to be nice, and the organization is making it clear that it does not care. A teacher who is paid the same whether the students learn anything or not may be a great teacher or may not be. You certainly can't say that the organization the teacher works for is concerned with the quality of the teaching. In fact, it may be just the opposite. Take Mary. She was shocked to learn that her son, after finishing the second grade, could not yet read.

Recognize the Effects of Teamwork

Because production goes on around the clock, each maintenance shift plays an important role in making sure everything on the line is running smoothly when the next shift takes over. One example of how this group pulls together in a difficult situation was evident when a wiring harness inside a robot went bad one night in late April. Several team members removed the bad harness while several others removed the good wiring harness from a robot not in use and reinstalled it in the other robot. "The problem occurred at about 3:30 A.M.", Dennis Waltz explained. "By the time the first shift came on at 6:30, we had the countermeasure in place." That took a lot of teamwork and hard work.

June 1990 issue of Toyota's monthly magazine, *Toyota Topics*.

She complained to the principal of the elementary school her son attended, only to find that the principal was very happy with test results that showed that the majority of the students finishing the second grade in this school could not read. Why was the principal so happy with this apparent failure? Because the low performance on the test meant that the school would get extra funds during the next year to help pay for more help in the teaching of reading. Although the first- and second-grade teachers had spent a little time on reading, they knew that if their students actually learned to read, they might have to take a cut in pay. I guess we should be amazed that any of the kids learned to read (they probably learned at home with their mothers and fathers).

Take the company that says it wants everyone to focus on the long-term health and growth of the company, then pays everyone on the basis of performance over a period of a few months. Bill is about to be moved, and so he uses up his supplies and allows his machine to go without maintenance in order to qualify for a special bonus given to low-cost producers. Of course, the machine wears out a lot faster, and the person who replaces Bill is in trouble for being a high-cost producer. The same thing applies to stockholders who demand that earnings stay high every quarter and then are shocked to find that the company has done no long-term planning.

Some experts would argue that compensation should be based on such factors as how much a person needs in order to live. The only problem with that is that it suggests that the company does not really care about a lot of things that the company probably does care about. People learn as children that if something is important, money will be involved. While we don't want to treat workers, or anyone, like circus animals, throwing them a treat if they do a trick, the truth is that money does talk. A school district that says it would like its teachers to get master's degrees but does not pay teachers with master's degrees any more money is saying that it really does not care if teachers get master's degrees after all. Companies that say they would like to see as many employees as possible with cross-training and specialized skills and then do not pay extra when employees master those skills do not really care about cross-training.

Let's imagine the average government agency. Sarah is an administrative assistant in Department X. She is nice to citizens who come in for help. Her coworker Sandy is not. Sarah actually tries to help citizens solve their problems. Sandy couldn't care less. Sarah goes out of her way to solve citizens' problems. Sandy leaves early whenever possible. Over months and then years, Sarah sees that Sandy receives the same pay, the same promotion opportunities, and the same recognition. Sandy then is promoted. How did that happen? It turns out that Sandy had found out that the department supervisor really liked apple pie and brought one every month like clockwork. Sarah has learned the lesson of this organization: It is not service to citizens that counts, it is doing nice things for the supervisor. Sarah changes her ways. The level of service in her department goes down, but no one measures the level of service or citizen satisfaction with her department, so no one knows it. Sarah takes a night course in accounting so that she can get a better job and spends as much time at work as possible studying for the course. Her work suffers even more, but when she finishes the course, she gets a promotion to another department that needs someone with basic accounting skills.

As far as possible, a team-based organization should provide some rewards to individuals on the basis of the level of their individual performance. Of course, that means being able to measure that individual performance in some meaningful way. Too often, this evaluation is left to the "boss," who bases it more on how he or she feels than on any objec-

The Free-Rider Effect

One problem with any group effort is that people working in groups tend to work less than they would if they were working alone. This is often called the *free-rider effect* because some people tend to try to take a free ride on the efforts of others. Ways to minimize the free-rider effect include the following:

1. Measure individual performance as well as group performance.
2. Allow group pressure to "encourage" everyone to pull his or her weight.
3. Seek information from group members about performance.
4. Use training to encourage effort.
5. Organize groups so that people do not have an opportunity to slack off from work.
6. Keep groups small enough so that no one can hide from other group members.
7. Provide incentives so that total group performance brings greater rewards.

Further reading: B. Latane, K. Williams, and S. Harkins, "Many Hands Make Light Work: The Causes and Consequences of Social Loafing," *Journal of Personality and Social Psychology*, vol. 37 (1979) 822–32; D. Forsyth, *Group Dynamics* (Pacific Grove, Calif.: Brooks/Cole, 1990).

tive factors. To the extent that objective factors can be developed, they should be used. A student takes a test and receives a grade. The test is an objective measure of individual performance that does not depend, hopefully, on the subjective goodwill of the teacher. The same should be the ideal in the world of adults.

Rewarding Teams

If a person is part of a team, then part of that person's reward should be based on the performance of the team. Often, teams are formed in organizations because it is possible to objectively measure the performance of a team in a way that would not be possible for an individual. Imagine the SUPER automotive company. In the SUPER Company, integrated teams of workers built automobiles. The SUPER Company was able to track each car and determine how much money had to be spent on warranty repairs during the warranty period. The SUPER Company had a good idea of the average cost of warranty repairs based on past performance, so it made a deal with each team: At the end of the warranty period, any money saved on cars produced by that team would be divided, half to the company and half to the team. The SUPER Company learned the hard way that if this was to make financial sense, it had to focus on groups of cars. When it provided this incentive on each car, without taking into account cars that went over the expected cost, it lost a lot of money. Only by looking at cars in blocks of one hundred produced by a team did it begin to make money and provide a meaningful quality bonus for the assembly teams. The assembly teams also received special bonus trips to exotic places if their record was significantly better than that of the average team. The SUPER Company was so pleased with the results of this effort in terms of increased quality that it used the system as the basis of a new advertising campaign. Teams decided on a mascot or symbol, such as the bear team or the tiger team, and put a letter in the glove compartment of each car they built, along with a group picture of the team that built the car. The teams began to receive fan mail from happy customers, which also were used in company commercials. An entire culture was created around quality and team spirit because the team members were allowed to know in detail how they were doing as a team and received a reward for better than projected performance. Oh, and they got a new batch of loyal customers who were even allowed to request the team that would build their new automobile. When a team built a real lemon, they were flown out as a group to listen to the customer's complaints and work, as a team, to fix the problems. To the extent that the problems were caused by poor design, the teams taking these "lemon trips" were allowed to make detailed reports to the design department.

Or imagine NEW City. In NEW City, each police precinct was given a target for reducing crime. City Hall did not care how each precinct reduced crime, it only cared that they did. Precincts that reduced crime to below the target received money bonuses for everyone in the precinct. Incentives for felons caught and convicted were also provided. Instead of prosecuting a lot of misdemeanors to get arrest numbers up, the precincts began to focus on felonies. Added incentives were provided for the conviction of felons who committed violent crimes, with special points for anyone who committed a crime using a gun. Soon the entire police force began to focus on what the citizens are most concerned about: violent felonies. In one precinct, violent domestic crime was reduced by offering family counseling in the precinct basement. Some members of the force took special courses to learn how to conduct the training sessions. Another precinct purchased more computers and used their database to predict the time and location of particular crimes, based on past history. Another precinct found that police began to take breaks and eat on the street so that they could keep watch on difficult neighborhoods. Seeing every member of the best precinct taking off for their free trip to Paris, all expenses paid, for two weeks that did not come out of their vacation was enough to inspire the worst precinct in the city.

Anyone who says that he or she cannot think of a meaningful way to reward a good team effort has not really tried. Of course there are intrinsic rewards from a job well done, but that does not provide specific goals and incentives. If a team has been structured around a coherent process, or area, in such a way that concrete performance feedback can be provided, then there should be no difficulty in coming up with some kind of reward for a good team performance.

This does not mean that individuals are not rewarded, but that individual rewards might be structured differently. What about a bonus every year, awarded by the team, to the team member who contributed the most to the success of the team? What about special prizes and recognition for people who provide services to the team such as seeing the humor in difficult situations or breaking up the tension in a crisis in a way that allows everyone to function in a more relaxed way? There really is no limit to the ways in which people can be rewarded for their team effort and team spirit if we just think about it.

Rewarding the Company as a Big Team

Every company says that its primary goal is ever-increasing profits. If that is the case, the profits should be shared in a meaningful way with the employees. A team-based organization that does not share profits is not really a team-based organization. It is only by sharing profits that people can begin to focus on the long-term major goal of the organization. One of the real morale busters of the 1980s was paying large bonuses to executives of companies that were laying off large numbers of employees. That certainly sent a message that employees are worthless and that managers who treat them as such are to be valued and rewarded. Sharing profits with everyone sends a very different message. Even if higher-paid workers and managers receive a large share of the profits based on their salary, they are still receiving a share of the profits just like everyone else.

Every company says that one of its primary goals is to see the price of its stock go up. If that is the case then stock should be given or sold to the employees so that they will want the same thing to happen. A participatory organization that does not share stock ownership with employees is not really a participatory organization. Stock ownership can be encouraged in many ways. In some organizations, employees are required to buy a certain number of shares when they come to work for the company (this is illegal in some states and countries). Other companies make it easy for employees to buy shares at a special reduced price. Others set up Employee Stock Ownership Plans that buy shares and hold them in trust for the employees until they quit or retire. Still others set up profit-sharing plans that buy shares for the employees with some of the profit-sharing money. There are dozens of ways to share ownership. The key is to make sure that everyone participates. An organization that shares ownership with the top executives and none of the other employees is not going to encourage everyone to feel like members of the same team.

The way compensation for individuals and teams is determined should be explained in detail. This is another type of communication that will be difficult for many organizations. The amount paid to particular groups of employees should be common knowledge. Organizations that think they are keeping this a secret are fooling themselves. This information leaks out of the payroll department, usually with a lot of misinformation. An organization that is ashamed to tell some of its people what it pays its people is probably not going to be a good candidate for a team structure. The salary of the top few executives may be kept secret without too much disruption. Salary information below that level should be available. Again, if information is not provided, people imagine far worse than the truth in most cases.

Hygiene vs. Motivation

Frederick Herzberg argues that people are motivated not to work if what he calls hygiene factors are low, but that the presence of high hygiene factors does not actually motivate people to work harder. What he believes do motivate people are what he calls motivators.

Hygiene Factors

Salary
Company policies
Working conditions
Relationship with supervisor
Relationship with peers
Relationship with subordinates

Motivator Factors

Achievement
Recognition
The work itself
Responsibility
Advancement
Growth

Further reading: F. W. Herzberg, B. Mauser, and B. Snyderman, *The Motivation to Work* (New York: Wiley, 1959); F. W. Herzberg, "One More Time, How Do You Motivate Employees?" *Harvard Business Review* (January-February 1968), 53-62.

Some have suggested that the goal of any capitalist organization should be to have about one-third of executive compensation based on performance bonuses and profit sharing. There is no reason why a similar goal could not apply to everyone in a profit-making organization. This kind of compensation system allows the organization to get away with paying employees lower than market wages in return for giving them the chance to make significantly more in bonuses and profit sharing. When times get tough, an organization that compensates people in this way can weather the storm without layoffs, or with fewer layoffs, and without having to cut pay. When times get better, the organization is ready to take advantage of the better times without having to hire and train a lot of new people. The trained people are ready to take up the slack and increase market share. People who operate under this kind of compensation system need to understand the risks and rewards, and some financial counseling might be in order.

Of course, the labor laws impose restrictions on what can be done. These laws were written in a period when workers were paid for putting in time, and they require that records of time worked be kept and minimum hourly wages be paid. However, the current minimum wage is so low that most organizations can comply with the minimum wage laws and still provide bonuses and profit sharing as a major part of a compensation package. Some team-based organizations have decided to take out the time clock. While that is a nice public relations and employee relations gimmick, the government assumes that there is a time clock; if there is not, any disagreement over how much time was worked will be decided against the employer who failed to keep accurate records.

Any organization that is trying to cope with business in the 1990s should be keeping an eye on new technology and the competition. In many cases, that means sending people on trips to see what is going on. A team-based organization uses these trips as a reward for top performance whenever possible. It is only sensible to send successful teams to see what they think of a new technology. If that means a trip to Germany or Japan, then why not? If the team writes up a report on the trip for the employee newsletter, then all the employees can both feel a little like they took the trip and see that top performance has a variety of rewards. Employees pay attention to this kind of report, whereas an official report would simply be thrown away.

As well as helping people to focus on what is important to the organization, rewards and compensation also tell everyone a lot about the organization. If the organization pays its people significantly less than other organizations for similar work, this tells people that the organization does not care about its people. It sees people as just a cost to be reduced to the lowest level. People are, of course, much more than just a cost to be reduced. People are people. Some executives do not seem to realize how much is communicated about an organization by the way compensation is awarded to the average worker. If people feel that they are not being treated fairly, they will not perform at the level required for any really successful organization.

Caring About People

The way people are disciplined and discharged is also part of the compensation system. If someone looking for a job is considering two organizations, and one of them guarantees that people will not be discharged without a peer review hearing, then that organization will be seen as a better place to work. If two similar jobs open up, but one is covered by a civil service system that provides some protection from arbitrary discharge, then the civil service job will be seen as providing extra compensation. Organizations seldom study the costs of providing reasonable discharge and discipline systems, but such systems certainly do have both a cost and a benefit.

Something intangible is also gained by any organization that communicates through its compensation system that people are important—that they are something more than machines that eat food. Often this is communicated through the employee handbook. An organization that has reasonable policies on issues such as family leave, sick leave, and vacation provides compensation of a very important kind. It communicates to people that people are important and that the fact that people have people problems is understood.

No one will believe that an organization really cares about people and is interested in their ideas and full contributions if people in that organization are paid less than people in other similar organizations. Participatory management often requires people to take on more responsibility and perform at a higher level. As a general rule, people are going to expect that an organization that really makes use of teams is saving money on supervisors and specialists. That should be the case. In return, these people who have been given more responsibility and more work to do expect to receive higher compensation. If that expectation is not met, and no information is forthcoming to explain why that expectation has not been met, then morale will suffer and the potential gains from teams may well be lost. Compensation systems that emphasize profit sharing can deal with these expectations in a way that causes everyone in the organization to focus on the bottom line.

The biggest mistake some organizations make is to spend a great deal of time and money introducing participatory concepts without examining the basic compensation and reward system of the organization. To tell the employees that they have more responsibility without discussing, and possibly changing, the compensation system can defeat everything that might have been gained.

Compensation in a Very Small Business

A very small business often is not in a position to reward team behavior. However, profit sharing and performance bonuses are possible even in the smallest business. Creating a compensation system that goes beyond paying people for the time they put in may be difficult for a very small business, but the time and money will be well spent if it helps the business grow and become more profitable.

Characteristics of Participatory Organizations

1. They provide reasonable compensation.
2. They provide bonuses that emphasize team performance.
3. They share profits and ownership with employees.
4. They recognize that discipline and discharge systems are a form of compensation.
5. They provide higher compensation to people who gain new skills that are important to the organization.
6. They provide reasonable and fair personnel policies and communicate them through the employee handbook.
7. They receive input concerning compensation policies from employees.
8. They communicate basic information about the compensation system to employees.
9. They use employee surveys and other methods to communicate with employees about compensation.
10. They make it clear that without profit, there can be no compensation for anyone.

Chapter 6

New Attitudes for Everyone

Participatory management requires a new attitude from everyone involved in an organization. The attitudes people bring to work are often overlooked when discussing why some organizations succeed and others fail, but this is a very important factor.

We are all familiar with the usual range of attitudes that we might find in any organization. The first, and most destructive, is the "boss" attitude. We all have some idea of what a boss is. By the boss attitude we mean the attitude that some managers have that they are in charge, on top, and responsible for the well-being of the organization. A boss gives orders, not praise. A boss makes decisions rather than helping others to make decisions. A boss gathers and uses information rather than sharing it with others. A boss tells people what to do and how to do it and reprimands people who do not do what they were told to do the way they were told to do it. A team-based organization cannot stand the drag of even one person with a boss attitude.

Creating the Coach Attitude

We will contrast the boss attitude with what we will call the "coach" attitude. Where a boss holds information, the coach acts as a conduit, passing information both up and down to those who need it. Where a boss makes decisions, a coach helps others to make decisions at the place most relevant to the particular situation. Where a boss tells people what to do and how to do it, a coach helps people to perform better, using the fine art of constructive criticism. A coach knows that people have already been told what to do by the goals and objectives they have been given, usually by someone other than the coach (in the case of football, the goal was created by the people who invented the game). A boss takes credit for everything good that happens and searches out people to blame for everything that goes wrong; a coach gives credit where credit is due and tries to explore ways in which failures can be avoided in the future. A boss orders people around; a coach teaches people how to do a better job. A boss waits while things get done; a coach helps to create an environment in which things get done.

Types of Leadership Style

Professors Vroom and Yetton argue that there are basically five types of leadership style, depending on how decisions are made. They argue that different styles are appropriate to different situations.

1. *Autocratic I*: The manager solves the problem by making the decision alone with the information available at the time.
2. *Autocratic II*: The manager solves the problem by making the decision alone after gathering information from subordinates.
3. *Consultative I*: The manager shares the problem with relevant subordinates individually, getting their ideas, suggestions, and information. The manager then makes the decision alone.
4. *Consultative II*: The manager shares the problem with subordinates as a group, getting their ideas, suggestions, and information. The manager then makes the decision alone.
5. *Group-oriented*: The manager shares the problem with subordinates as a group. The group generates and evaluates alternative decision outcomes and attempts to reach a consensus on the best choice. The manager does not try to influence the group decision and is willing to accept and implement any solution that has group support.

Further reading: V. H. Vroom and P. W. Yetton, *Leadership and Decision Making* (Pittsburgh: University of Pittsburgh Press, 1973).

Getting executives to change their attitude from boss to coach is probably the hardest part of moving an organization toward teams. People have grown up with the hope that one day they will be the boss, only to be told that bosses are obsolete.

There is more mental baggage that goes along with the boss attitude. Bosses usually do not have much respect for workers. They think of workers as lazy, stupid creatures who, if they are not performing, should be kicked in the rear. A coach asks first what he or she could do differently if workers' performance is below acceptable standards. Bosses spend a lot of time playing power games with people. Bosses tell people when they are a minute late. Bosses enjoy making arbitrary decisions based on a personal whim. Bosses like to bark orders and watch people jump to attention.

Coaches think first of the objective and then of how they can help other people achieve that objective. Coaches help other people obtain the information they need to make a decision. Coaches expect their highly trained and trustworthy employees to do a good job and ask what could have been done differently if there is a failure. Coaches are teachers first and cheerleaders second. Coaches come to work early to get things ready for the workers. Coaches help others to learn from mistakes.

One of the problems in making the transition from boss to coach is that someone who is half boss and half coach is not doing anyone any good. Someone who gives orders part of the time and tries to help others make decisions part of the time drives everyone crazy very quickly. There is no real middle ground. Organizations that think they can turn bosses into coaches overnight have found this to be the worst miscalculation of all. Bosses can be turned into coaches, but it takes a lot of training both on and off the job.

Union Relations

We believe that all people want to be involved in decisions that affect them, care about their job, take pride in themselves and in their contributions, and want to share in the success of their efforts. By creating an atmosphere of mutual trust and respect, recognizing and utilizing individual expertise and knowledge in innovative ways, providing the technologies and education for each individual, we will enjoy a successful relationship and a sense of belonging to an integrated business system capable of achieving our common goals which ensures security for our people and success for our business and communities.

From the labor contract between the United Auto Workers and Saturn Corporation.

In the real world, the only way to turn bosses into coaches is to reward coach behavior and punish boss behavior. In other words, people who are at the top of an organization must learn to ask those in the middle how a decision was made. If the answer is, "I made it," then the decision must be sent back to be made by those who actually do the work. If a major problem comes up, the people at the top must ask what kind of task force they should form to deal with it, rather than make the decision themselves. If something isn't working, the people at the top need to ask what kind of training will solve the problem.

As may be apparent, the key is to think in terms of pushing information and decision making down the organizational ladder. If those at the bottom are not prepared to deal with this, then the issue is what kind of training to give them. If those at the bottom do not have the right kind of information, then the question is how information can be pushed down to them. If those people at the bottom do not have the right mix of experience and skill, then perhaps some people who do have the right mix of experience and skill should be hired. In an ideal world, decisions are always made by the people who will have to implement them. While this may take longer in the decision phase, the time is usually made up in the implementation phase.

Bosses have people working under them who are not having fun. Coaches consider having fun to be one of the purposes of the whole enterprise. If people are not having fun, then coaches know something is wrong. Bosses are primarily concerned with their own ego needs. Coaches are primarily concerned with the ego needs of those around them. Bosses spend a lot of time fixing blame on people. Coaches try to find things about people to praise. Bosses love to play bureaucratic politics. Coaches don't have time for bureaucratic politics. Exhibit 1 provides a summary of the differences between bosses and coaches.

Exhibit 1

A Boss:

1. Hoards information
2. Makes decisions
3. Takes credit

4. Tells people how to do things
5. Ridicules people
6. Blames people
7. Satisfies his or her own ego
8. Plays politics
9. Makes people miserable

A Coach:

1. Shares information
2. Helps others to make decisions
3. Shares credit
4. Helps people learn how to do things
5. Supports people
6. Praises people
7. Satisfies other people's egos
8. Points out goals
9. Makes people happy

Bosses rule by fear. People do what bosses say because they are afraid of what will happen if they don't. Bosses may or may not know what they are doing. It doesn't matter to anyone other than the organization, which will suffer in the long run if the bosses don't know what they are doing. Coaches rule by competence. They are listened to and respected because they actually know what they are talking about. Coaches are facilitators who make it possible for other people to excel.

Of course, if people are to be good coaches, they have to be measured in terms that are appropriate to good coaching. Coaches should be rewarded when their people gain the necessary training and skill, when their people learn to operate in a team-based environment, when their people are meeting goals and hitting targets. A coach should never be rewarded for something he or she personally did. That misses the whole point of being a coach. A coach is rewarded if the team wins. It would make no sense to say that a football coach was great but the team lost. All football coaches know this. Coaches in business and government need to learn it.

When a boss is trying to become a coach, the first lesson is to relax and let other people do it. Bosses worry at night. Coaches sleep well because they know that they have created conditions in which other people can perform. They don't have to worry about what they will do each morning. Someone else is doing that—namely, the person who has to accomplish the goals. The coach can come in late and see if the arrows are hitting the center of the target. If they are, the coach can focus on what is most important for the long run.

Stephen R. Covey, in his book *The Seven Habits of Highly Effective People*, argues that the things we spend our time on can be broken up into four categories. There are important things and unimportant things; there are urgent things and nonurgent things. If we see these as a two-by-two box we see:

	Urgent	**Nonurgent**
Important	I	II
Unimportant	III	IV

Stephen Covey discusses these four quadrants. People who spend a lot of their time in quadrant I are spending their time dealing with crises; they suffer from stress and burnout. People who spend a lot of time in quadrant III are spending time going to meetings, answering phone calls, and writing letters, not accomplishing anything of importance. They get some work done, but no one thinks of them as making a real contribution to the organization. People who spend a lot of time in quadrant IV either are spending their time with people who are known as time wasters or are time wasters themselves. They eventually get fired. The ideal is to spend as much time as possible in quadrant II. People who spend a lot of time in quadrant II are planning, building relationships, looking for new opportunities, and helping others to meet long-term and important goals. They become leaders. Bosses spend a lot of time in quadrant I. Coaches spend a lot of time in quadrant II. Bosses get ulcers. Coaches get ahead.

Bosses like to know what their people do after work and like to interfere in people's personal lives. Coaches couldn't care less, as long as it does not affect the team effort during the workday. Bosses love to find people doing something stupid so that they can yell at them. When coaches find people doing something stupid, they view it as a chance to help people solve a problem. Why are they doing that in this way? What is the result? How can they get the information and training needed to turn a stupid activity into a productive activity? What should the coach have done differently to avoid this stupid activity in the first place?

The Do-It-Yourself Syndrome

The hardest thing for executives at participatory organizations to avoid is the "do-it-yourself" syndrome. Executives are used to making decisions and getting things done. At a participatory organization executives do not make decisions or get things done. They help others make decisions and get things done. There is a very important difference. It may be easier to do it yourself rather than to show someone else how to do it in the short run, but not in the long run. This is where the coach analogy can be useful. Coaches are not allowed to run out onto the field and begin playing the game. In the world of sports, coaches coach and players play. The same should be true in any participatory organization. Executives in a participatory organization should be able to say with pride:
I DON'T DO ANYTHING AND I DON'T MAKE ANY DECISIONS.

Bosses blame everyone other than themselves. Coaches do not blame anyone except, in rare cases, themselves. Bosses try to find fault with people. Coaches try to find fault with everything else: information, training, equipment, company policy, the environment. If the problem is a people problem, then coaches deal with it by working to help the people involved solve the problem. Bosses fire people who do not jump when they bark and bow down to them as they pass. Coaches fire people for only three reasons: They really cannot do the job after a great deal of effort and training, they are not trustworthy, or they simply cannot function in an environment with low supervision and lots of teamwork. An organization built on trust can deal with a few incompetent people. It cannot stand untrustworthy people.

Creating the Player Attitude

As for the employees, there are a dozen possible attitudes that they might have. The best is the player attitude. Just as we would like bosses to become coaches, we would like workers to become players. Players realize that this is a game with a variety of goals, such as increasing profits, raising share prices, cutting costs, meeting quality and quantity goals, and so on. Players work as part of one or several teams to help meet these goals. Players come to play, not to sit on the sidelines. Players tell the coach when they are hurt or otherwise need some special attention. Players join in group activities and try to convey information when possible. Players work to play their positions so that the rest of the team will not be let down. Players try to come up with ideas to improve things and get those ideas to the people who can make things happen. Players work to improve their skills and to get more training when necessary. Players ask for training from the coaches and give the coaches feedback concerning the effectiveness of the training. Players try to have fun, and if something is not fun, they say so. Players help other players out when they need a hand and give them the benefit of their knowledge and experience.

Players work to improve themselves when they are not playing. They take community college courses that might help at work. They get rest, relaxation, and exercise when they are not at work. Players do not do anything away from work that would harm the team. They keep their eyes on the goals and do not spend time on things that will not help to achieve the goals. Players cheer on the other players when they meet a goal and comfort players who have made a mistake. Players can sit on the bench, but they would rather play. They say to the coach, "Send me in, coach."

Of course, there are a lot of other attitudes besides that of player. One attitude is that of time waster. This is probably the worst of all attitudes. Time wasters have decided, for whatever reason, not to play the game and to keep others from playing as well. They come into other people's offices to talk about nothing in particular and everything in general. Time wasters have decided either that the game is not worth playing or that the goals are not worth achieving. Having come to this conclusion, they try to convince others that they are right. They are often seen walking around with coffee cups in their hands, engaging others in meaningless conversation. Picture someone doing that on a football field to see how ridiculous this kind of behavior really is. The first question for someone dealing with a time waster is: Can the time waster be convinced that the game is worth playing and the goals are worth achieving? A long talk with a time waster can usually help answer these questions. Why has someone with skill, intelligence, native desire to excel, training, and motivation become a time waster? In many organizations people have become time wasters because no one treats them like players and trying to accomplish something only gets them into trouble. If any action is more likely to result in negative feedback than positive feedback, time wasters simply engage in as few actions as possible. On the other hand, some people seem to be born time wasters. If a time waster can be turned into a player, great. If not, he or she has to be gotten rid of as quickly as possible. Time wasters not only accomplish nothing, they keep others from accomplishing anything.

Another attitude is that of the shadow. Shadows are not time wasters, but their goal is to stay in the shadows and do as little as possible. Shadows play their positions a little bit, but not enough to help achieve the goal. Shadows do not waste other people's time, but they waste the resources that have gone into getting them ready to be players. Shadows do not volunteer, do not speak up in meetings, do not get enthusiastic about anything. Shadows have gotten so much negative feedback that they ask for guidance at every opportunity and do not make a move on their own. They think in terms of light and shadow and stay out of the light, even if the light is where everything is happening. Shadows have learned over time that people who stand out get in trouble sooner or later. The lights are too bright on a football field for anyone to play the shadow, but most other organizations have at least one shadow. Again, shadows may become players if they can be convinced that playing in the light really is better and more fun than staying in the shadows. A coach has to take them into the light and teach them that playing and losing is a lot better than not playing at all.

Another attitude is that of the cheater. Cheaters try to cheat their way to success. Often, they found that that strategy worked in school, and they have continued it in life. Cheaters try to get ahead by taking credit for other people's accomplishments and putting the blame for their mistakes on others. Cheaters do not contribute original ideas, and they do not do much in the way of actual work. Cheaters usually do not pay attention in training sessions and do not worry about actual results. Cheaters are concerned with how they look, not with what they accomplish. Cheaters usually say yes to everything the boss says and no to everyone else. Cheaters are not trustworthy and usually cannot be reformed.

Another attitude is that of the uninterested. Uninterested people are simply not interested in work for any one of a thousand reasons. They may have so many personal problems that work simply seems unimportant in comparison with the difficulties at home. Uninterested people come to meetings and concentrate on their problems away from work. They do not contribute ideas or input because they simply are not interested. If they could straighten out their personal lives, they might become interested if work was actually made interesting to them. They are not interested in doing small things, and we can hardly blame them. They might be interested in playing the game if the goals were worthwhile and they were surrounded by a lot of players who were really having fun. Absent these kind of circumstances, they remain uninterested.

Another attitude is that of the cowboy. Cowboys like to ride hard and shoot their guns a lot. They think only in terms of themselves. "What's in it for me?" is the question that is always uppermost in their minds. They find it hard to be part of a team, any team, because their focus is on what they can do to show themselves off. Cowboys on a football team run great, but never block for the other guy. Cowboys may produce a lot by themselves, but they usually make everyone else so miserable that it is not worthwhile having them on board. Cowboys hog the limelight, which makes it hard for everyone else to see what they are doing. Cowboys breed distrust because whenever they offer to do something for someone else, the assumption is that there is something special in it for the cowboy. This makes it hard for other players to relax and have fun, since they know that the cowboy is going to ride away with the glory at any moment. There may be a place for cowboys in some organizations, and if there is, they can be very useful. Their inability to be team players, however, makes it hard for everyone else to focus on the long-term goals that are important.

Another attitude is that of the waiter. Waiters are waiting to see what happens. Waiters are from Missouri; they have to be shown. They will give people, and organizations, the benefit of the doubt, but they have to be convinced. Waiters pay attention but do not volunteer ideas. They master a skill but wait to use that skill until they are asked. Waiters don't say much. Waiters can be turned into players, but they have to be encouraged to speak up and get involved. Waiters need a coach to help them get their head into the game.

How can an organization tell if someone is a cowboy, a time waster, etc.? One way is to describe these different attitudes to potential employees and ask for a self-evaluation. Many people know exactly what they are and will tell you if you ask them. A team-based organization needs to make it clear what kind of attitude it is looking for and ask people why they think they can be real players. Selecting as high a percentage of players as possible is key to the success of any team-based organization. Often, the only way to see whether someone is a player is to put the person into a game situation and see what he or she does. That is why team-based organizations make use of simulations and role playing—both to show people what the work will be like and to find out how potential employees will react to the games that the organization plays.

All the tools of internal and external communication should be used to emphasize that coaches and players work at the organization. The CEO plays a key role because he or she has to be the head coach, not the chief boss. The CEO has to both act as a coach and check up on other people to make sure that they are acting like coaches. If they are not, the CEO has to either coach them to be better coaches or fire them. The CEO has to be willing to turn important decisions over to a task force or a relevant team and overrule their decision only if he or she is sure that disaster would result if he or she did not. This takes a lot of self-control and personal confidence on the part of the CEO.

One of the most difficult lessons for team-based organizations has been that people who are not sure of their own abilities have a great deal of difficulty being good coaches. Coaches have to be sure they know what they are doing and then be willing to teach rather than do. People with inferiority complexes do not make good coaches. People who cannot communicate do not make good coaches. People who do not like people do not make good coaches. People who cannot take and give constructive criticism do not make good coaches.

The employee newsletter can help by playing up people who do a good job coaching or playing. Talking about how a coach helped a new player gain confidence goes a long way to encourage everyone to be coaches and players.

It is sometimes difficult for us to forget that when we are talking about people in an organization, we are not talking about rats. "People are not rats" should be our motto. What do we mean by that? When we deal with rats, we reward and punish behavior in order to get the behavior we want. When we deal with people, we do the same thing; however, if we want ours to be a team-based organization, we tell the people that is exactly what we are doing. There are no secrets. We tell people that this kind of behavior will be rewarded because it is what a team-based organization needs. Anyone who does not agree should write an article for the employee newsletter explaining why he or she feels this way.

Scientists become scientists because they are curious about the world. They do experiments because they want to see what happens. A team-based organization has to have the same attitude. Trying something new should be valued by the organization. If a player wants to try a different play, he or she should be allowed to do so whenever possible. Of course, not every new play can be tried, and factors such as cost have to be taken into account, but whenever possible, new ways of doing things should be experimented with. Whether the experiment is a success or a failure, the person making the experiment should be rewarded for trying and should be asked to write it up so that others can learn from what he or she has done.

A team-based organization needs people that think and act in ways that encourage everyone to follow the philosophy of participatory management. It is just that simple, and just that complex. People who cannot or will not play the game cannot be on the team, or teams. Players and coaches win games. Cowboys should be herding cattle and waiters should be waiting on tables, not getting in the way of players. And no one has time for a time waster if the team is going to win.

New Attitudes in a Very Small Business

Becoming a coach is often the most difficult part of creating a team-based organization for the small-business owner. It requires being willing to make a real effort to change the way employees are treated. It is also difficult for the owner of a very small business to take the time to find and hire real players. However, once the owner of a small business has become a coach and hired players, he or she should have more time to spend on the important/nonurgent issues that Covey tells us people need to be spending more time on. It is the small-business owner who has the time to deal with those important issues who becomes the owner of a big business.

Characteristics of Team-Based Organizations

1. They have coaches, not bosses.
2. They have team players, not cowboys and time wasters.
3. They make it clear that only players need apply.
4. They encourage the player attitude by letting everyone see the game plan.
5. They ask the players who is not playing the game.
6. They reward people who act like coaches, not people who act like bosses.
7. They reward people who act like team players.
8. They have training for both coaches and players on how to be coaches and players.
9. They listen to players.
10. They tell everyone what the score is.

Chapter 7

The Meaning of Democracy

A fundamental question is the extent to which empowerment requires democracy. Before we can begin to answer that question, we have to explore what we mean by democracy. If democracy means being allowed to choose between two candidates for an office that has little or no impact on our daily lives, that is probably something that private organizations should not try to imitate.

Political Equality

Democracy has many aspects. One aspect is the idea of political equality. In a democratic society, people may not all make the same salary, but they all have the same vote, at least in theory. They are all citizens as opposed to barons, dukes, and serfs. They all, at least in theory, have the same access to important people, such as the leaders of the country. They all should look the same on the street and be treated as equals by their fellow citizens. To the extent that this is not true, you do not have political equality.

Can a business or government agency have political equality? Of course, but it requires a major change in the culture and the look of some organizations. The executive washroom and the executive dining room must go. After all, if we want to encourage communication among all levels of the organization, then these institutions simply make that task harder. If everyone eats together and talks together we can expect them to begin to feel differently about one another. Special parking places and special perks like a company car should also go. Everyone has to drive; why should some people have a company car? Of course, if someone actually does a lot of driving as part of the job, that would be very different.

FREEDOM

Another aspect of democracy is personal freedom. In a democracy, people are allowed to make their own decisions about how they will live and what they will do for a living. In an empowered organization, this kind of freedom comes in the form of being free to control the details of everyday work life—along with fellow team members, to be sure. This freedom is of course limited by the demands of the work and the technology used to perform the work.

In the workplace, personal freedom means being allowed to make decisions that primarily affect the way you do your work. For example, employees of Reuther Mold in Ohio who will have to work with a machine are allowed to make decisions concerning which machine the company will buy. When the president of the company, Karl Reuther, was asked about this policy, he pointed out that if he made the decision and there was a problem, the workers would simply stop working and say, "I told you so." If the workers make the decision, then they will find a way to make the machine work for them.

If people are given goals to achieve, rather than detailed instructions of what to do, personal freedom goes up, as does a sense of real accomplishment. If part of democracy is personal power, then the more people can control their own work environment, the more personal power they feel as if they have, and the more they actually have.

DEMOCRATIC LEADERSHIP

During the 1930s, Professor Kurt Lewin conducted a series of experiments using boys between the ages of ten and twelve. He had the boys attend a kind of summer camp. At this camp, they were put into groups (teams) and given various tasks to do. They did things like building model airplanes and other toys. The boys were put into a situation in which, in order to produce a product, they had to work as a team. Professor Lewin then rotated the kind of leader each group was exposed to. There were three types of leaders: autocratic, anarchic, and democratic.

An autocratic leader brought in the supplies and plans for the project and told everyone what to do in great detail. The autocrat did not show the plans to the boys or make any effort to listen to their ideas.

The anarchic leader arrived with the same supplies and plans and put them on the table. He made no effort to direct the boys' actions or guide them in producing the product. He would answer questions if asked, but otherwise he simply stood by while the boys did whatever they felt like.

The democratic leader brought in the supplies and plans and showed the plans to the boys. He explained what was to be done and asked which boys were interested in doing what kinds of work. The democratic leader gave guidance rather than orders and tried to create an atmosphere in which the boys asked questions.

Professor Lewin measured a number of things. He found that the democratic and autocratic leadership styles produced about the same results in terms of quantity and quality of product, but that the boys said they enjoyed the democratic style much more. The anarchic style did not produce much more than confusion. While Professor Lewin did not write a book on this series of experiments, he did produce a film that can still be found in the film library at many universities. We can see the boys reacting to the changes in leadership style. We can see the boys throwing things at each other while the anarchic leader stood by. We can see the confusion on the boys' faces as the autocratic leader came in and started giving orders. The most interesting finding was what happened when the leader was not present. When the boys were working under autocratic and anarchic leaders, all work would stop when they realized that the leader was out of the room. When the boys were working under the democratic leader, they would actually continue to work on the task when the leader was gone. Even for ten-year-old boys, the difference between autocratic, anarchic, and democratic leadership styles really mattered. Even ten-year-old boys responded when they were treated as if their ideas and concerns mattered.

Letting people in on the plan is part of democracy. What are we trying to achieve, and how are we going to achieve it? Those are questions that citizens ask their elected leaders and workers ask their supervisors. To the extent that they do not get an answer, we do not have democracy.

Having direct input on important policy decisions is another aspect of democracy. In most cities, states, and countries, we use opinion polls to find out what the average citizen thinks about important issues. The same technique can be used by any organization, from a private company to a government agency. A survey of opinions on issues that the average employee should or might have an interest in can and should be a part of any team-based organization. Often it does not make sense to conduct such a poll because there is too much information involved. In that case, a randomly selected group of employees can be brought together to go through the information and give an opinion. For example, suppose an airline was considering the purchase of some new airplanes. Given the obvious needs of the airline, the choices can quickly be narrowed down to two or three. Why not randomly select a group of employees, making sure every work type is represented, to make the decision? The people who will maintain the airplane can see how difficult maintenance will be for each option. The pilots who will fly the plane can examine each choice for how it will fly. The stewards and stewardesses who will work inside the planes can examine the possible cabin configurations to see how difficult or easy they will be to work with.

Two things are gained by this kind of decision procedure. First, if the employees who will be working with the plane actually make the purchase decision, or have a lot of input into the decision, the decision may be a good one. Second, if the employees understand that employee representatives were involved in making the decision, they should be more willing to accept it and work with whatever problems come up.

Making decisions about leaders is what many people think of when they think of democracy. Here is another area where any organization can consider making more use of democracy. Once a highly skilled team has been assembled, why not let the team decide who the team leader will be? Of course, an employee-chosen leader will need some special training, but the employees will be more likely to work with the leader if they were involved in making this decision. Compare this with the usual procedure, where highly skilled team players are given a leader. There is usually some resentment because many of the team players may feel that they should have been made the leader. If the leader has been chosen by someone else, these players can come up with a lot of ways to make sure the leader fails, which would make it possible for them to have a chance at the job. If the team has chosen the leader and will choose the next one, then the team members know that they will have to exhibit a very different set of behaviors. They will want the leader they have chosen to succeed. They will want to be seen as cooperative team players so that if and when a new leader is chosen, they will have a chance at the job.

Representation

In business corporations, another aspect of democracy would be to allow the employees to elect representatives to the board of directors. This idea is generally rejected out of hand in the United States. In Germany large corporations are required by law to have employee representatives on the board of directors and Germany has a very strong economy, so the argument that this idea simply cannot work carries no weight. When we ask people why they would not want employee representatives on the board of directors, the answers usually involve not wanting the employees to be able to provide information to the other board members. Of course, in a real team-based organization, that is something we would want. Another reason is that people do not want the employees to have the same kind of information that the board of directors has. Again, in a real team-based organization, that should also not be the case.

While the employees may have elected representatives on the board of directors, the stockholders, of course, will also have elected representatives on the board. If the two groups most interested in the long-term health of the corporation are the employees and the stockholders, then why shouldn't they elect the members of the board of directors?

One of the problems with conventional democracy as practiced by governments around the world is the problem of trying to give people who have a greater interest in a particular decision more input into that decision. That has proved to be very difficult and has resulted in the creation of interest groups and a thousand and one organizations intended to bring pressure on government decision makers. In a business organization, this should be easier to accomplish. The people who will work with a particular machine should have the most input into deciding what machine to buy. The people who will never have to see or use the machine should have little or none. If everyone is trying to achieve the same goal, a profitable company, this should make perfect sense. Democracy in such an organization will seldom mean giving every employee an equal vote on every decision. Democratic governments do not do that. They give everyone an equal vote when it comes to deciding who the leaders will be, but when it comes time to make policy decisions, different interest groups have more or less influence, depending on the decision to be made.

Democracy should be easier to accomplish in a private company with profit sharing than in the typical city, state, or country. In most governmental units, there is little agreement about what the unit should be trying to accomplish. In a private company, everyone should agree that the primary goal of the organization is to make money. If it does not make money, there can be no wages for the workers and no dividends for the stockholders. Of course, the major conflict that people suppose will arise between these two groups is over how much each should receive. That is much easier to solve than is generally imagined. We know what similar organizations pay for wages, and we know what kind of dividends the average company provides. If we pay those average wages and average dividends and split the remainder between the two groups, everyone should be better off than he or she would be if he or she had not gone to work for, or invested in, a democratic company. Whether you split the remaining profit fifty/fifty or sixty/forty, both groups will be better off than would otherwise be the case, and both groups will have an incentive to work toward the long-term health of the company.

Of course, there are many different kinds of democracy. Direct democracy means that people have a direct input into a decision. Indirect democracy means that people have some influence on the choice of who will make a decision. Information democracy means that people have input into the kind of information that is considered by the people making a decision. Random democracy means that decision makers are chosen at random from a group of people with the kind of information and expertise needed to make the decision. This is the way the United States makes decisions concerning which people will be sent to jail or put to death, and the system seems to have worked pretty well. Few companies seem willing to try the same procedure.

Democracy comes in all shapes and sizes. There is no easy blueprint for an organization that wants to make better use of democratic procedures. Every organization is different, and every decision is different. However, a team-based organization tries to make use of democratic procedures whenever possible.

Democracy in a Very Small Business

Small-business owners often cannot imagine having any kind of democracy in their business. They imagine that democracy would mean having to stop and vote on everything in the course of a business day. But there are many aspects of democracy that even the smallest business can take advantage of. For example, nothing hurts morale in a small business more than special treatment for one or two special employees. A little equality can go a long way. Allowing employees to control their immediate work environment can also help improve employee morale. Letting employees in on the plans for the business's future can also be very helpful. And, yes, in some cases some decisions can be made by allowing employees to vote without the world coming to an end.

Characteristics of Team-Based Organizations

1. They make use of democracy when possible.
2. They use employee surveys when appropriate to gather information and opinions.
3. They use randomly selected groups of employees to make decisions or provide input into major decisions.
4. They allow employees to have control over their work environment.
5. They allow teams to select their team leader whenever possible.
6. They allow employees to select a representative to the board of directors.
7. They share profits with the employees and set wages so that everyone has an incentive to increase profitability.
8. They treat all employees equally when that is possible and appropriate.
9. They provide information to employees.
10. They listen to employees.

Chapter 8

Symbols and Signs

When we think about what has to be changed to bring about the development of a real team-based organization, we tend to think of a lot of things: communications channels, training, and so on. We often overlook a very important factor, the use of symbols and signs. Long before a real participatory management environment has been created, symbols can be used to help point the way.

If every employee is important—and in a team-based organization, every employee is important—new approaches to wardrobe are in order. Do some people come to work in an assembly-line worksuit, with no metal that could scratch the finish? If so, shouldn't the white-collar workers also have a uniform that is comfortable and designed to help them do their job? The need for new ways of dressing in every part of the organization must be pointed out at the top. What that new way will be must be decided at the bottom, through the use of surveys, randomly selected groups, and all the rest. When the decisions have been made, everyone must come on board, including the CEO. Lee Iacocca turned a lot of people into believers when it came to the rebirth of Chrysler. He did it wearing a suit and talking into a television camera. What impression would it have made if he had worn a new uniform, designed by the white-collar workers to be functional and comfortable?

We know that in many organizations, the workers talk about the "suits"; the suits did this and the suits did that. In these organizations there is not one big team. The suits are obviously on a different team, and everyone else resents it. The suits are aristocratic; the workers are not. The suits stick to themselves, while everyone else has a beer after work in the bar across the street from the plant (or the mine or the store).

Real CEO Behavior

Henry Mintzberg studied the actual behavior of CEOs and found that they spend most of their time doing three things:

1. Developing interpersonal relationships
2. Exchanging and helping others exchange information
3. Making and helping others make decisions

Each of these tasks requires a CEO to fill a number of different roles.

As a developer of interpersonal relationships, a CEO must be

1. *Figurehead*: Filling the symbolic role of ribbon cutter
2. *Leader*: Filling the role of final decision maker
3. *Liaison*: Helping others interact

As an exchanger of information, a CEO must be:

1. *Monitor*: Seeking out and sifting through information
2. *Disseminator*: Spreading information to those that need it
3. *Spokesperson*: Speaking for the organization to the outside

As a decision maker, the CEO must be:

1. *Entrepreneur*: Taking responsibility for and creating change
2. *Disturbance handler*: Dealing with problems
3. *Negotiator*: Negotiating with groups to achieve desired goals

Further reading: H. Mintzberg, *The Nature of Managerial Work* (Englewood Cliffs, N.J.: Prentice-Hall, 1980).

In some high-technology firms, the suits have been replaced by shorts, and a new feeling pervades the entire organization. Everyone wears shorts to work in the summer, from the CEO on down, and everyone sees that this is the case. Suits are still fine for board meetings and funerals. Otherwise, even the CEO wears casual clothes. People who sit in front of computer terminals all day don't need to wear a suit and tie, or high heels, or a tight dress, or any of the other trappings of high fashion.

Some organizations produce expensive products that many of the workers cannot afford. That provides a bad symbol and reminds us of the days when workers slaved in sweatshops for the right to subsist one more day. In most cases, given wholesale costs and the cost of transportation, it should be possible to allow every worker, from the lowest to the highest, to own the product. In fact, that could become a symbol for an advertising campaign: "We build them so good that we use them ourselves" or "We buy them ourselves so we have to build them good; we wouldn't want to end up with a lemon." Blue Bell Ice Cream tells the world, "We eat all we can and we sell the rest." There was a time when you could go to the parking lot of any American automaker and see a large selection of Japanese cars. There was no better symbol of the faith the people who built American cars had in their own product. That kind of symbol works on everyone at a subconscious level. As people came to work every day, they could think to themselves: "Hey, we make junk that is so bad we wouldn't even drive it ourselves."

Calling people associates instead of employees is a small thing, but it seems to fit into the basic empowerment philosophy, and it symbolizes the change in attitude that everyone in management is supposed to be undergoing. Associates are people who deserve respect. In a university, "associate professors" have demonstrated that they can teach, publish, and fulfill the other duties of a university professor. They are no longer assistants, they are associates. In a university, they may eventually become full professors. This kind of language, and the symbols that go with it, can be put to good use by other organizations. People can go from assistant, to associate, to fully cross-trained and ready to teach others. These kinds of terms and stages work well if an organization is trying to compensate people for who they are and what they know rather than for the particular job they may be doing on any given day. A "full" might be teaching a new person one day and doing a dirty job the next. He or she can do this because of the symbols that the organization has used to encourage its people to put themselves where they are most needed at any given moment in time.

What could symbolize a participatory style of management better than a CEO taking time out to ride a plane (if the company is an airline) or walk through the plant or do whatever it takes to get close to the "associates" and find out what is on their minds? The CEO might also talk to some customers while he or she was at it. Any organization has to serve customers if it wants to succeed over the long term. Every organization has to encourage all the employees to get close to and communicate with customers. In fact, that should be something that sets a team-based organization apart from many other organizations. What could be more symbolic than to see the CEO getting up close and personal with the customers? What a wonderful symbol it would have made if Lee Iacocca had made a commercial in which he rode around with someone who had just bought a new Chrysler and asked what the customer liked and didn't like about the new car.

CEOs need a larger office. Do they really need one the size of a football field? Top executives need assistants. Do they really need an army of secretaries and receptionists? If everyone is looking for ways to cut costs, shouldn't the top executives be expected to find costs that can be cut in what they do every day? If people are being laid off, shouldn't top executives forgo their usual bonus? The giving of large bonuses to executives while workers are being laid off is perhaps the worst signal any company could send. If we are all equal, how come some are more equal than others? It would be much more in line with the principles of participatory management if executives took a cut in pay, even if it was small and symbolic.

Nothing sends a stronger positive signal than for the workers to see themselves and their fellow workers in a television commercial for the product they produce. A commercial in which employees talk about why they think their product is better than the competition is both convincing to the customer and convincing to the workers themselves. Research suggests that the best way to get people to have an attitude is to get them to express that attitude. If people are put in a situation in which they have to say "I like Ike" often enough, they will actually start to like Ike. The same goes with products and services. If employees are given a chance to express their positive attitude about the product or service, they will come to have a positive attitude. If people say that "quality is job one" often enough, they will come to believe it. If they see their fellow workers saying it in television commercials, they will have that attitude reinforced.

While some people think of the use of symbols as simply a way to manipulate people, they are a powerful part of what enters our subconscious. If employees are allowed to paint their work area whatever color they want, this becomes a symbol of the kind of freedom employees have in the organization. When it came time for Ricardo Semler, the president of Semco in Brazil, to pick the site for a new factory, he turned the decision over to the employees who would be working in the new factory. As he describes in his book *Maverick*, they came up with a decision that he did not personally like, but he went along with it. Once the new factory was built, it stood as a symbol of the company's commitment to participatory management.

Many of the things that have been discussed up to this point can also double as symbols. The monthly employee newsletter is both a means of communication and a symbol of the company philosophy. An employee representative on the board of directors is both a way to bring more democracy to the organization and a symbol of the company's commitment to empowerment. Whereas special parking places for top executives stand as a symbol of separate and not equal, the lack of such special parking places is a symbol of the desire to be more equal. Whereas executive washrooms are a symbol of elitism, the lack of special facilities for executives is a symbol of the desire to treat everyone as an equal contributor to the company's long-term success.

Suggestion programs can provide a set of very important symbols. If the program provides real rewards, then those rewards may become symbols of what comes from going that extra mile and making a suggestion. That is why suggestion programs should reward both the individual who makes the suggestion and the facility where he or she works. If all the employees can watch the new color television in the employee lounge because one of them made a good suggestion, that television becomes a symbol of the company's desire to reward good suggestions. Concrete changes made as a result of employee suggestions become symbols of the concern with employee ideas.

Companies that introduce some type of employee ownership can put a sign over the entrance that tells everyone it is the "owners' entrance" and change the name of the human resources department to the "owners' resources department." They can also make a point of employee ownership in commercials. Weirton Steel Corporation, an employee-owned steel company in West Virginia, runs advertisements in magazines that point out that Weirton has 7,952 quality control experts, 7,952 delivery expediters, and 7,952 sales representatives because all 7,952 of its employees are also owners. Companies that introduce some kind of employee ownership and do not make use of these kinds of symbols are not getting the full benefit of sharing ownership.

The fact that everyone wears casual clothes or uniforms is a symbol of equality, just as ties and suits were a symbol of inequality. Having everyone eating in the same cafeteria and going to the same bathrooms is also a symbol of the company's desire to treat everyone as a person. The way the lowest-paid employee is treated when it comes to benefits is also a powerful symbol of how the organization intends to operate.

Of course, having symbols without substance is a waste of time and money. While a homeowner may be able to get away with placing a sign on a window that says there is a burglar alarm, a company that says it wants empowerment and does nothing but add a few symbols is probably going to do more harm than good. If employees come to learn that the company is not worthy of trust, they will act accordingly. Just as team-based companies need to trust employees, employees must be able to trust the company. If they cannot, there is no point in trying to introduce employee participation.

Symbols and signs that reinforce the team philosophy are often overlooked by companies that are trying to move in the direction of more employee participation. That is a mistake. A few symbols that emphasize the new direction of the company can go a long way to convince everyone that real changes are in the works.

Characteristics of Participatory Organizations

1. They use symbols to reinforce participation.
2. They have commercials that emphasize average workers.
3. They use signs that emphasize the importance of employees.
4. They get the most out of every substantive change by combining it with symbols.

Chapter 9

Institutionalizing Participation

A new CEO can do a lot to bring participatory management to any organization. The real trick is to institutionalize it so that when another CEO comes along, there will be a structure that forces him or her to continue it. In fact, the first real test of whether or not an organization can sustain participatory management comes when there is a change at the top. If employee empowerment has really become a part of the culture, then changes at the top should make no difference. If it has not, then changes at the top can mark the end of a noble, but failed, experiment.

The first major institutional change is in the human resources department. The HR department and the HR director are the key to beginning to institutionalize participation. The HR department will spend more time and money on training than was formerly the case. New employee training in team-based organizations will include training in how to function in a participatory environment, how to perform in a team structure, and how to both receive the additional information that will be forthcoming and provide more information to decision makers at all levels. Once this training has become institutionalized and internalized by the HR department, it will be much more difficult for the company to abandon the participatory management philosophy.

The HR department will become used to surveying employee opinions about issues such as holidays and other personnel policies. An organization with empowered employees should have an annual survey that every employee at every level participates in, and employees will come to expect the annual survey of their opinion. Making a companywide opinion survey of all employees an annual event will help to institutionalize the practice. Once the survey process has been set up, it can be used to do random-sample surveys from time to time on any issue on which the top executives wish to have employee input. Just as a nation with 240 million people can get a pretty good idea of what those millions of people are thinking by talking to about a thousand people, so a large corporation can make use of random survey techniques to get feedback from employees on everything from the state of customer complaints to employee opinions concerning how a new process or procedure is working for them in their work environment. The more executives and everyone in the organization come to expect survey data to be a part of any major decision, the more everyone will come to accept participatory management as a part of the institutional landscape.

Likert's Organizational Systems

Rensis Likert's research suggests that there are four basic types of organizations:

1. *System one (Exploitative-Authoritative).* A system one organization uses authoritative management styles in an attempt to exploit workers. In system one organizations, managers do not trust workers. The organization is used to control people and limit communication. Employees become suspicious, resist organizational change, and develop informal systems of communication.
2. *System two (Benevolent-Authoritative).* A system two organization is run like a system one organization, but with a more paternalistic attitude toward employees. Employees are still suspicious and still resist organizational change.
3. *System three (Consultative).* A system three organization has a strict hierarchy of decision making, but employees are allowed to provide input into higher-level decision making. Employees feel more involved in the organization.
4. *System four (Participative).* A system four organization uses participative management techniques. Managers trust their employees and allow them to be involved in decision making. Communication is encouraged to travel both up and down the organization. Employees are given the power to make real changes in their work environment.

Further reading: Rensis Likert, *The Human Organization* (New York: McGraw-Hill, 1967).

The HR department should also be holding an annual employee suggestion contest. If the suggestion program is an annual contest of some kind, it will become part of the institutional process. Everyone from the top to the bottom should come to look forward to the fun and excitement of the suggestion contest. It should be a time for meeting new people from other areas of the company and exchanging ideas. Again, new employee training should include training in how the annual suggestion contest works and what will be expected of them when the time comes. An annual suggestion contest works better than a simple suggestion box because it becomes a part of the institutional process. Many organizations have a suggestion box, and nothing ever comes of it. An organization that really cares about employee ideas has to spend a significant amount of time and money asking for those ideas.

The HR department should also have people who do nothing but help teams be better teams. In a large organization, the need to continually provide support for team structures can be significant. Every team has some problems with the team structure and will need some kind of help maintaining the team and keeping it performing at maximum efficiency and effectiveness. Doctors do not take out their own appendixes, and teams cannot minister to their internal group dynamics problems. A large organization can afford to have people in the HR department who specialize in performing this function. Smaller organizations might have an ongoing relationship with a consultant who performs the same function.

Annual retreats should also be a feature of any team-based organization. In a small organization, everyone should participate in the retreat. In a large organization, there may be retreats at different levels to deal with different long-term problems. At least once a year, the members of the board of directors should have to spend a few days with the top executives and a randomly selected group of employees to discuss where the company has been and where it wants to go. Many companies try to function without a company philosophy. A team-based company cannot really function without such a philosophy or statement of goals and values, and examining this philosophy should be a part of the annual board of directors' retreat.

The company that plays together stays together. Company sports teams should be a part of every team-based company. If a company wishes to emphasize teamwork, then it should encourage people to be part of teams both at work and away from work. Uniforms may cost a little, but it will be an investment worth making. Support for company teams will become part of the institutional structure and reinforce the team philosophy. A company may also wish to have a company charity or to adopt a local public school. This will allow the employees to work together away from work. This will reinforce both formal channels of communication and the informal channels that are so important to a team-based organization. Participation in these activities by top executives is very important. It allows everyone in the organization to see and interact with top executives in a common activity where everyone is on an equal footing. Employees will be more willing to provide input to top executives and listen to orders from them if they had a chance to know those executives in an informal setting, away from work.

Creating institutional programs that facilitate contact between the top executives and the rank-and-file employees is important. In an organization with a lot of locations, this might mean a regular, annual visit from one of the top executives, during which the employees can get to know the person and talk to him or her about anything and everything. When Publix Super Markets in Florida opens a new store (it has over 250), all the top executives attend a banquet for the new employees before the opening. They make a point of wanting to hear from these new employees now that they are part of the Publix team. Then, when the new store opens, the top executives are right there working beside the new employees, doing everything from stacking shelves to bagging groceries. This sends an institutional message that everyone values the work done by the organization and that every job is important, from the simplest to the most complex.

Regular institutional forms of communication are also important. The monthly or biweekly newsletter with everything from birth announcements to a letter from the CEO and answers to letters from employees by top executives helps to institutionalize the kind of communication that a team-based organization needs in order to be a success. While setting up a newsletter will cost something (less now that small computers are readily available), it is money well spent. If a large organization wants everyone to feel like part of a big family, then everyone has to know what the members of the family are doing.

The way employees are disciplined and discharged is another important part of the institutional structure. When Robert Owen set out to change the way employees were dealt with at the giant cotton-spinning mill he ran in New Lanark, Scotland, in the early 1800s, one of the major changes he made was to allow employees to appeal managers' decisions in these areas to him. This was a major innovation, and it helps explain why the employees believed Robert Owen when he told them he was serious about a new style of management. Having some kind of peer review or executive review of management decisions in this area creates an institutional procedure that everyone becomes used to. Even common criminals have a right of appeal; why shouldn't employees have the same right? The right to some kind of hearing before discharge may cost something in time and money, but it will provide a major payback in terms of employee relations. Once the idea that everyone has a right to a fair hearing before being dismissed sinks in and becomes a part of the institutional landscape, everyone will begin to think differently about how people should be treated. Managers do not make snap judgments if they know those judgments are going to be reviewed.

Providing financial information to employees so that they can see if the big team is winning the game is another important part of the institutional structure of a team-based organization. Once the organization prepares an annual report to the employees, the idea that employees are entitled to know the score will become institutionalized. The annual report to the employees might contain the results of the annual retreats along with the basic financial statements. The employees' annual report might have more detail than the stockholders' annual report because it might break out information for the different profit centers so that everyone can see how their mid-level team is doing as well. A letter from the CEO to the employees in an employees' annual report might discuss very different issues from the CEO's letter to the stockholders in the stockholders' annual report.

Setting up profit-sharing and employee ownership programs also helps to institutionalize participation by employees. Once the organization sets up a system to share profits every year or to share ownership, that will become a part of the institutional structure. At the end of every year, employees will find out how many shares their fellow employees have acquired or how much of the profits have been shared with the employees. Once an organization begins to treat employees like owners and partners at a financial level, it is easier to do so at other levels.

An annual employee awards banquet is another idea. Marion Laboratories holds quarterly meetings with employees that are called Move meetings. At these meetings, individual employees are given stock in the company to reward them for such things as perfect attendance or winning suggestions. Providing rewards at an annual or quarterly banquet makes this a part of the regular routine of the organization. Pitney Bowes holds annual employee meetings with groups of two to three hundred employees that are structured much like a stockholders' annual meeting. At these meetings, the employees receive the annual employee report and hear from top executives. Any employee can ask any question of top management, just as a stockholder can at a stockholders' meeting.

Allowing employees to control their immediate work environment, within reasonable limits, also can become a part of the institutional structure. Once every workspace is unique and people are allowed to set their workspace up in a way that makes them feel comfortable, it is usually impossible to go back to the old army way of painting everything the same color and making every workspace look like every other workspace. At a warehouse facility, the coming of participation might be marked by something as simple as allowing the employees to vote at the beginning of every week on what radio station the radio will be tuned to for the week. That simple employee decision, made at a short meeting held every Monday to kick off the week and make announcements, sends the important message that employees are adults and are entitled to control their own work environment.

Stress is the major enemy of many modern workplaces. Any organization can set up institutional ways to help employees avoid or minimize stress. Walt Disney knew how stressful drawing cartoons was, so he instituted a daily exercise break, during which everyone stopped for a few minutes and got together to talk and move around. A daily ritual such as this can form the basis of an institutional program that emphasizes prevention rather than illness, and wellness rather than sickness. Having a program that pairs any sick or injured worker with another worker who is responsible for checking to see if there is anything the company can do to speed the recovery of the sick or injured worker can help morale and actually speed recovery. No one likes to feel forgotten when he or she is sick or hurt. While some people think the informal social system should take care of this, institutionalizing a "wellness partner" program can help a lot to emphasize the organization's commitment to the well-being of all employees.

Every organization should have an employee handbook that every new employee receives. For participatory organizations, this handbook will be longer and should contain a basic explanation of what participatory management is and how the organization is trying to live up to its principles. Every section of a team-based organization's employee handbook will be longer and contain more detail. In a sense, the employee handbook will let the new employee in on all the secrets that are kept hidden in other organizations. Employees who read the handbook will feel that they are being introduced to an organization where their efforts and ideas really count for something. They will learn about the profit-sharing or employee ownership program. They will learn that they have rights, such as the right to appeal a discipline or discharge decision. They will read about the wellness partner program and the annual retreats. They will be introduced to every aspect of the participatory management philosophy and the way it has been structured at this particular organization.

A team-based organization should have policies that communicate that the organization recognizes that every person is different. This means allowing people to set their own work schedules if that is possible or allowing for flexibility concerning working hours and holidays. There might even be a bill of rights for employees that guarantees that they will not be punished for bringing bad news or for demanding that the proper company procedure be followed.

The point is that a participatory organization has to do more than just say that the organization is committed to participation. Participation has to be institutionalized at every level in every way possible in order to convince people that the organization is serious about employee empowerment. Rules, structures, and handbooks are necessary if participatory management is going to make the kind of contribution it can make to any organization.

Ways to Institutionalize Participation

1. Change the human resources department to reflect the new philosophy.
2. Institute training in empowerment and teamwork.
3. Have an annual employee survey and random surveys of employee opinion when necessary.
4. Have an annual employee suggestion contest.
5. Have an annual retreat for everyone.
6. Have company sports teams and a company charity.
7. Have a monthly or biweekly employee newsletter.
8. Have an annual employee report and employee meetings.
9. Set up profit sharing and employee ownership.
10. Have an extensive employee handbook that explains how the organization intends to make use of participatory management.
11. Provide due process rights to employees before they are discharged or disciplined.
12. Allow employees to control their immediate work environment.
13. Institute wellness programs that emphasize employees looking out for employees.
14. Have personnel policies that fit with the theme of participation and empowerment.
15. Give employees rights to go along with their duties.

Chapter 10

Knowing the Difference

What is the difference between a regular company and a company that uses participatory management? Can we be specific enough about what we expect to find at a team-based company to produce a checklist and a rating system? That is the idea behind this chapter. Given everything that has been said in the first nine chapters, what sort of list of questions can we use to give any organization an empowerment rating?

The first and most important characteristic of a participatorily managed organization is the basic way the workers are treated. In his best-selling book *Working,* Studs Terkel gives us the results of interviews he conducted with over a hundred people about their experiences at work. These working people tell stories of a life filled with daily humiliations. They describe adult workers being treated in ways that no ten-year-old should have to put with. Kurt Lewin proved in the 1930s that even ten-year-old boys will respond positively to being treated like adults and negatively to being treated like children.

The key to treating people like adults is to trust them to make decisions that affect their working life. Giving people the power to control some of the basic characteristics of their work environment, empowerment, is the most important characteristic of an organization that hopes to reap the benefits of participatory management. Giving working people power is not as easy as it seems. In most organizations it means changing the basic structure of decision making and the fundamental nature of the organizational culture.

Once the change has been made, life is usually easier for top executives. They no longer have the entire weight of decision making on their shoulders. They can delegate decisions to the appropriate person or group in the organization. Their function becomes one of delegating decisions

Toward Adult Behavior

Chris Argyris has argued that large organizations have a tendency to treat people like children rather than like adults. He believes that as people go from being children to being adults, they go

1. From passivity to activity and increased initiative
2. From few ways of behaving to many ways of behaving
3. From dependency to independence
4. From shallow interests to deep interests
5. From a short time focus to a long time focus
6. From subordinate relationships to equal or superordinate relationships
7. From lack of self-awareness to self-awareness

Organizations that treat people like children will receive childlike behavior as a result. Only organizations that treat people like adults can expect to have employees who act like adults.

Further reading: Chris Argyris, *Personality and Organization* (New York: Harper Brothers, 1957).

and making sure that the people making the decisions have all the information and tools they need to make the best decision. Top executives have to learn to delegate decisions, review decisions, facilitate decisions, and support lower-level decision making. This is often more work than making the decision, but it is very different work.

Trust is the other side of the empowerment coin. An organization that intends to give employees more power has to be able to trust those employees. This means hiring employees that are worthy of trust and providing them with the training they need if they are to come up to expectations. People cannot be trusted to make major decisions if they do not have the basic knowledge necessary to make such decisions. They also have to be provided with information, or given the power to gather information, that will allow them to make the right decision.

Whether or not an organization has given its employees power is usually easy to spot. If there is a small group of executives making most major decisions at the top, then the organization is not a participatory organization.

1. The first major characteristic of a participatory organization is that the employees have been given the power to make, and are trusted to make, decisions that have a major impact on their work life.

The second thing a real participatory organization should excel at is communication. Every organization has communication flowing up and down the hierarchy. A participatory organization has a significantly greater amount of information flowing. This should be one of the major advantages of such an organization. However, real communication takes time and costs money. Employees have to be told things that most employees in most organizations would never be told, and top executives must be seen to receive information from lower-level employees that top executives in most organizations would usually not be privy to.

This communication should be very visible. There should be a variety of institutional forms of communication, from newsletters and group meetings to informal chances for people from all levels of the organization to meet and interact. The open door is not necessarily a sign that communication is taking place. The question is: Has anyone walked through the door with some useful information lately?

Employees in a real team-based organization will know things about their own work and the entire organization that most employees would never know. They will know a great deal about the financial health of the entire organization and their small part of the organization. They will know a lot about the quality and quantity of the output of their team and their group. They will know from routine communication how close they are to hitting the quality and quantity targets.

Most important, employees in a team-based organization will have a variety of ways to communicate their ideas and opinions to others in the organizations. We would expect to find random groups of employees called together to discuss anything and everything. We would expect surveys of employee opinion. We would expect a real suggestion program that has achieved real results. The real test of a participatory organization is the extent to which information developed in one section has been shared with other sections that could make use of the same information.

2. The second major characteristic of a participatory organization is a high level of communication among all levels and sections of the organization.

The third aspect of a participatory organization is the way people interact with one another on a daily basis. Attitude is often more important than any other factor. People working in a participatory organization should be having fun. Employees should generally be glad to see a manager or executive because most of the time that manager or executive should be bringing them information they need or helping them to perform their job better. Most interactions between people should be friendly and positive.

As a general rule, a team-based organization spends more energy catching people doing something right than trying to find them doing something wrong. The way mistakes are handled is a key characteristic of a participatory organization. Mistakes should be seen as a chance for everyone to learn, not as an opportunity to belittle someone and make him or her feel bad. Criticism should be constructive and positive and should deal with the specifics of the problem at hand. It should not be mean-spirited or personal. It should lead to real improvement and positive change. Arguments should be over how to improve the situation, not over who to blame for the mistake. Discussion should focus on what can be learned from a mistake, not on whether or not it was a mistake.

3. The third major characteristic of a participatory organization is the positive attitude everyone has about himself or herself, their work, and fellow workers.

Organizations that intend to make use of participation should appear to be an ever-larger conglomeration of teams. Teams have many advantages. A participatory organization should be using teams to the fullest advantage. People on real teams know the score every minute of the game and are trying to improve it. People on real teams have a real impact on the team's efforts and are trained to perform in a team setting. Teams have leaders that are either chosen by the team or would have been chosen by the team if the team had been allowed to choose. In a team-based organization, someone who cannot function in a team is sent on his or her way. The brilliant star is not allowed to outshine the work of the group.

An organization that is dedicated to teams has people in teams at work and encourages people to participate in team sports outside of work. Teams should exist at all levels, from the executive team at the top to the production or service team at the bottom. While some teams may have players who function alone a great deal of the time, there should still be a team structure. A great swimmer or tennis player can still be on a team.

4. The fourth major characteristic of a participatory organization is the use of teams.

An organization that is dedicated to treating people like adults and allowing them to participate fully in the life of the organization is going to structure rewards very differently from other organizations. While people may still receive a basic salary, there should be very significant efforts to share profits or ownership with the workers.

People who are really playing the game receive some kind of reward if they win the game. People who are not really playing do not receive a reward if the team wins and usually couldn't care less what the outcome of the game is. Rewards and compensation should reinforce the organization's desire to have team players and to encourage everyone to work together. An organization that bases all compensation on individual performance is not a participatory organization.

5. The fifth major characteristic of a participatory organization is the use of profit sharing, employee ownership, and bonuses to reward team and organizational performance.

It is often easy to tell whether or not an organization is really a participatory organization by looking at the executives in the organization. Are they bosses, or are they coaches? Bosses limit information and make decisions on their own. Coaches share information and help others to make decisions. Bosses blame people and take credit for any success. Coaches praise people and give credit where credit is due. Bosses try to micromanage everyone and everything. Coaches provide guidance and set goals. Bosses are rewarded for what they accomplish. Coaches are rewarded for what their team accomplishes.

6. The sixth major characteristic of a participatory organization is that such an organization has a lot of coaches and no bosses.

An organization that is serious about participatory management uses the signs and symbols of participation. People at different levels of the organization should dress alike and eat alike. There should be a lot of associates and no employees. Better yet, there should be a lot of owners and no employees. While people with different skills should receive different salaries, everyone should be eligible for a bonus or profit-sharing. Equality should be emphasized, not inequality.

Another aspect of any organization that is trying to encourage everyone to participate is fairness. A participatory organization treats people fairly. That means listening to the employee's side of the story before making a decision concerning discipline or discharge. That means providing some kind of appeal from discharge decisions that gives employees a real chance to win and be reinstated. Adults should not be subject to the arbitrary whims of anyone.

7. The seventh major characteristic of a participatory organization is that everyone is treated equally and fairly.

The human resources department of an organization that is dedicated to participation will be very different from the human resources department at a "normal" organization. The human resources department at a participatory organization will provide extensive training for new employees on everything from how to do the job to how to function well in a team environment. It will conduct employee surveys and publish an employee newsletter; and it will provide consulting services to teams that need help. The director of the human resources department will be the equal of every other top executive in the organization except for the CEO.

The human resources department of a participatory organization will work to help everyone become familiar with and comfortable with the basic structure of participation. It will conduct suggestion programs and publish an annual employee report. It will conduct annual employee meetings and retreats for everyone in the organization. The human resources department will select employees who are capable of functioning in a participatory environment. Everyone in the organization will recognize and acknowledge the important role the human resources department plays.

8. The eighth major characteristic of a participatory organization is the existence of a human resources department with the authority and resources to hire, train, and facilitate participatory employees.

Some experts have argued that it is difficult to tell whether an organization is really a participatory organization. That is not really true. Anyone interacting with an organization should be able to tell in a few minutes whether it is a participatory organization. It should be as plain as the smiles on the employees' faces.

Part II
Practice

Introduction to Part II

Much has been written on the theory of team-based management, employee empowerment, and participatory management. For many people, there is often a very real gap between theory and practice. One often hears, "OK, what do I do next?" That is a very good question, and of course the answer is different for every organization. It is often particularly difficult for small-business owners to know how to apply what they have read about the practices of large corporations such as Toyota and IBM.

The chapters in Part II of this book are an effort to begin to provide an answer to that question, or, rather, to help people to answer it for themselves. It is often only by looking at what people have done and what the consequences of those actions have been that we begin to see how theory becomes practice. While the chapters that follow are fiction, they are inspired by the real-world problems that organizations face every day.

One thing that any organization should do if it is serious about introducing the principles discussed in this book is to provide some basic training for the employees. For a small business, this may mean having everyone read the same book and then discuss it. Many people find a discussion of principles uninteresting. It is hoped that employees and managers could read this book, particularly the chapters that follow, and discuss the implications these fictional events might have for their own organization.

Each of the chapters in this part is followed by ten questions for thought and discussion. These are intended to provide a framework for group discussion. Each of these stories is intended to illustrate potential problems that any organization might have and how those problems might be dealt with within a framework of participatory management.

They are not intended to teach the "right answer" or to provide specific answers for particular problems.

Some readers may find some humor in some of the stories. This is not intended to suggest that any of the problems presented here are trivial, just that there can be a lighter side to any problem. It is hoped that a group of employees and managers reading and discussing the following chapters would have as much occasion to laugh as to cry.

Chapter 11

The Gary and Glenda Story

Introduction

To what extent can a very small organization take advantage of the principles of participation and empowerment? How can an organization with only half a dozen employees have teams? Those were the issues that faced Gary and Glenda, the owners of the Center for Participation Studies. They decided that such a small organization could not really take advantage of the principles of participation. Their employees believed differently, which led to conflict. Ultimately Gary had a change of heart.

The Gary and Glenda Story

When Wilbur arrived at the Center for Participation Studies in Washington, D.C., he could not have been more excited. He felt as if he had found the Holy Grail. Here, at last, was a center dedicated to spreading the word about participatory management. No longer would he feel as if he were shouting in the desert. Finally he would have people to work with who believed as he did, that the future of America depended upon participation in the workplace. Of course, he did have some misgivings. When he had met the two people who ran the Center, he couldn't help feeling uneasy. It was a husband-and-wife team, Gary and Glenda. Gary wore an old rugby shirt with a hole in the back, while Glenda wore a smart blue suit. The interview turned into a debate between the two of them about how the Center was run and what its major goals were. Still, the Center was what he had been looking for, and he wasn't going to look a gift horse in the mouth.

Gary and Glenda had started the Center on a shoestring several years before, after they had both lost their jobs as management consultants. In the seven years since then, the Center had grown to eight employees, including Gary and Glenda. Gary and Glenda always included themselves as regular employees in every calculation, even though they owned the Center and certainly had every right to consider themselves much more than just employees. Wilbur wondered why they didn't use a term such as associate for everyone, but they didn't. Everyone was an employee, including the owners.

When Wilbur first saw the office setup, he was a little uneasy. Instead of individual offices, there was just one big room with metal tables for desks. Against the one wall that had no windows there were two tables with three personal computers and a printer. The room occupied half a floor of an old office building. Gary had his "nest" in one corner, and Glenda had taken over the other corner. The other six work areas were spread around against the three walls that had windows. Gary had his own personal computer and printer as part of his work area. This meant that he could call up information from the various databases without leaving his desk. The other employees, when talking to people who called asking for information, had to take their phone and move to one of the computers in the middle of the room in order to access information. The phones had very long cords to make this possible. Wilbur wondered why there wasn't a computer at every desk, but he didn't want to make waves by asking too many questions the first few days.

The other five employees were an interesting group. Mary, the office manager, was small, with short, brown hair. Like many people, she had moved to Washington, D.C., looking for a change in her life after her divorce. She ended up at the Center when a friend told her they needed someone to manage the office. Sandra was right out of business school. She was tall and lean, with long, dark hair. She was a true believer. One of her professors had preached participatory management, and she felt as if she had found a new religion. The professor was a friend of Gary and Glenda's and had recommended her for the job. Robert had started as a summer intern while a philosophy student at a university in the Washington, D.C., area. When he graduated, he simply gravitated to the Center. Linda was the resident computer genius and a lesbian. She wore men's clothes and at first it was difficult to tell which sex she was. She maintained the computers and updated the database information. Dawn, small and blond, was the real dynamo of the place. She was involved in every project, and her energy and enthusiasm were contagious.

Wilbur, as the new guy, got the metal table next to Gary. This was supposed to help Wilbur learn the ropes by being able to watch Gary, but Wilbur felt like he was the one being watched most of the time. That first morning was a very strange experience. The operation of the office was not anything like what Wilbur had expected. Instead of laughing and working together, the eight people seemed to work separately on their own individual projects. There was very little communication, and that was carried on in a very low whisper. Of course, since the place was one big room with no room dividers, anyone making much noise would soon disturb the others. After a few minutes, Wilbur felt the tension run up his back and into his brain. He could feel that everyone in this big room was uptight. This seemed strange to him, given that they all were working for something they believed in. The first day all the employees except Gary and Glenda took Wilbur to lunch. It seemed that Gary always brought his lunch from home and Glenda always spent her lunch hour shopping, mainly for shoes. The group went a few blocks to a small restaurant that had become the regular lunchtime spot for the Center's employees. Everyone ordered their usual, and the waitress brought iced tea for everyone without asking. Linda was the first to speak.

"What'd you think of the setup? Not what you had expected, I'll bet."

"What do you mean?" Wilbur asked.

"Oh, come on. The last thing you expected to find at the Center for Participation Studies was a group of uptight people sitting at their little metal tables whispering and walking on tiptoe around the office." Linda seemed exasperated.

"Hey, leave him alone. He only arrived this morning," Sandra shot back. "We should let him spend a day before we start pouring our problems down his throat."

"If we let him stay here a whole day without clueing him in, he'll go crazy," Robert replied.

"I think we should let him have a few days to make up his own mind," Dawn said. "Maybe we're the ones who have gone crazy."

Wilbur felt like a football being tossed around from one to another without a chance to get a word in. Finally he cut in. "Make up my own mind about what?"

"This place, of course," Linda answered.

"What about this place?" Wilbur asked.

"Oh, come on. I watched you looking around," Linda said. "What did you expect? Be honest. Did you expect that everyone would tiptoe around and whisper to each other? Did you expect that everyone would be working alone on individual projects with almost no communication except when we get out of the office? Did you expect that Gary would have a computer at his desk, but the rest of us would have to use the pool of computers against the wall, even though it makes us much more inefficient?"

"So, Gary's cheap," Robert jumped in. "He learned to be cheap when the Center was running on a shoestring, and old habits die hard."

"He was born cheap," Linda responded. "He rides his bike to work and brings his own lunch because he's cheap. He won't spend a few thousand dollars for each of us to have our own computer at our desk because he's too cheap, even though we lose so much time waiting to get a machine that they would pay for themselves in no time. And what about the copying problem?"

"What copying problem?" Wilbur asked.

"Each month we ask for some kind of copying machine for the office, and each month Gary says we can't afford it. Of course, in the course of an average day, we make half a dozen trips to the copy shop three blocks from the office for one thing or another," Linda answered.

"But I like that," Dawn said. "It gives me a chance to get out of the tension. Sometimes I just pretend that I need to copy something so that I have an excuse to take a walk and breathe some fresh air."

"Now that you mention it, I have noticed that the tension level seems high. It's as if an invisible layer of tension settled over the office after I arrived. Is it always like that?" Wilbur asked no one in particular.

"Only when Gary is there," Sandra responded. "When he goes away, Glenda plays hooky most of the time and we laugh and sing and have a very good time. But Gary doesn't like any noise. He needs absolute quiet to concentrate on his work."

"If he needs absolute quiet, why doesn't he get himself a private office?" Wilbur asked.

"Oh, that's easy," Robert said. "If he had a private office, he wouldn't be able to keep an eye on everyone. He likes to be able to look around the room and see everyone with their nose to the grindstone. When I first got here, I resented that, but now I just accept it as a fact of life. Gary doesn't trust anyone, including Glenda."

"Especially Glenda," Linda jumped in. "Glenda has turned doing nothing all day into an art form. She shuffles papers, checks everything we write for spelling and punctuation, and looks out her two windows a lot. We each have our own theory about Glenda. Personally I think she was a prostitute when Gary found her and gave her a job."

"My theory is that she started out as a nun but lost her belief in God and then became a chorus girl. Some rich management type took her out of the chorus line and gave her one of those jobs with a big title and no work. Somewhere along the line she married Gary, and she just does what she has always done—nothing, with style and grace," Sandra said.

"No, I think she convinced Gary that she was pregnant, and then after they got married she pretended to have a miscarriage," Robert threw in.

"You're all wrong. I think Glenda is the real brains behind this Center. She doesn't do or say anything during the day, but when they get home, she reports on everyone and everything to Gary. Haven't you noticed that Gary will come to work mad at one of us for something, and it will be something only Glenda could have known anything about?" Dawn added.

"Boy, you make it sound like working in a concentration camp," Wilbur said.

"Oh, you'll see for yourself soon enough. Glenda will probably give you some training this afternoon. Then you'll see," Linda said.

The conversation turned to politics, the pastime of people who live in Washington, D.C., but Wilbur couldn't help but feel uneasy. He had assumed that a center dedicated to teaching people about participatory management would be run on participatory principles. The tension and obvious lack of trust were not what he had expected.

Back at the office, Glenda announced that as the new person, Wilbur would need some training. Anyone who wanted a refresher course on the mail system could of course sit in. No one wanted a refresher course, so that left Glenda and Wilbur on their own. They moved to the mail processing section of the large room. Here there were stacks of books and shelves with various forms. Wilbur learned that the Center made money three ways: by selling publications, by putting on workshops, and by signing up companies and consultants as members of the Center. Member companies got the monthly newsletter and a discount on publications and workshops and could order custom-made workshops. Member consultants got a lot of cheap advertising and participated in the workshops when appropriate. Glenda explained to Wilbur that for every phone conversation and every letter, a form was to be filled out. All forms were placed in the mailroom in-box to be processed after lunch each day. Every day one of five employees would have mailroom duty. Gary, Glenda, and Mary did not do mailroom duty, so Wilbur would be one of the five and have his day of the week to do it. Glenda then proceeded to explain a very complex form that covered everything and a very complex system that involved putting little initials on everything and on the form as each step in a very complex process was completed. Wilbur asked politely if they had thought of using a computer to keep track of all this instead of the form and all the other slips of paper, but Glenda simply said that they didn't trust computers. Wilbur soon figured out that beyond doing a little simple word processing, Glenda didn't know how to use the computers and was unable or unwilling to learn. When she explained that filling an order for a Center publication would take six different pieces of paper, which were placed in six different files, Wilbur burst out laughing.

"Who invented this crazy system?" he couldn't help asking. It was the wrong thing to say. Glenda began to cry. Instantly Gary was out of his chair with a hand on Wilbur's arm. Wilbur found himself out in the hall with Gary and Glenda before he knew what was happening.

"What did you say to her?" Gary asked.

"Nothing; I just asked how the publication system got so messed up," Wilbur answered.

"What's messed up about it?" Gary asked through clenched teeth.

Wilbur realized that these two had created this crazy system and obviously felt personally threatened by any criticism of it. Wilbur tried to recover some balance. "Oh, nothing really. I just thought that perhaps, with a computer, we could keep track of the orders without the need for so much paperwork, that's all."

"He said it was crazy," Glenda added through her tears.

"I don't know how they behaved where you worked before, but we don't call people crazy around here, mister," Gary continued in a way that suggested that if Wilbur didn't do something right away, he was going to get punched in the nose.

"Oh, I didn't mean to say anyone was crazy," Wilbur added quickly. "If I said the wrong thing, I'm sorry. I can see now that before I make any suggestions for changes, I should live with the system for a while."

Glenda stopped crying instantly, as if she could just turn off the tears, and Gary relaxed. "I can handle it, honey," Glenda said to Gary. "You go back to your desk. I'm sure Wilbur and I will get along famously."

As Gary walked back to his desk, Glenda took Wilbur by the arm and led him back to the mail processing area of the big room. Wilbur felt the same way he had felt as a small child when he had been made to see the error of his ways. For the rest of the afternoon, as Glenda trained him, he did not criticize or make suggestions or even ask questions. He just listened and did as he was told. Glenda took obvious pleasure in being the person with all the answers. She liked being the teacher, but more than that, she liked being the boss. You did it her way or she would tell Gary or, worse, burst into tears.

At the end of the first day, Wilbur left a minute after five and Sandra followed him out. As they walked to the nearest subway station, Sandra tried to help.

"I know what you're thinking, but we do a lot of good work at the Center. We've helped a lot of companies discover the advantages of participatory management."

"Look, Sandra, you don't have to be an expert on participatory management to see that the Center for Participatory Studies doesn't practice what it preaches. You have mailroom duty once a week; you know how silly that system of theirs is."

"That's just it, it is their system. They started this Center with nothing, and it's only because of their hard work and financial investment that there is a Center at all. When you go out to do workshops or work with member companies, you'll have a lot of freedom to say and do what you want. When you're at the Center, you have to play by their rules, even though their rules are not very participatory."

"I get it; do as I say, not as I do," Wilbur responded.

"Is that so unusual?" Sandra asked.

"Well, I didn't expect to find it in this context, that's all. I guess I thought that a center dedicated to participatory management would actually be run along participatory principles."

"You'll see that it just doesn't work that way. I've used the things that happen at the Center to advantage when doing workshops. When I want to discuss what not to do, I only have to explain some process at the Center. Wait until Friday."

"What happens Friday?" Wilbur asked.

"The last Friday of every month is suggestion day. During the usual Friday staff meeting, we go through the suggestion cards in the suggestion box. I think you'll find the process interesting."

"I can't wait," Wilbur said as he headed down for his train. Sandra waited on the other side of the station. Wilbur wondered what the next day would bring.

The next day, Tuesday, was very different in many ways. First of all, Gary showed up in a suit and looked a lot like a normal business type. Wilbur learned that Gary never wore a suit unless he had to, and then only for as long as he had to. He had on a suit that day because he would be spending most of the day with some potential new members. Wilbur arrived a few minutes after nine o'clock and Gary took him aside.

"Look, we all arrive before nine and stay at least until five. For every minute used on lunch, you have to stay an extra minute unless you bring your lunch and eat it at your desk," Gary explained.

Wilbur made the mistake of asking where the time clock was. This resulted in a long stare from Gary, who then looked at his watch and left. The minute Gary left the room, it was as if a great weight had been lifted from everyone. The change was most noticeable in Glenda. She took out a pair of ballet shoes from the bottom drawer of her desk. Glenda had a real desk, while everyone else, including Gary, had metal tables for desks. She put on her ballet shoes and began to dance around the middle of the room. Various members of the staff complimented her on how well she was doing. Wilbur could hardly wait for lunch to find out about this.

Lunch was at the usual place, at the usual time, with everyone sitting at what was clearly the usual table.

"OK, what's the deal with the ballet dance this morning?" Wilbur asked even before the usual iced tea had a chance to arrive in its usual way.

Mary, the shy office manager, spoke up. "Glenda is taking dancing lessons, tap and ballet, at the community college near where she lives. When Gary leaves, she invariably puts on either her ballet or tap shoes and gives us all a recital."

"I see," Wilbur responded, trying not to say what he was thinking, which was that he had fallen into a nuthouse.

"Glenda does many of the things she does because she's not a very happy person," Mary continued. "I think she married Gary because she figured no one else would marry her, and I don't think she likes him very much."

"I see; so I've come to work for a husband-and-wife team where the wife is not happy and the husband is a nut," Wilbur said to no one in particular.

"We don't use the word *nut* around the Center," Dawn jumped in. "We all think Glenda has been in the nuthouse more than once, and we assume that all you have to do to get fired is make some crack about being nuts. The person who had your job before you did just that and was fired on the spot."

"I did a little study when I first arrived," Mary joined in. "It seems that the average employee only lasts three months at the Center. Of course there are exceptions, like Robert and Dawn, who have both been here more than a year, but on average I think three months is about it."

The group kept talking, but Wilbur sank into thought. Glenda was not happy. Obviously, if you added to her unhappiness in any way, she would turn on the tears and Gary would come down on you. Gary was a not very communicative fellow who found himself running a center for participatory management. While he might have liked to be more participatory, he was trapped by his own personality. Are participatory managers born or made? Perhaps the answer was that there is a limit to how much you can make out of some people.

Over the course of the week, Wilbur tried to interact with Gary. Gary seemed to love to talk on the phone, but he did not like to talk to people in person. Also, Gary loved to work at his computer screen. When people came up to Gary to talk to him, he would continue to stare at his computer screen while talking to them. Wilbur found this to be the most maddening thing about Gary. He never looked you in the eye, and he never really seemed to care much about what others were saying. He was clearly very uncomfortable around people. He might have been perfect as a watch-maker or at some other job that required long hours of concentration without having to deal with people. Gary was not a people person. Glenda was more of a people person, but she was so insecure about her own knowledge and abilities that anything and everything threatened her.

That first week Wilbur became fascinated by the way everyone worked with Glenda. Glenda had the final say about everything, from the color of a brochure to the spelling of a word. Everything that went out of the Center had to have her final approval, even a form letter to a potential new member. This gave Glenda a lot to do, and it allowed her to feel powerful. At the same time, it made a tremendous amount of work for everyone else. Since everything had to go through Glenda, people often had to make several trips to her desk or to the copy shop. For example, Sandra was preparing a brochure to announce a new publication. She walked to the copy shop and got a sample of the six colors available that day. She then walked back and showed them to Glenda. Glenda took a while and eventually decided on gold. Sandra then showed Glenda the final version of the brochure. Glenda had already seen several drafts and had made changes in every draft. In some cases Glenda would change things and then change them back in the course of this review process. The joke was that if you wanted a particular result, if you ran the draft by Glenda enough times, you would eventually get what you wanted. All this meant that it took Sandra twice as long to get the brochure ready for the copy shop that did most of the Center's printing.

The Friday afternoon staff meeting rolled around, and Wilbur could hardly wait. A week before he had imagined what a really participatory staff meeting might look like. Now he knew that he was not going to see a really participatory staff meeting. The employees brought their desk chairs into a circle in the middle of the room. The routine was that each employee told what he or she had done during the week and what he or she planned to do in the coming week. Most people could point to progress on writing a publication or preparing a workshop. Mary simply reported on the kinds of supplies she had ordered, and Glenda couldn't say much except that she did her usual thing. Then Dawn took the notecards out of the suggestion box and read them to Gary. There was no group discussion. For each suggestion, Gary explained why it would not be possible. In some cases he pointed out that the idea had been tried before and failed. In others he simply rejected the idea as not fitting in with the philosophy of the Center. Wilbur began to wonder what the philosophy of the Center was, but of course he knew better than to ask a question like that. There was no group discussion, just a dialogue between Dawn and Gary. Glenda stared off into space, and Mary worked on something in her lap.

The next week Wilbur was introduced to the workshop preparation routine. Gary, Glenda, Sandra, Dawn, and Wilbur would present workshops. Mary, Robert, and Linda were not asked to participate in this for one reason or another. The five workshop presenters had a special meeting in the middle of the room on the next Monday afternoon. The main purpose of the meeting was to help Wilbur learn about the process. The main workshops were given in the spring and fall, with a variety of special workshops in the summer. Gary had learned that people did not sign up for workshops in the winter, but the winter was a good time to prepare. There were twenty workshops in twenty cities planned for the coming spring. Gary picked the four cities he wanted to do workshops in, and Glenda did the same thing. Then the other people picked their workshops in order of seniority. Wilbur was stuck with the four that were left. These four cities were in four very different regions of the country. Wilbur pointed out that it would make more sense economically for each person to take a region instead of flying great distances, but Gary explained that the Center had so many frequent flyer miles that it didn't make much difference. He felt that people should be able to go where they wanted to go. Of course, by people, he meant himself and Glenda. Everyone else got the leftovers.

Putting together a workshop involved many different steps. Hotels had to be contacted to see which would offer the best deal. The management consultants in that region who belonged to the Center were contacted to see if they wanted to join in the workshop. Potential members had to be contacted and personally invited to the workshop in their area. Wilbur found it strange that each of the five workshop people worked alone on his or her four workshops. He couldn't help wondering whether the work would not have been easier and faster if one person had dealt with hotels, another with consultants, another with potential members, and so on, but he knew better than to suggest a major change in the way workshops were prepared.

Wilbur did ask about expenses on the trip. There was a schedule for food. People were allowed six dollars for breakfast, eight dollars for lunch, and ten dollars for dinner. At the next staff meeting, Wilbur asked if this could be changed to twenty-four dollars a day for food. Gary exploded.

"What's wrong with the way we already do it?" Gary asked.

"Well, I know how it is on the road," Wilbur answered. "Sometimes you have to skip a meal, and in these big hotels you are not going to find a ten-dollar dinner. I would just like the flexibility to be able to skip lunch and then have dinner in the hotel instead of having to wander around a strange city at night trying to find a cheap meal."

"How much do you think you'll need to spend on dinner?" Gary asked in a sarcastic tone.

"Well, in my experience," Wilbur said, trying to stay calm, "dinner at a large downtown hotel might run fifteen or twenty dollars with tip. I'm not saying I would always spend that much, but I'd like to be able to do just that without having to make up the difference out of my own pocket. After all, when the Center spends money on this kind of stuff, it's a tax deduction."

"Oh, I see; if it's something we can deduct, the Center should pay, no matter how much it costs," Gary said, yelling at the top of his lungs. "I'll have you know that when I give workshops, I take carrots and sandwiches and never spend more than ten dollars a day for food bought on the road. What do you think of that?"

Wilbur thought about actually telling Gary what he thought about that, but Sandra gave him a nudge in the side with her elbow and a wink that said, "cool it." Wilbur decided that he could live with the food expense plan as currently written.

"It was just an idea, never mind," Wilbur said.

That evening, as Wilbur and Sandra walked to the subway station, Wilbur asked how she could stand it.

"Oh, I just try to put myself in their shoes," Sandra said. "Gary and Glenda failed at a lot of things in their life, and then they created this Center. It's their baby. When you criticize something about it, you're criticizing their child, a child they created piece by piece without a blueprint."

"It seems to me they created a monster," Wilbur said.

"Oh, it may seem that way to you, but you'll get used to it. Wait until you meet some of the people at the member companies. They really live, breathe, and eat participation. It's great to meet them at the workshops and exchange ideas. Most of our publications have grown out of those conversations. Once you get out and away from the Center, you'll see things differently. Everyone will look to you for answers on how to run a participatory company, and you'll have the answers if you've read all our publications."

"Oh, I've read most of them, and I agree with everything they say. What I don't understand is how Gary and Glenda can say what they say in the publications they've written and then do what they do day in and day out." Wilbur was still upset by his latest interaction with Gary.

"I've wondered about that myself, but they just don't seem to make the connection. When it comes to talking participation, they do a good job, as if they have memorized every catch phrase and basic principle. They don't seem to be able to live it in their own lives for some reason."

"I think the reason is insecurity," Wilbur responded. "Gary and Glenda both seem very unsure of themselves. I guess my first lesson from the Center is that people who are not sure of themselves cannot give others the freedom to try and fail. The fear of any kind of failure keeps that from happening."

"Yeah, I think that's a big part of it. Glenda knows her spelling and punctuation. When you want to talk about anything else, she just changes the subject. I think she might be really happy as a proofreader at some publishing firm or something like that. Wait until you see her give a speech in front of a lot of people."

"If she is so bad, why does she do it?" Wilbur asked.

"I think Gary makes her do it. After all she is the co-executive director of the Center for Participation Studies. People expect her to give talks and so on."

"That's another thing," Wilbur said. "They act like this is some kind of nonprofit organization when everyone knows it's a corporation and they own all the stock. Why don't they just make that clear to people?"

"I think they're afraid that if people realized how much money they make at the Center, they would object to all the things Gary and Glenda ask them to do free or at low cost. Gary and Glenda got a lot of mileage out of their poverty in the beginning, and now they want to have their cake and eat it too."

Sandra went toward her train and Wilbur his.

The next week, Wilbur had to get ready for his first set of workshops. He would be in four cities in five days, and he would be flying to every region of the country. Glenda got Atlanta; he got Birmingham. Gary got New York, he got Hartford. Dawn got Los Angeles; he got Phoenix. Sandra got Dallas; he got Oklahoma City. This seemed like such a stupid way to run a business that he couldn't help but fume about it. At the second stop he couldn't find any place to eat dinner except the hotel, so he ordered a real meal and put it on the hotel bill. The meal came to just over twenty dollars. He had not had a chance to spend any money on food that day, and he thought about a system that let him starve and then asked him to pay for half the cost of a real meal out of his own pocket. He pictured Gary with his bag of carrots and sandwiches eating in his hotel room every night. As he did so, he began to hate Gary. He began to hate Gary's rugby shirts and Gary's inability to look people in the eye. He began to hate Gary's assumption that Glenda was always right and everyone else in the Center was always wrong. He didn't hate Glenda. He viewed her as a mental case who should be in an institution somewhere, under medication. Gary was different somehow. Gary was bad or mean or something that deserved to be hated. Wilbur hated him.

The next Monday everyone went to the usual place for lunch and had the usual meal. "I've begun to dream about killing Gary. I don't know what to do about it," Wilbur said.

"Do about it? Why do anything about it? We all have dreams about killing Gary," Linda responded. "Let's compare notes. Recently I find myself imagining that I'm trying to talk to him and he is talking to me and looking at that damn computer terminal of his and all of a sudden I just take his head and smash it right into that computer terminal."

"I always imagine that I'm walking to work and I see Gary fall out of his window to the sidewalk at my feet," Robert joined in. "I see him lying there having fallen twenty flights, and the blood just runs out of every part of his body. What a mess."

"I always imagine that I very calmly take a gun out of my purse and shoot him right between the eyes," Sandra added.

"Yeah, me too," Mary said. "I just shoot him right in the head. There is no blood in the dream, just a nice little hole in his head."

"I always use an ax and just cut up his body while he keeps sitting there looking into his computer screen," Dawn said. "When I have cut off his legs and one arm, he looks up at me and asks in that usual 'how stupid can you get' tone what I think I'm doing. I just tell him I know exactly what I'm doing and cut off the other arm. Then he falls to the floor and bleeds to death."

"So, at least I'm not alone," Wilbur said. "I was beginning to worry."

"No, you're not alone," Linda said. "I began having dreams about killing Gary the first week I came here. I guess one of the reasons I don't just quit is that I keep half expecting to actually see one of us crack and do him in. I don't want to not be here when that happens."

"But why do we hate him so?" Wilbur asked.

"I hate him because if you ask him something, he has this way of putting you down for not knowing the answer," Robert said.

"I hate him because he never looks you in the face," Linda said.

"I hate him for the way he treats Glenda," Mary said.

"Treats Glenda? What do you mean?" Wilbur asked.

"Well, you got to see right away that Glenda does this crying number on him and he just goes crazy. If he stopped doing that, she would have to deal with us as people. Glenda was raised in the South, and she learned to manipulate men with tears and a smile. Gary just encourages her when he jumps to defend her at every moment," Mary said.

"I see; so you hate Gary because he lets Glenda manipulate him," Wilbur responded.

"I guess that sounds strange, but I don't see how women are ever going to progress as long as men like Gary encourage women like Glenda to act the way she acts."

"I hate him because he is so self-righteous about everything he does," Sandra joined in. "He makes such a big deal about the fact that he takes carrots to eat on a workshop trip and makes us all feel guilty that we actually sit down in a restaurant once in a while and have a real meal. It's such a small part of the expense of these trips that I don't see the point, except that it is some kind of power trip for him."

"I thought you were the one who understood this kind of behavior," Wilbur said. "Isn't that what you told me?"

"Oh, yeah, I can understand it in the abstract, but when I was on the road last week, I found myself unable to enjoy any of the food I had bought because all I could think about was how Gary was going to act when I paid the difference between the food allowance and what I spent on a couple of dinners. What a pain."

"Oh, I had a real meal at one hotel. I put it on the hotel bill," Wilbur said.

"You did what?" Sandra asked.

"I put the dinner on the hotel bill."

"Have you filled out a form and given the extra money to Glenda yet?" Sandra asked.

"No, I figured they might not notice," Wilbur responded.

"Oh, brother, did you do the wrong thing," Linda joined in. "I tried that once, and they took me out in the hall and yelled at me for an hour. You would have thought I had stolen the crown jewels. Man, you'd better fill out that form and get it on Glenda's desk with some cash when we get back from lunch or your name will be mud."

"But we're talking about ten bucks. I spent a week on the road, and on one meal I spent an extra ten bucks. They're going to make a federal case out of that?" Wilbur asked.

"Federal case? Brother, you'll wish your only problem was that J. Edgar Hoover was after you before they get through," answered Linda.

Wilbur rushed back from lunch and grabbed a form. He left the form and the cash on Glenda's desk. She was not yet back from her usual shopping. Glenda walked in a minute later and saw the form and the money. She motioned for Wilbur to come over.

"So, they told you I would catch that dinner you charged to the room in Birmingham?" she asked.

"What? Well, they told me what was the proper procedure to follow in cases like this," Wilbur answered.

"Yeah, I bet. Listen, no one gets anything by me. I know what you think of me, I know what they all think of me, but I'm not just a pretty face. I know my stuff. I go over those bills with a fine-tooth comb and nothing gets by me."

Wilbur imagined the hours she must have spent going over everything with a fine-tooth comb in order to catch a dollar here and ten dollars there. Given her salary level, how many thousands of dollars had been spent in order to catch, at most, a hundred dollars of expenses? Wilbur imagined the amount of bad feeling this tactic had caused among the staff. What a waste.

What Wilbur and the other employees did not know was that Gary was sitting two booths down in the corner of the restaurant during lunch that day. He had forgotten to bring his lunch and decided to surprise everyone. Instead, it was he who got the surprise. He had heard them all discussing their dreams of killing him. His first thought was to fire everyone. His second thought was to visit the office of his old friend Bill.

Bill was the best consultant in the country when it came to employee participation. He and Gary had gone to business school together.

"Hey, Gary, what's happening?" Bill asked as Gary walked into his office without an appointment. Bill knew that Gary was not the kind of person to just walk in without an appointment, so something must be very wrong.

"I just overheard my employees discussing how they dream about killing me," Gary answered.

"I see. Just a minute," Bill said, getting up to close his office door. He told his secretary to hold all calls and returned to his desk. "Now, tell me about it."

"I was sitting in the restaurant—you know, the one where they always go for lunch—and I overheard them comparing notes on how they would like to kill me," Gary said.

"I see. How do you feel about that?" Bill asked.

"Very angry," Gary responded.

"Why do you think they want to kill you?" Bill asked. "Be honest."

"I can't imagine," Gary said.

"Do you think it's because you don't practice what you preach?" Bill asked.

"What do you mean by that?" Gary asked.

"Well, I think it's time for you to take your own participation inventory," Bill said, reaching into his desk for a small booklet. "Remember when we wrote this ten years ago?"

"Of course," Gary answered. "It was the Center's first publication." Gary picked up the booklet as if it were fine china and would break if handled roughly.

"Let's turn to the list at the back and see how the Center stacks up," Bill said. "The first thing on the list is teams. Have you broken up the Center staff into teams?"

"Hey, there are only eight of us," Gary said.

"Yes, and you could have teams. What are the major functions of the Center?" Bill asked.

"You know the answer to that question—workshops and publications," Gary answered.

"OK, then there should be a workshop team and a publications team. That would be possible, wouldn't it?" Bill asked.

"I guess, but some people would have to be on both teams," Gary said.

"That's all right. How about employee input into policy? Have there been any conflicts over Center policy recently?" Bill asked.

"Well, there has been some discussion about the meal reimbursement policy. Wilbur thinks there should be an amount for the day rather than an amount for each meal," Gary said.

"And what do the other employees think?" Bill asked.

"I really don't know," Gary said.

"How much more would you spend if you made the change Wilbur wants?" Bill asked.

"Oh, perhaps a hundred dollars more a year," Gary answered.

"I see; for the want of a hundred dollars, a highly paid employee's effectiveness is being destroyed," Bill said.

"Well, I hadn't thought about it like that," Gary said. A light bulb was going on inside Gary's head. "What else should I change?"

"You really want to know?" Bill asked.

"Of course," Gary answered.

"You have to fire Glenda," Bill said.

"Fire Glenda!" Gary exclaimed, jumping into the air.

"Yes, fire Glenda," Bill responded. "Glenda doesn't like her work, and she takes it out on everyone else. I see that when she runs a workshop. Everyone knows that but you, and I think it's time for you to face the facts. In fact, I think if things continue on the same course, you two will probably be divorced inside of a year. Do you want that?"

"No, of course not, but I can't run the Center without Glenda," Gary said.

"No, my friend, you couldn't have run the Center without her three or four years ago, but times have changed, and you have to change," Bill said. "It's time for Glenda to retire and for you to set up the teams, with team-elected leaders. I can imagine you meeting with the two elected leaders to go over major policies and to discuss what the teams want you to do."

"What the teams want me to do!" Gary screamed.

"That's right," Bill responded. "You have some very good people over there, and they all know what your strengths and weaknesses are. Let them tell you how they want you to play to your strengths. I think you'll be happier in the long run. They won't ask you to do anything you don't like doing, and you can get rid of some of the things you hate to do, like writing articles for trade magazines."

Gary thought for a minute. "You mean I never have to write one of those silly articles again?"

"That's right, and you'll never have to hire another new employee, and without Glenda there will be more money to buy things like a computer for each staff member," Bill said.

"How did you know the staff members wanted to have their own computers?" Gary asked.

"I've been in your offices and seen them carrying their phones over to the computers," Bill said. "It was sad to see, given that you have such a nice computer setup on your desk and wouldn't think of doing that yourself."

"But I started the company," Gary said.

"That's exactly right, and you would like to see it grow and get involved in more international projects, wouldn't you?" Bill asked.

"Yes, I would," Gary said.

"That's not going to happen unless you and perhaps one other staff member devote a lot of time to it," Bill said. "Don't you think that is the kind of thing you should be spending your time on at this point?"

"Well, won't the other employees resent it if I don't do some of the grunt work?" Gary asked.

"I think you know how they feel about you right now," Bill said. "I think you need to concentrate on what you like to do and what you can do that serves the growth needs of the Center. I think if you turn most of the routine stuff over to the other staff members, everyone will be happy."

"But, fire Glenda?" Gary said. "I can't do that."

"Look, make her a consultant," Bill said. "Let her stay at home and come in once or twice a week to proofread things, or perhaps you could take stuff home for her to work on. I've talked to her, and frankly, she hates being at the office all day. She would be much happier if she could work at home, and there's no reason why she can't. Of course, if she's working at home, she can't be the big boss anymore."

"Yes, I see what you mean," Gary said.

"Look, do you want me to come over and discuss this with the employees?" Bill asked.

"No, I have to do it," Gary answered, walking out of Bill's office.

The walk back to the Center was the hardest four blocks Gary had ever had to walk. He had created the Center with his own hands, and now it was time for him to give up some control in order to allow it to grow and prosper. It was time for him to practice what he had been preaching. Sure, his was a small operation, but he had told the owners of small businesses hundreds of times that they could use the principles of participatory management and charged them for booklets that tried to tell them how to do just that. Now it was his turn. As Gary walked into the office, he told everyone to bring a chair into the center of the room.

"I have a few announcements to make," Gary began. "First of all, from now on Glenda will work at home, and her duties will be reduced to proofreading things before they leave the Center. Second, I am forming two teams, which will elect their own team leaders. I will not be a member of either team. I will continue to do workshops, but I will not be involved in most publication duties. I want to devote more time to international projects. It is four o'clock now. I want everyone to go home now, take an hour to write down the Center policies that they would like to see changed, and bring their memorandums on the subject to work tomorrow. I have finally realized that we are now big enough to take advantage of the theory that we preach, and I think it's high time that we started to do just that. That's all. See you all tomorrow." Gary turned and walked out of the room. That had been the hardest speech of his life, and he felt shaken. He went to the bar across the street for a drink.

Glenda began packing up her stuff as if nothing of much significance had happened. The other employees walked out in a group and headed for the subway station. They all had just one thought. Tomorrow really was just a day away.

Questions for Thought and Discussion

1. How should the owner of a very small business—one with less than a dozen employees—introduce participatory management?
2. How can a small number of employees be organized into teams?
3. Who should pick the team leaders?
4. How can policies be reviewed and changed without undermining the authority of the small-business owner?
5. What kinds of decisions can be made only by the small-business owner?
6. How should goals and objectives be set in a very small organization?
7. What principles of participatory management would not work in a very small organization?
8. How can the small-business owner make a distinction between "giving in" and "being participatory"?
9. What information can the small-business owner allow the employees to have?
10. When is the best time for the small-business owner to introduce participatory management?

Chapter 12

The Vacation of a Lifetime

Introduction

Charlie Watson inherited a small hotel but could not get anyone to work for him, for reasons that you will soon discover. He turned to his friends to help him through the crisis. They agreed, but only on the condition that he give them some stock and use participatory management techniques. Charlie Watson learned a lot of lessons about how to handle people during the next few months. The main lesson involved where to draw the line between control and empowerment. He also learned which team structures worked in his situation and which did not.

The Vacation of a Lifetime

Charlie Watson was a frat boy. His father before him had been a frat boy, as had his father before him. The fraternity they belonged to at Old Miss was not one of those dedicated to academic success. It was dedicated to fun, fun, fun, and more fun. Every year it won the award for best frat party of the year. Charlie was president of the fraternity his senior year of college, and the big party was better than ever. His grandfather would have been proud. Charlie's father had died when he was young, and he had spent his summers with his grandfather, who owned a small resort hotel in the Virgin Islands. Charlie had great vacations and also learned the business. The day Charlie graduated from Old Miss, he got the telegram. His grandfather had died, and Charlie was the proud owner of the fifty-room Jefferson Davis Hotel. Charlie's grandfather, a true son of the Old South, had named it Jefferson Davis to attract the southern business. In the more recent days of political correctness, this had cost him some business, and many of the people living on the island refused to work at a hotel named for Jefferson Davis.

Charlie flew south to accept his inheritance and arrived in the office of attorney Walter Frenfroe. Walter Frenfroe was at least seventy years old, with a long, gray beard. He appeared to be a mixture of black and white and perhaps other races. He laid it on the line.

"Son, there's a new, fancy highrise being built just up the beach from your place. The word has gone out that they intend to put you out of business. No one will work at the old Jefferson Davis any more, not that they wanted to much in the first place. This summer is your make-or-break summer, and I'll tell you, the place needs some fixing up before the big crowd arrives."

"Don't worry," Charlie answered. "I'll get the place on its feet again."

Charlie took the old Jeep that he had also inherited and drove to the Jefferson Davis Hotel. The roof had fallen in on part of one wing, and the whole place badly needed a coat of paint. Most of the rooms looked to be in pretty good shape but Charlie would need a good plumber, a good electrician, and a couple of good carpenters, not to mention a staff to run the hotel. He would need maids, desk clerks, gardeners, cooks, waiters, and all the other people that a hotel needs. If no one on the island would work for him, what was he going to do? Easy: he had friends and something better than friend—he had frat brothers.

Charlie flew back to Mississippi and started calling people. He figured he needed at least twelve people to work like dogs all summer to keep the hotel going. He managed to line up six fraternity brothers and six sorority sisters, but he had to promise each of them a 1 percent share in the hotel if the summer was a success. There was Bill, the big football player. He had spent some summers doing basic carpentry work. There was Sarah, the math genius with long stringy hair and thick glasses. She promised to read up on basic wiring and electricity. There was Fred, the physics major. He was sure he could do basic plumbing with a little help. There was Jane, beautiful Jane, with her long blond hair. She had a lot of experience waiting on tables in the summer. Her tips were twice what everyone else received. John, Joe, Walter, and Sam each brought his own unique talents to the project, as did Susan, Cindy, Carol, and Connie. They were all sure they could repair and run the Jefferson Davis Hotel. How hard could it be?

There were three wings off the center lobby and a large restaurant area. The second floor of the wing with the fallen roof was chosen to house the new staff members of the Jefferson Davis Hotel. Charlie figured that if they lived there, everyone would have an extra incentive to fix the roof as quickly as possible. The first day Charlie told everyone what to do, and at the end of the day he had a rebellion on his hands.

"Hey, who died and appointed you God?" John asked. John was an accounting major, and he knew how to add two and two and get four.

"What do you mean?" Charlie asked.

"Look, we all agreed to come here and work hard for a stake in this broken-down hotel, but we didn't agree to be your slaves," Cindy joined in.

"But someone has to be in charge," Charlie answered.

"Look, we've all read the book on participatory management, and that's what we want to practice around here," Sam joined in.

Everyone nodded in agreement. Charlie knew a potential mutiny when he saw one. "OK, where do we begin?" he asked no one in particular.

"Great," Cindy said as she pulled out an old blackboard she had found in the basement. "I'll be the facilitator. First, we need to list every job around here. I'll put the ones I can think of on the board." Cindy listed things like maid, clerk, cook, and waiter. Other people began to yell out jobs that were obvious and some that were not. Sam thought that one job should be called Dirty Work; it would include everything that no one wanted to do, like cleaning bathrooms. Connie thought one job should be called Find It because there were always things that had to be found at a hotel. Sarah felt that one job should be called Interface, because everyone knew that at a hotel one person should have the job of interfacing with the guests. Beautiful Jane thought that any self-respecting hotel should have some kind of entertainment at night, so Entertainer should be on the list. As the list grew longer and longer, Charlie jumped in.

"Look at this list," Charlie said. "There are thirty jobs on this list and only thirteen of us. How are we going to do all this stuff?"

"Easy, frat brother of mine," Bill answered. "Job rotation. First, we need to come up with thirteen jobs because there are thirteen of us. I think we can do that. Every job on this list has its advantages and disadvantages. The only fair way to handle this is to rotate the jobs. There are seven days in a week. We need to group together the jobs that fit together, and then in the course of two weeks everyone gets to do everything."

"But everyone doesn't know how to do everything," Charlie objected.

"Then we need to have a giant training session before the first guests arrive," Connie answered. "Jane can show us the basics of waiting tables; I can cover the essentials of using a cookbook, and so on. How hard can it be?"

Charlie laughed and agreed. Since he owned 88 percent of the hotel, everyone seemed to accept that he had some kind of veto power over major decisions, but that went unsaid. The ideal of any participatory organization is a group of fully cross-trained individuals sharing the bad and the good jobs. But he could see a problem.

"What about tips?" he asked everyone and no one.

"What do you mean?" Sam responded.

"I mean some of us are going to get more in tips than others, and that will cause resentment," Charlie answered.

"Look, I think if we share the jobs that get tips, the fact that some people will make more than others on those jobs is just a fact of life," Jane chimed in.

"Easy for you to say," Sarah said. "You get tips for just walking across a room."

Everyone laughed. Sam was serious. "We all know that this kind of thing can build into resentment pretty darn fast. I think we should put a note in every room explaining that this is a different kind of hotel and that if people would like to leave a tip, they should leave it with the manager to be divided up among the staff. Otherwise they should not leave a tip during their stay at the hotel."

There was some discussion of this, but a consensus soon developed that this was the best approach.

"We should also explain to the guests that each day during their stay, a different person will be in charge of dealing with problems and complaints. We need some symbol that will tell them who to talk to," Connie said.

"You mean the Interface person needs a uniform," Sarah added.

"I know, a tie," Charlie joined in. "No one wears a tie here, so if they see a person, male or female, wearing a tie, they know that that is the person to talk to."

"Let's make it a red tie so that no one will make a mistake," Connie added.

"A red tie with big white spots," Bill added as he left the room. He returned a moment later with just such a tie. "It was a present from my Aunt Mae. She loves to give me stuff like this."

Everyone passed the red tie with big white spots around and had a good laugh. For the next couple of days, everyone attended the cross-training sessions. Jane explained how to wait on tables in a southern friendly way, while Sarah discussed guest interface. Cooking and cleaning and basic gardening rules were covered. While the group didn't know everything, among them they had a basic grasp of most things. They had all spent time in good hotels, and each person had an idea or experience to add to the mixture. The day before the first busload of guests was due to arrive, the repairs had been completed and everyone was relaxing by the pool. Suddenly Charlie jumped up and screamed, "Shopping!"

The one thing they had not put on the list was shopping. Two buses with over sixty tourists would arrive in the morning, and there was not enough food for that many people. Shopping would have to be done every day once the guests arrived. Their simple version of job rotation was not good enough. Shopping would take several people many hours. And how would they allocate the use of the Jeep?

"Relax, Charlie," John spoke up. "We just forgot to put teams into the picture."

"Teams?" Charlie asked.

"Yeah, teams," John responded. "Each day each of us will be a member of one of three teams. There will be the food team to deal with everything to do with the restaurant. There will be the room team to deal with cleaning and repairing the rooms, and the lobby team to deal with the pool, the grounds, and the lobby things like registering people and carrying luggage. If we have four people on each team and one person to act as coordinator to move people from one team to another during slack times, things should work out."

"Teams, yeah, of course. Why didn't I think of that?" Charlie laughed. "So each day each of us will look on the job rotation list to see what our basic job is. Then we report to our team leader. But who is the team leader?"

"Each day the first thing the team will do is elect a team leader for the day," John answered.

"Elect a leader each day? Come on," Charlie responded.

"No, it will work," John shot back. "You just have to trust everyone to vote in the interest of getting the team's job accomplished. For example, we all know that some of us know more about some things than others. On any given day it will probably be obvious who the leader should be. And of course, some jobs will rule people out. No one doing the toilet-cleaning job could handle that responsibility and still be the room service leader. You get the idea."

"It can work; give it a chance," Sarah added.

"We can do it," Connie joined in.

"Sure, it will be fun," Jane said.

"Well, with this kind of enthusiasm how can we fail?" Charlie said. But Charlie was thinking to himself that this was probably going to be a disaster.

On Sunday at about noon, two buses pulled up at the Jefferson Davis Hotel. Thirty-two rooms would be filled by thirty-two couples, most of them from Atlanta. Charlie, wearing the red tie with white spots, asked everyone to take a seat in the restaurant or the lobby for a minute while his "staff" sorted luggage and took it to the rooms. Of course, his staff had never done this before, and nothing short of chaos ruled at the front door. Was putting the luggage in the rooms the job of the room team or the lobby team? After some negotiation, it was decided that since this would generally be a problem only on Sunday, when most people would be arriving and leaving, both teams would work on this. Everyone agreed that the restaurant team had enough to do on any given day, even Sunday. The room and lobby teams came up with a way to decide who got what room right away. People with heavy luggage would have rooms on the ground floor near the lobby. People with light luggage would have rooms on the second floor away from the lobby. Meanwhile Charlie gave his welcoming speech.

"I just want to welcome you to the Jefferson Davis Hotel. My grandfather built this hotel, and I am proud to say that it has been in continuous operation since 1946. You may notice that the staff is made up of young people from Mississippi. I have asked some friends to help me out for the summer. They all own stock in this hotel and have every reason to want your stay here to be as pleasant as possible. Each day a different person will be doing any given job. Each day one person will be wearing this red tie with white spots. If you have any questions or problems, it will be that person's job to solve them. Also, we ask that you not tip people during your stay. If you wish, you may leave a group tip with the red-tie person at the end of your stay. Are there any questions?"

There were several questions, and Charlie did his best to answer them. Just as Charlie ran out of things to say, Bill, the lobby team leader for the day, arrived with room keys and a list.

"As I call your name, please come up and get your room key," Bill announced with as much authority as he could, wearing green shorts and a T-shirt. Bill called out the names and people took their room keys and went off to find their rooms.

The guests settled in and began to explore the pool and the beach. At the pool they found the pool master, and at the beach they found the beach master. Bill was the lobby leader and the beach master for this first Sunday. Connie was the pool master and she looked very good in her swim suit and T-shirt. People complimented her on the T-shirt and she got an idea. Why not have T-shirts printed up with Jefferson Davis on them and sell them to the guests? She had always assumed that there was a big markup on such things, given that she could get shirts for three dollars at the corner stand in Gulfport and they cost fifteen dollars at the sportswear stores. She went to Charlie and told him her idea.

"Great idea," Charlie responded. "We need a suggestion box where people can write down ideas when they come up. We can discuss them at the weekly staff meeting."

"Oh, are we going to have a weekly staff meeting?" Connie asked a little sarcastically.

"Sure, on Sunday morning," Charlie responded. "Hey, I'm entitled to make that decision. I'm the coordinator for the day, aren't I?"

"Yeah, I guess so," Connie said. "Listen, coordinator, when you have a free minute, why don't you make some phone calls and see about getting some special T-shirts down here pronto."

"I know just who to call," Charlie answered.

Charlie, as president of the fraternity, had on occasion dealt with a T-shirt company in New Orleans that produced specialty art on T-shirts. He made a few phone calls and negotiated a price. He would pay four dollars per shirt and order them by the dozen in assorted sizes. The hotel could sell them for twelve dollars each and make a good profit. Who wouldn't want a T-shirt with a drawing of the hotel on one side and a picture of Jefferson Davis on the other? Charlie felt that things were really cooking when it hit him: cooking. It was only a few hours from the first big meal, and the restaurant staff was still gone with the Jeep. They had hooked an old trailer to the back and gone off hours ago. Where could they be?

Of course, the restaurant team was making its way through a market that was not like any market they had ever had to deal with in Mississippi. The chickens were alive, and the fish was very fresh. Some of the fruits and vegetables looked like nothing they had ever seen before. Sarah was the team leader for the day, and she had calculated how much food they would need to serve dinner to seventy-seven people. The only way to do that was to prepare a few big dishes and have chicken done Jefferson Davis style. She wasn't sure what Jefferson Davis style would be, but she was going to come up with something. The team had pored over the cookbooks they found in the kitchen before leaving and had decided that the only way to handle so many people was to have a salad bar. One member of the team became the salad bar master, while the rest negotiated prices for fish and chicken. Sarah decided to pay more and get chickens that had already been killed and dressed. Limes were cheap and in abundance, and so she decided that lime would play a big part in the first dinner.

The restaurant team returned to find things running fairly smoothly. They needed help unloading the trailer and chopping up stuff. It was too much for four people. Sarah went to Charlie, the coordinator.

"What, you want more people to help?" Charlie asked.

"Look, mister coordinator, part of your job is to move people around when special problems come up. We can't get everything unloaded and chopped in time without one or, better yet, two extra people. I don't care where you get them; just get them." Sarah stormed back to the kitchen.

Charlie looked around at the lobby team. They all had their hands full dealing with guest problems of one sort or another. He went to Joe, the room team leader.

"Look, Joe, we have a problem," Charlie said. "The restaurant team is going to need some help every day about this time unloading the trailer and getting the food ready. I need two of your people for a couple of hours. I don't care who, just send some over."

Joe thought for a minute. He couldn't go, since he was the room team leader, and he couldn't send the toilet person, since that job was so dirty and time-consuming. He called the other two members of the room team and explained the situation. The beds had all been made and most of the room preparation had been done, and they were needed in the kitchen. They didn't like it, but they understood the need. They reported to Sarah for kitchen duty and found themselves chopping and mixing and pouring and baking. At one point a small food fight broke out, but Sarah put a stop to that with the declaration that the next person who threw anything would get toilet duty for a solid week. The idea of team leader authority was born. Toilet duty would be the standard punishment for major violations of the rules. Jane couldn't help throwing a handful of chopped lime at Sarah, and Sarah marched off to see Charlie. A moment later she returned with Charlie in tow.

"Jane, as coordinator for this day, I think that what you did deserves punishment," Charlie said. "You will have toilet duty for the next week."

"But you can't decide that for yourself," Jane screamed. "That kind of thing should be decided at the staff meeting."

"I'll tell you what, you can appeal the decision to the staff review panel, which will meet tonight after dinner."

"Who's on the staff review panel?" Jane asked.

"We'll pick three people at random who did not see the incident," Charlie said. "They can hear everyone's testimony and decide on the proper punishment. Sarah's recommendation of one week's toilet duty will be reviewed by them, and their decision will be final."

Jane figured that with three randomly selected people, some of them would be men, and her face and figure would get her a lighter sentence.

"OK, I agree to that," Jane said as she went back to chopping limes.

"Sarah, I think this is the best approach," Charlie said. "We don't want anyone to make snap decisions like this."

"Well, I guess you're right," Sarah said. "But Jane had it coming."

The restaurant had twelve tables for four, so only forty-eight people could eat at any one time. That meant two sittings. It was agreed that dinner would be served at seven and eight and that the staff would eat with the eight o'clock sitting except for the restaurant team, which would eat after everyone else. It was also decided that there was no way to print menus, so the choices for the night were listed on the big blackboard. The first night the choices were lime chicken à la Sarah, lime fish à la Sarah, lime pork à la Sarah, and Jefferson Davis fried chicken. People would help themselves at the salad bar, and the vegetables would depend on what there was and what the kitchen staff hadn't run out of. No promises. To drink, there was iced tea, water, or something from the bar.

The bar was a problem that first night. They had not thought to list bartender as one of the jobs. A quick decision was made that the gardener would do garden work in the morning and be bartender the rest of the day. That seemed to satisfy everyone.

That evening, as the kitchen team was eating, the staff held their first peer review panel. Three names were picked out of a hat. Bill, Connie, and Walter formed the first panel. Walter was ROTC and he knew something about court-martial procedure, so the panel elected him to be the president of the court. The panel asked questions of everyone involved. Sarah presented her side, and Jane said it was just a joke. The panel went to a private room and came back with a verdict delivered by Walter.

"As president of the court, it is up to me to deliver the verdict. It is unanimous. First of all, we decided that the person would be presumed innocent until proven guilty. If the person was proven guilty, the punishment recommended by the team leader would be presumed to be appropriate. We find Jane guilty, and we sentence her to one week, seven consecutive days, of toilet duty. That means she will wear the toilet uniform and clean bathrooms all day every day for the next seven days. Her offense was serious, in that the only way we are going to get anything done is to follow team leader directions."

"But seven days—have a heart," Jane said.

"We do not think it is too much, given the serious nature of your offense," Walter answered. Everyone headed for bed.

"Wait a minute; we can't all go to bed. What if something happens in the night?" Charlie asked.

"I think the red-tie of the previous day should stay on duty until midnight, and then after that guests can wake someone up," Bill said as he stood up. "All those in favor say aye." Everyone yelled "aye," and they all got up to hit the sack. They were certainly bone tired.

The next morning, William showed up bright and early. William was tall, slim, and some kind of cross between black and white.

"Hi, I'm William. My uncle the lawyer sent me to help you folks out," he said in polite Virgin Islands English.

"Your uncle the lawyer?" Connie asked. She was the red-tie for the day.

"Yeah, he was, uh, is the lawyer for this place. He said you folks really got took at the market yesterday, and you might need some help."

"Just a minute," Connie said as she rushed to find Charlie. Charlie was pool master and available.

"Charlie, come in here," Connie said as she grabbed Charlie by the arm and started dragging him into the lobby. "This is William. His uncle is our attorney."

"Oh, are you William Frenfroe?" Charlie asked.

"That's right," he answered. "My uncle said you probably needed some help negotiating the local market and things like that."

"But Charlie," Connie said, "how will we deal with another employee? We have everything set up."

"Look, Connie," Charlie responded, "we'll just deal with it. William can get paid a wage just like a regular worker. That's what you had in mind, I assume."

"Getting paid," William said. "Yeah, I did assume I would get paid."

"And you don't expect to live at the hotel, do you?" Charlie asked.

"No, thanks. I have a home."

"Well, that's perfect. William will be our interface with the island, buying everything we need, leading the shopping group, and so on, and providing some local color." Charlie shook William's hand. "Welcome aboard."

Connie took Charlie aside.

"Look, I don't think you or you and I should make this decision alone. I think we should ask the group."

"We don't have time. You're the coordinator for the day, what do you think?" Charlie asked Connie.

"Well, I guess we probably are being taken at the market and we will need to buy things, so maybe it's a good idea, but I think we should ask everyone else."

"Look, we can't call a staff meeting every time something like this comes up. William isn't going to wait until our Sunday morning staff meeting. We have to act now." Charlie obviously felt that this was someone sent from heaven. "Besides, if he doesn't work out, we can fire him at the staff meeting. Let's give him a tryout."

Charlie didn't wait for Connie's answer. He grabbed William and started explaining how things worked. The job rotation and so on was spelled out as they walked to the kitchen. Sam was the team leader for food that day because his father owned a restaurant, but he didn't really know much about food. He had worked seating people at tables, but he had never been in a big kitchen before.

"Sam, this is William," Charlie said. "He's going to help with the buying and community interface. Until the shopping is done, he's on your team, so take him with you to the market."

"Hey, I thought Connie was red-tie for today," Sam said.

"These orders come straight from her," Charlie responded.

Sam, William, and Carol went off to do the shopping while Bill and Cindy set up the kitchen. They fed people cereal for breakfast, and soup, salad, and sandwiches for lunch, and so the only meal that required a lot of cooking was dinner. Once the soup and salad was set up, one person could manage the sandwich line, which was mainly do-it-yourself, while the other cleaned tables and the rest of the food team went to market. Bill was the sandwich king for the day. Cindy had a crush on Bill, so she was happy to clean tables and keep an eye on him.

At the market, William was a big hit in that he saved a lot of money. He knew how much was fair for everything, and Sam was very glad to have him along. William knew something about the local recipes, and he could add some local color to the evening menu. Sam was glad of that as well. William was a godsend as far as Sam was concerned.

However, Jane was not happy. As they put on her the black wetsuit and white goggles that was the uniform for the toilet person, she screamed bloody murder.

"Ouch, that hurts," Jane yelled at the top of her lungs. Sarah had been elected team leader for the room team that day, and she took pleasure in forcing Jane's ample body into the tight-fitting wetsuit.

"Don't worry, Jane, it will only hurt for a minute," Sarah responded. She and Carol had the job of getting Jane into her uniform as Walter began pulling sheets off the beds and changing towels. He was sheet and towel man for the day. Jane would do bathrooms, and Carol would do basic dusting and cleaning. Sarah would make sure every room had new towels and toilet paper and soap. It worked pretty well. They had to work hard from about ten to two, but then two of them could help the kitchen staff for a while when the rooms were finished.

"I don't know anything about cleaning toilets," Jane protested.

"Then it is my duty as team leader to train you," Sarah said, with glee in her voice. "Here is your toilet brush. Whatever you do, you must not lose your toilet brush. It goes in this bucket, which is your toilet bucket. You take this bucket everywhere you go. And this is the dolly with your other bathroom cleaning supplies. Here is Comet cleaner and another brush. I bet you'll get the hang of it in no time."

Sarah and Carol helped Jane to stand up. She really did look like something from the Black Lagoon. Everyone laughed except Jane, who just yelled some more.

"What about my feet?" Jane asked with a whine in her voice.

"That's right," Sarah said. "We can't have you cleaning bathrooms without something on your feet. And I have just the thing." Sarah pulled out two orange flippers and put them on Jane's feet before Jane could stop her. "That completes the picture rather nicely, don't you think?" Sarah said.

"I can't walk in these," Jane protested.

"Sure you can, give it time. You'll be walking like a duck when this week is over," Sarah said.

Jane waddled down the hall and into the first bathroom of the day, pulling her toilet bucket behind her and pushing her dolly with supplies. It was quite a sight.

The rest of the week went fairly smoothly. The first week's guests got on the buses early Sunday for their trip to the airport. A few hours later the same buses would return with more guests. Every guest was asked to fill out a card with suggestions.

The group sat in the restaurant for the first Sunday morning staff meeting. "As red-tie for the day, I call this first staff meeting to order," Bill said. "We've passed an agenda around, and there are several things on the list. First, the hiring of William. Is there anyone who doesn't know about William? Good. Well, then, what do you think? Should we keep William?"

"I think we should," Sarah said. "The prices I paid at the market were much higher than what William got us. I think he pays for himself."

"And I think the guests expect someone like William to be around singing songs at dinner and telling jokes," Jane added. "With William we get a chief of procurement and an entertainer all in one."

"Are we agreed that William stays?" Bill said. "OK, on to the next item. Carol, what did the guests say in their report cards?"

"They say having different people doing different things all the time is too confusing," Carol said. "They wish there was one beach master, one pool master, and so on."

"I've been thinking about that," Charlie added. "I think we've taken things a little too far. I think we should rotate every week, not every day. You would be on the room team one week, the lobby team the next, and so on. That way, the guests would work with a set group during the week they are here."

"What about toilet duty?" Jane asked.

"I think we'll have enough people to do toilet duty for punishment," Charlie answered. "We have the next three weeks taken care of, as I understand it."

"Yeah, that's right," Walter said. "It seems that some people have a real problem following their team leader."

Everyone looked at Jane, who just frowned.

"The next order of business is the cook problem," Bill continued. "Sarah, do you want to speak to that?"

"Yes." Sarah stood up. "As you know, we've tried to rotate every job, and for most things that works. It does not work for cook. The food is great one night and terrible the next. Since we've hired William, I think we should also hire a cook. William says his Aunt Sue would be willing to come to work for us, and I suggest we take her up on it."

"I agree," Charlie joined in. "I think we can afford to pay another professional person, and one of the reasons people are going to come back every summer is the food."

The group decided to hire Aunt Sue if Charlie could make a deal with her. Carol stood up.

"The other major complaint from the guests is that they expected to get swimming and sailing lessons. We should think about getting some kind of small sailboats. I've asked around and four of us can give swimming lessons."

"That's a good idea," Jane joined in. "I could teach sailing if we had a boat."

"I've done some sailing, and so has Charlie," Bill added.

"It seems to me that we need to take these special skills into account in our job rotation," Charlie said. "I move that Bill be assigned to work out a new rotation that takes all this into account."

"I second that," Cindy said, looking longingly at Bill.

"OK, everyone in favor say aye," Bill said. "The ayes have it. I'll have a new weekly rotation schedule up in an hour or so. Now I think we'd better take a break. The buses will be here sooner than we think."

Charlie walked out the door and toward the beach, with Connie hot on his trail. Charlie sat in the sand and Connie sat down beside him.

"Penny for your thoughts," Connie said.

"I was just thinking that I never thought this would work when we started," Charlie answered.

"Never thought what would work?" Connie asked.

"Oh, you know, job rotation, peer panels, voting at staff meetings, teams, and all the rest."

"Why not?" Connie asked.

"That all seems like something that works in a book, but when you try to put it into practice, everything goes wrong," Charlie answered.

"But everything hasn't gone wrong," Connie said. "Even Jane is working out, and she's got toilet duty for another week."

"I have to admit it was worth it just to see her in that outfit they came up with," Charlie said.

Just then they heard the bell ringing, calling everyone back to the lobby. They found Bill at the blackboard with the jobs for the week. Charlie would be pool master, Connie clerk, Jane toilet duty, and so on. Bill had called Aunt Sue, and she had agreed to cook five days a week, so on the weekends they would still be on their own. When the buses pulled up, the next group of people were from South Carolina and mainly Baptists. That would mean very little bar work and a lot of extra cleaning. After the new guests had been told how things worked, they went to their rooms and then to the beach. Even though this was just the second group, the staff was beginning to feel that they knew exactly what the guests were going to do and ask. They had heard the questions before and felt easier about giving the answers.

The summer moved along, and groups came and went. The Dallas group drank more than any other and left bigger tips. The New Orleans group complained about the food. The Memphis group asked a lot of questions about everything from how they were running the hotel to why they wanted to spend their summer doing this. The Nashville group found fault with everything, while the group from Washington, D.C., couldn't believe how good everything tasted and how well the staff performed. Expectations had a lot to do with how each group responded. Aunt Sue's cooking was a big hit, and William's singing at dinner kept the noise level down. By the time mid-August rolled around, Charlie was beginning to think that they had made it. There was enough money in the bank to pay all the bills and do needed repair work over the winter. He was sure that with William's help he could get some locals to work once the college group left to go back to Old Miss. Then the unexpected happened. A hurricane was reported headed their way. The group from St. Louis canceled, and everyone had to get ready for the storm. The Sunday morning staff meeting was not routine.

"I think we should get out of here and come back when the storm is past," Sarah said when everyone was quiet.

"If we leave, there may be nothing here when we come back," Walter said.

"I don't want to drown, but I sure don't want to see these toilets wash away after all the work I've done cleaning them," Jane added.

"I don't think we can vote on this," Charlie said. "Those that want to go should go, and those that want to stay should stay. But if you go, you lose your share."

"That's not fair," Sarah said.

"The deal was very clear," Bill joined in. "To get the share, you had to work the whole summer. I think that if people leave now, they haven't worked the whole summer, and they should lose their share. A deal is a deal."

"I agree," Jane said.

After some heated discussion, they voted, and eight voted to require those who left to give up their share. The same eight voted to stay through the storm. John, Walter, Sarah, and Susan voted to leave by the Sunday plane. The rest would stay. The discussion turned to getting ready for the storm.

"There's a lot of plywood in the basement for the windows that can't be covered with shutters," Charlie said. "I think Bill should be in charge of that, since he knows the most about carpentry." There was no objection. "I'll lead a team to get as much of the furniture as possible to the second floor, if that's all right." No one said anything. "We'll need supplies, and I think William should buy what he can on the way back from taking our four lost members to the airport."

John, Walter, Sarah, and Susan packed their bags and climbed into the Jeep. William drove them to the airport. Along the way, the four talked about how they didn't think the group would be able to get along without them.

As they got to the airport, Sarah said, "I can't leave them."

Everyone looked at everyone else and nodded. William turned the Jeep around and headed for the market. The wind was already beginning to pick up. They bought some vegetables and fruit and the last of the fish and headed back to the Jefferson Davis Hotel. When they got back, they saw everyone boarding up windows and moving furniture. Everything in the basement that would be harmed by water was being carried to the second floor. As the Jeep pulled up with the four lost comrades, everyone cheered. They jumped out of the Jeep and started working. William had a family to worry about, so he got on his bicycle and headed home. The original group would be on its own.

As dinnertime came around, they realized that they had not picked a food team, so everyone stopped and headed for the kitchen. Sarah took charge and prepared a ton of lime fish à la Sarah, just as she had done the first Sunday night. After dinner they sat around the big radio and listened to the weather report. The wind was picking up outside, and the bulk of the storm was expected to hit before morning. They all got flashlights and candles and headed to their rooms. Since their rooms were on the second floor and the roof had just been rebuilt, it was likely that they would be better off there.

After an hour Charlie came around and knocked on everyone's door. He called them into a meeting in the hall.

"Look, I think we need to form into emergency response teams. I think I should be coordinator, if everyone agrees," Charlie said. No one objected. "Good. I think we need three teams, one for each wing. If the lobby has a problem, I'll call on a team that isn't busy. I've pulled names out of a hat, and the three teams are listed on this paper. Form teams and elect a leader right away. I think from the sound of that wind out there that this is our night."

The list was passed around, and the teams formed up. Bill would lead one team, Connie a second, and Walter a third. Each team drew out of the hat for its wing and headed off. Charlie moved to the lobby. The electricity was out, so everyone had a flashlight. Each team got rope and tools and began discussing what its most likely problem might be. Charlie sat down in the lobby where he could look at the portrait of his grandfather over the desk. He wondered how many big storms his grandfather had been through in his half century of owning the hotel. Connie, Bill, and Walter sat down with him.

"My team is ready for anything," Bill said first.

"Same for mine," Connie added.

"Me too," Walter said.

"Good," Charlie said. "You know, whatever happens, I couldn't have done this without you guys and everyone else."

"It's OK, Charlie," Bill said. "We've loved every minute of it. It was worth the summer just to see Jane in her toilet duty outfit." Everyone laughed.

One by one the other members of the group came into the lobby, having done their particular jobs. As they sat on the couches that were too heavy to move upstairs or on the floor, everyone could hear the wind howl outside. They all thought of the paint they had splashed on and the nails they had driven when they first arrived. Would it hold up? Just then the french doors to the pool exploded inward. A tree had been picked up and slammed into the doors. There was no plywood protection because they had all assumed they would be protected by the porch that hung so far over them. Charlie jumped up and ran to the doors. Bill and Connie began sending team members for tools and supplies. A couple of canvas tarps would have to do the trick. Everyone got very wet pulling them across the opening where the french doors had stood. Ropes and nails held them in place. After half an hour of hard work, the water was no longer coming into the lobby. Walter and his group were mopping up the water before anyone could say anything. A loud noise at the far end of the west wing sent Bill and his team running. Something similar at the east wing sent Connie and her group to answer the call. Charlie just sat and watched as everyone worked through the night to save the group's investment.

As the dawn broke, the rain let up and the wind slacked off. While there would be another day of rain, the worst was clearly over. Everyone ran into the front yard to survey the damage. A few windows were blown out and a few rooms were soaked, but nothing major. The little sailboats they had bought and fixed up had been smashed against the dock and the Jeep was on its side, but a group soon had the Jeep on its wheels again.

"Boy, that must have been some storm to turn a Jeep over like that," Sarah said.

No one answered.

"Hey, I'm hungry. Who has kitchen duty today?" Charlie called out.

"I'm sure I don't know," Bill said.

Just then, out of the front door, everyone saw a strange sight. It was Jane in her toilet-cleaning outfit, complete with orange flippers. Everyone just laughed, including Jane.

"I'm sure I did something wrong last night. Which toilet should I start with, Mr. Coordinator?" Jane asked.

"Hey, look what I found," Connie yelled as she pulled the red tie with the white spots out of the mud. She put it around Charlie's neck and gave him a big kiss.

"I'm sure you did something wrong, Miss Toilet. But before we start, let's see if we can't convince Sarah to prepare lime eggs à la Sarah just one more time," Charlie yelled above the noise of the storm.

Sarah was way ahead of him. She had already put on the cook's hat and was standing at the front door.

"Come and get it," Sarah yelled.

Everyone went through the front door and headed toward the kitchen. They didn't mind eating on the floor, and they didn't mind sitting in a layer of mud. Years later they all agreed on one thing: That was the best breakfast they had ever had, limes and all!

Questions for Thought and Discussion

1. To what extent can a participatory organization listen to the customers and make changes based on their opinions?
2. How should these "customer-caused" changes be introduced to empowered employees?
3. How can the team structure of a participatory organization be changed without harming the principle of participation?
4. How should team-based organizations make decisions in a crisis?
5. How can teams deal with different members having different skill levels?
6. Where do we draw the line between decisions that teams should make and general policy that the whole organization or the business owner should make?
7. What information about the business should empowered employees not be given?
8. How can a participatory organization deal with some employees who are owners and some who are not?
9. How should a team-based, participatory organization deal with employee discipline?
10. How can the owner have a veto over major decisions without harming the culture of participation?

Chapter 13

The Creative Computing Consortium

INTRODUCTION

Billy Watson was given the chance to create a new organization, and he organized it along classic hierarchical lines. That did not work. Jim Buchanan was sent in to find out what had gone wrong. He found highly intelligent and highly educated employees being treated like assembly-line workers. He found an organization where employees were not trusted and where credit was not given where credit was due. He found team leaders who did not understand the most basic principles of how participatory teams should be managed.

THE CREATIVE COMPUTING CONSORTIUM

Jim Buchanan had a reputation for taking unusual jobs for a management consultant. His offices in Boston were filled with the small mementos of someone who had traveled all over the world to advise businesses and governments large and small about everything from currency reform to cafeteria design. His secretary, Mary Worth, was as unusual as his office. She was somewhere between the ages of fifty and ninety, and she always wore her long hair in a bun with a bright bow. Her old-fashioned clothes suggested that she had just stepped out of the pages of a 1920s magazine. It was generally assumed that Jim had assistants, but they were "confidential" and nowhere in evidence in the small suite of offices that he and Mary occupied. Jim was of middle height and middle age, with brown hair and very normal features. The fact that he seemed so normal and unthreatening probably allowed him to blend into the woodwork when necessary in order to study an organization.

One beautiful fall morning, the leaves were just beginning to turn as Jim left his office in an old building near the center of the city and walked a few blocks to a high-rise office tower. He entered and rode the special express elevator to the top floor. As he entered the reception area, the receptionist recognized him from pictures that had recently been in the newspaper and ushered him straight into Walter Jackson's private office. Walter Jackson was a computer genius turned business tycoon who had turned a small idea into a billion-dollar company. His Wordeaters Corporation had become one of the standard suppliers of word-processing and other software. While other companies were shrinking in the face of competition from Microsoft, his company was growing by filling special software niches that Microsoft was either unwilling or unable to fill. Walter Jackson was very tall, very thin, and very bald, which made him stand out in a crowd as much as Jim Buchanan blended in.

"Come in, Jim. Have a seat," Walter Jackson said, showing Jim to a large couch near a large window with a wonderful view of Boston and the bay beyond.

"I came as quickly as I could," Jim responded. "What's up?"

"I want you to do a confidential job for me," Walter answered.

"How confidential?" Jim asked.

"Well, let's put it this way: If you are captured the Secretary will disavow any knowledge of your existence," Walter said.

"I see," Jim responded. "Do I have to kidnap some Latin American dictator and convince him that he has died and gone to heaven so that he will give me the combination to the safe?"

"In fact, you don't even have to leave New England," Walter said. "Have you heard of the Creative Computing Consortium, or CCC for short?"

"I think so," Jim answered. "Isn't it some kind of think tank down on the Cape?"

"That's right," Walter replied. "There are several hundred computer geniuses in one big building thinking about the next generation of hardware and software, or at least that's the story."

"You don't believe it?" Jim asked.

"Let's just say that we've been members for four years and we don't have much to show for it," Walter said.

"Why'd you join?" Jim asked.

"For the same reason most countries in Europe joined the Common Market: We joined to keep an eye on our competitors," Walter answered. "Of course, we had some hopes that we might also get some real ideas out of the place."

"I don't know much about it," Jim said. "Fill me in on the history."

"There isn't much to tell," Walter said. "A few years ago Billy Watson came to me and other CEOs of large technology companies with the idea of starting a consortium to do research on advanced computer technology. His idea was that if the Japanese continued to cooperate and we continued to compete, they would leave us in the dust in the next century."

"Sounds reasonable to me," Jim said.

"Oh sure, in theory, but American companies are not Japanese companies," Walter said. "We're not used to cooperating. Anyway, Billy Watson convinced a dozen major companies to sign on for at least ten years. The idea was that the CCC would concentrate on doing research somewhere between the basic research done at universities and the ready-for-market research done in companies. He hoped that this would enable American companies to get ideas conceived in the United States to market faster than is usually the case."

"Well, that sounds pretty good to me as well," Jim said. "It seems to me, just reading the newspaper, that the ideas are invented here and the Japanese cash in on them before any American company can get into the market. By the time they do, the Japanese have everything all sewed up."

"Oh, yeah, it's a great idea in theory," Walter replied.

"I take it things have not worked out in practice," Jim said.

"Let's just say that four years later we have very little to show for our investment, and my board of directors wants some answers given the fact that we're locked in for another six years," Walter said.

"What do you want me to do?" Jim asked.

"Every member company has two liaison people at the CCC," Walter replied. "One of ours has just retired, and I want you to take his place for a few weeks."

"How can I do that?" Jim asked. "I don't know anything about high technology."

"Neither did the guy you're replacing," Walter responded. "Look, the purpose of the liaison people is to keep their ears and eyes open and ask a lot of questions. We want someone who can think in terms the average person might understand, not a computer nerd."

"I see," Jim said. "Well, I should be able to do that. But what if someone recognizes me?"

"They won't," Walter said. "These people don't read newspapers or watch television. They live in their own little world. You'll be perfect."

"Tell me about this Billy Watson who runs the place," Jim said. "How did he end up heading a project like this?"

"That's a good question," Walter answered. "Billy Watson was born in 1940, first in his class at West Point, ten years in Vietnam. He went to Vietnam a captain and came out the youngest three-star general in American history. He went on to be the head of the CIA, and then retired to start the CCC."

"I think I remember some stories about him during the war," Jim said. "Isn't he the one who had all his men killed or badly wounded and was down to six bullets in his revolver and six Viet Cong but he killed each one with one bullet?"

"That's him," Walter said. "The pistol was an exact replica of the ones General Patton wore during World War II. It was given to him when he finished at the top of his class."

"This guy sounds like a tough customer," Jim said.

"Yeah," Walter responded. "And the funny thing is that the guy is so small. I don't think he's over five feet eight inches, and he can't weigh more than a hundred and forty pounds. He still wears his hair very short like he's ready to jump into a combat uniform at any minute and hit the beach."

"How did he go from the jungles of Vietnam to the CIA to head of this CCC thing?" Jim asked.

"You know, I haven't got the foggiest idea," Walter answered. "I guess he got the idea for the CCC and things just took off from there."

"Does the government have any stake in the CCC?" Jim asked.

"Not officially, but there are several former CIA types on the payroll and I can't believe that anything of importance discovered at the CCC doesn't end up on a desk at the CIA in a matter of minutes," Walter said.

"So what do you want me to do exactly?" Jim asked.

"I want to know if we should pull out of this thing, break our contract, and take our chances in court or if you think we might actually get something useful out of this place at some point in the future," Walter said.

"I don't know if I'm your man," Jim said.

"You're my man, all right," Walter said. "I want someone without a bias. I want someone to go in and see how things are organized. I want a management consultant's report, but I don't want anyone there to know you're a management consultant. And, of course, I have hired you because I know you will find out everything I need to know, not just the obvious. I want to know about the dirt and the things that crawl out from under the rocks at this place. I know you're the man for me."

The rest of the conversation was about fees and expenses. Jim would need to use two of his operatives on this job, and their cost and expenses were worked out. Jim would send his two key operatives to the Cape to see if they could get jobs at the CCC. Joe was a refugee from Vietnam. Joe and Jim had gone to high school together after Joe's dad came over to work in the United States early in the 1960s. He used the name Joe because he got tired of trying to help people to pronounce his real name. Joe had classic Vietnamese features. Since he had a black belt in karate and a master's degree from MIT in electrical engineering, he was a good man to have on your side. Joe had much of the CCC building bugged by the time Jim arrived. The other operative, Candy, was blond and twentysomething. She had a B.A. in English from Harvard, but her looks suggested that she was a relative of Jean Harlow. Candy could play the part of the dumb waitress real well, and she never had any trouble getting a job in the cafeteria of a place like CCC. She was hired on the spot and began working the executive floor. While even the executives went through a regular cafeteria line, many of them brought their trays back to the top floor to eat. Candy went around with a cart serving drinks and providing desserts in the executive dining room. She received three propositions during the first day. Those that involved dinner and conversation she accepted.

By the time Jim arrived as the new man from Wordeaters, Candy had been on the top floor for a week and Joe had been a janitor for three days. Wordeater's threw a party for him at a famous restaurant with all the main players from CCC in attendance. There were, of course, Billy Watson and the two vice presidents, Hanz and Fritz. Both Hanz and Fritz had heavy German accents. Jim began to wonder how CCC was going to keep any secrets from the Germans with these two reading every report and attending every meeting. There was Donny and his combination girlfriend and assistant, Suzie. Donny had one of those pear-shaped bodies that suggested that he had never raised one foot more than three inches off the ground in his life. Suzie was drinking a lot and clearly was trying to be the life of the party. Donny was some kind of genius concerned with software. It was common knowledge that in a world of so-called equals, Donny was the fair-haired boy. He had a special contract that gave him a percentage of any money made on his project. No one else had that. There was Freddy, head of the universal translation project. His project was trying to build software that would allow all languages to be translated by computer. Freddy was already drunk by the time Jim arrived. There were Willie, Charlie, and Jackie. These three were brilliant hardware men. Each of them headed a team trying to greatly increase the speed at which computers worked.

Jim moved around the room and made small talk. When he got to meet Billy Watson, he could understand how this guy had gotten so far. All you had to do was look him in the eyes. Something told you that he was a genius and a killer wrapped up in one. Jim came away with a combination of awe and fear. After the party, he went back to the furnished apartment he had rented. Joe and Candy had apartments in the same building.

The next day was Jim's first day at CCC. He put a few things on his desk to make it look like he intended to stay a while and had a long talk with the other liaison man from Wordeaters. Jeff Golden was fat and blond and about forty. He didn't like to say anything negative about anyone.

"So, what can I tell you about the operation?" Jeff asked.

"Well, how does it work?" Jim asked.

"The basic operation is simple," Jeff responded. "There are a dozen teams of about a dozen people each. Each team is working on a different kind of technology problem. Everything from faster computing to new computer programs is being developed."

"How were the team leaders chosen?" Jim asked.

"Oh, by Watson, I guess," Jeff answered. "They all have long-term contracts. Everyone else is here until they get fired or quit, which happens quite regularly around here."

"How would you describe these team leaders?" Jim asked.

"What do you mean?" Jeff responded.

"I mean, are they prima donnas or open to new ideas or what?" Jim asked.

"Oh, I see," Jeff said. "Prima donnas—yes, definitely prima donnas. If they didn't think of it, then it can't be any good. You know the type. I think that's why we have so much turnover here. Brilliant people are hired to work on projects they already know a lot about, only to figure out over time that their idea either will have the leader's name put on it or will never see the light of day."

"I see," Jim said. "Tell me, if the teams had an election, do you think any of the current team leaders would be elected to head the teams they currently head?"

Jeff laughed a hearty laugh. "Are you kidding? I think they would all be fired if their teams had any say in the matter. You remember when you had the basic course in industrial psychology and they described the traits of a good group leader—open to new ideas, facilitates communication, listens a lot and says little, gives credit to subordinates, encourages innovation, and so on?"

"Yes, of course," Jim responded.

"Well, think of these so-called team leaders as the antimodel of that ideal. They do just the opposite. They are all giant egos who can't stand for anyone on their team to shine or for any idea to go up without their name on it. I can't imagine what we might have gotten out of this place if these egos had not gotten in the way. But, of course, they are all the best in their field. I guess to get their ideas we have to give up something."

Jim just nodded and sat in silence. He spent the first day wandering around the building. It was beautiful. A design competition had been held for the sole purpose of coming up with its design. From the air the building must have looked like a giant wheel. The spokes were lined with offices, and the center was an atrium with the cafeteria at the bottom. Every office had a window to the outside and yet was only a few steps from the central atrium. Every floor had a refreshment section with free drinks and a salad bar. Obviously people were encouraged to live in this place almost all the time, and many of them did. Many of them seemed to have no personal life, just their research.

At the end of the first day Jim found himself sitting at the little dinette set in his apartment eating pizza with Joe and Candy.

"I can tell you this, there's a lot of sexism in that place," Candy said. "Many of the top executives have a mistress working in the building somewhere. Many of them boast openly that a condition of their coming here was the promise to hire their mistress and give her a nothing job."

"There seem to be about twenty top executives who all wear suits and huddle together on the top floor around Watson's office," Jim said. "What do they do?"

"As far as I can see, they are all yes men for Watson," Candy responded. "They all have long resumes and fancy titles, but there isn't much for them to do in a place like this. The few I have gotten to know something about all have some personal connection to Watson from either his army or CIA days. While most are in their fifties, I'm sure Watson could launch a covert operation from that top floor if he ever wanted to."

"The same goes for the bottom of this organization," Joe added.

"What do you mean?" Jim asked.

"There are a lot of people at the bottom who have some kind of connection with Watson," Joe responded. "I blend into the janitorial staff because most of them are former generals from the South Vietnamese army who Watson sponsored after the South collapsed. They all would do anything for him. The kitchen staff has a lot of people from either Vietnam or Japan or Germany, all places Watson was stationed during his rise to the top of the army brass. They have some connection to him. And they all would do anything for him."

"I see," was all Jim could think to say. "What about morale among the researchers?"

"From what I hear just listening to their conversations in the lounges and in the cafeteria, I would say it was terrible," Candy said. "They all came to this place thinking they would be able to work on research in their field of expertise. They soon discovered that they were really hired to be glorified assistants to the great men. The twelve great team leaders are clearly in charge of their projects, and they rule with an iron fist. If you disagree with them or suggest a new approach, you are gone by the end of the week."

"Yeah, I would say the personnel records support that," Joe added. "I took a look, and most people come, spend a few months figuring out how things work, and then start looking for another job. Three-fourths of the team members have been here less than a year, even though the place started with a full complement four years ago."

"That kind of turnover can't be good for the research," Jim said.

"I assume not," Joe answered. "I would guess that about the time they figure out the system, they start spending as much time looking for another job as doing research. Also, since any good idea they have is going to get the name of one of the twelve great men put on it, I would bet that many of them keep their best ideas to themselves until they leave."

"You know, it's a funny thing, but if you listened to the conversations of the top executives, you would think everything was just great," Candy added. "They are called the suits by the researchers, who, of course, all wear casual clothes. The suits play with budget numbers and put out press releases and give interviews and fly around the world. It doesn't seem to matter to them that in four years, this place has provided the member companies with almost nothing of value."

"I guess with those ten-year commitments from the member companies, they don't have to worry about a paycheck for a while," Jim said.

Candy, Joe, and Jim talked into the night. Clearly, an organizational culture had developed that was not very conducive to actually getting major research done. After just a few days on the job, that had become obvious to Joe and Candy. That night Jim had trouble getting to sleep. Was the CCC set up this way because Billy Watson thought this was the best way to set it up, or was he getting some bad advice? The more he thought about it, the more he felt that the answer was in Billy Watson's military background. His years in Vietnam must have taught him that with a few good officers you could move mountains. It didn't matter much what kind of troops these officers had as long as they did what they were told and didn't make waves. Perhaps in setting up the CCC Watson had simply been the victim of his own experience. What had worked in fighting a war would not work in fighting the Germans and Japanese for dominance in the high-technology arena. Of course the computer Ph.D.'s they hired did not like being treated like young recruits fresh out of boot camp, and the whole point of having them together in the woods on the Cape was being defeated. Jim decided to focus on one team, the group trying to come up with a universal language translator. He had already met the leader, Freddy, and several of the team members. As a representative from Wordeaters, it would seem perfectly natural that he would be particularly interested in this research project.

Over the next few days, Jim talked with each team member alone and in small groups. He watched them as they had brainstorming sessions together, and he asked them questions as they ate lunch together. The team was made up of six men and six women. The men were paid more (he had Joe check the payroll records), even though they had less experience than the women as a group. Often the lunchtime conversation degenerated into sexist jokes or stories about the "dumb blonde." Freddy and two of his male team members, Terry and Frank, had noticed Candy and never missed a chance to make a remark after Candy passed by their table. Jim decided to focus on Terry and Wilma. Terry was working on the African languages, while Wilma concentrated on the major European languages.

Terry was big, about six foot two inches, with a lot of thick black hair and a scar down one side of his face. He wouldn't say where he had gotten the scar. He had grown up in South Africa, where he became an expert on African languages, but he had left South Africa in protest over the race policies. He had lived and worked in England for a while and then was hired to work at the CCC. While many people had come and gone, Terry had been with the project from the beginning. The easy way he joked with Freddy suggested that either he liked working with Freddy or he had figured out how to stroke Freddy and was willing to do just that to keep his job. Jim asked Terry to have a beer after work, and Terry agreed. Terry, it turned out, liked beer very much and was much more willing to talk freely after pouring down a few. They went to a local hangout called Mom's that John Kennedy had made famous when he was president. It seems he had had a little too much one night and hit someone's car in the parking lot or something like that. There was nothing much to it, but the media had made a big deal out of it, and Mom's had lived off the glory ever since. Jim and Terry took a booth in the corner away from the pool tables and cigarette smoke. Jim ordered first one pitcher and then another. Terry was talking freely fifteen minutes after they entered the bar.

"So, what brought you to CCC in the first place?" Jim asked.

"The same as everyone else, I suppose: the chance to really get deep into my research without the constraints of a university," Terry responded. "I don't have to publish—in fact, I'm not allowed to publish—and of course I don't have to teach courses. All I have to do is my research. And I don't have to find jobs for my graduate students. While I liked teaching at Edinburgh, I didn't really fit into the Scottish scene. Here, in the States, people are freer to do and say what they want, if you know what I mean."

"Sure," Jim said. "Tell me, is the CCC what you expected?"

"Well, I guess I'm luckier than most," Terry responded. "I had known Freddy for many years, and he told me straight out that we would operate under his command."

"Did he use that word, command?" Jim asked.

"Yeah, that's what he said," Terry answered. "He said that as long as I didn't get too far away from the theories he felt would be useful, I could pretty much do what I wanted. That sounded pretty good to me. Of course, Freddy gets joint credit for anything good I come up with, but that's a small price to pay to be able to live out here with a good salary and no hassle. I lived in London for a while, and it took forever just to get to work. Out here I can ride my bike on a good day and I can go sailing whenever the weather is right. Because we have so much freedom I can come in and work on Sunday and then sail on Monday. No one cares as long as you put your hours in and meet your targets."

"And have you met your targets?" Jim asked.

"Yeah," Terry replied. "Oh, you're wondering why we don't have more concrete to show for our work, aren't you? Hey, I understand. I guess Wordeaters is more interested in our project than any other. I'll tell you if you promise to keep the source to yourself."

"Sure," Jim said as he poured more beer into Terry's glass.

"It's really pretty simple," Terry said. "When we first started four years ago we were all excited. I spent months trying to use transformational grammar to help create a universal translation grammar, only to find that it was useless. Well, I thought the member companies would be interested in that. After all, it was one rathole they wouldn't have to go down. And I learned a lot about what we would need to develop in the process of going down the rathole. Well, I gave a presentation and everyone seemed really interested, that is, everyone from the member companies working on this kind of software. After the meeting Hanz, or was it Fritz—have you met Hanz and Fritz?"

"Yes," Jim replied.

"I can't tell them apart," Terry said. "They seem to be Watson's hatchet men. Anyway, whichever one it was called me into his office and made it very clear that the CCC was not in the business of discussing failure. I tried to explain to him how much I had learned from this particular failure, but he was very convincing, in a Germanic kind of way, if you know what I mean."

"Yeah, I know," Jim said.

"Well, anyway," Terry continued, "I got the message. From then on I only talked about success. Of course, in this kind of basic research business there isn't a lot of success as such, so that meant I had a lot less to say. But Hanz or Fritz talked to me after the next presentation and let me know how happy he was with what I said. Of course, I had said very little, but they seemed to like that. You know, trying to work in this area between basic and applied research is not easy. In fact, it is very difficult. I don't think anyone realized how difficult it would be when we started this place. Still, it beats working for a living."

"How would you say your project was going?" Jim asked while pouring more beer into Terry's glass.

"As well as can be expected, given that Freddy is an insecure little bastard who wouldn't know a good idea if it jumped into bed with him," Terry answered. "You've seen the way he talks to the women in the project. What a bastard. Everything to him is tits and ass. These women have Ph.D.'s from places like Harvard and Yale and he treats them like dirt. Every chance he puts his hands on them or makes some kind of sexist remark."

"And that bothers you?" Jim asked.

"Yeah. I left South Africa to get away from racist and sexist bastards like Freddy," Terry said. "Oh, I go along with it. Remember, I'm the only one of the original dozen still left in the group. Don't you find it odd that I'm the only one left?"

"I guess I do, now that you mention it," Jim said.

"Damn straight," Terry said. "I love phrases like that. You Yanks love to say things like damn straight and right on and kiss my grits. English people don't say stuff like that. You know, as a person growing up in South Africa, I could tell that most of the new words and phrases in English were coming from America, not England. That was when I made up my mind to get to the United States if I ever had the chance. And here I am."

Terry's speech was becoming slurred by the beer. Jim drove Terry home.

A few days later, Jim repeated the process with Wilma. After a few beers, she was just as anxious to talk as Terry had been. Yes, she was disappointed about the sexist jokes and remarks that she and the other women had to endure from Freddy. Yes, she was disappointed that many of her ideas were never allowed to see the light of day. Yes, she was looking for another job. No woman had lasted more than two years in her group, and she was approaching the two-year anniversary. Yes, that was a shame because they usually left at about the point where they were really making a contribution, but if the top brass was unhappy about it, she couldn't tell. Surely they knew about Freddy's sexist mouth and roving hands, and surely they knew that the group was a revolving door where women were concerned. What could she do? During her two years she had tried to make a contribution, and now she would be leaving as soon as word came from New Haven that her grant had come through. She had a Ph.D. from Yale, and she would be glad to get back there. At least she could publish the results of her research and she wouldn't have to share credit with a pig like Freddy.

The next Saturday Jim, Joe, and Candy met in Jim's apartment to compare notes.

"What about security?" Jim asked Joe.

"There isn't much really," Joe answered. "Oh, there are security guards at the entrances and everyone has to have a pass to get in, but there is no real effort to check things. Particularly on the weekends, people bring their friends and family to look around and the guards just accept that they are who they say they are. Also, when someone quits or is fired, that person just packs up all his or her stuff and carries it out in boxes. The guards don't check."

"The files on the top floor contain everything, and nothing is locked up," Candy added. "I've had a couple of dates with Hanz and he laughs about it. Apparently he used to work for West German intelligence, and he thought it was pretty strange. When he asked Watson about it, he was told not to worry, so he stopped worrying. He trusts Watson completely. He figures that anything that needs to be kept secret is being kept secret by someone, and it is not his business."

"Just out of curiosity, what is his business?" Jim asked.

"I don't think he really knows," Candy answered. "He just does what he's told and walks around in expensive suits. From time to time he travels to Germany to check on something, and sometimes he translates a technological report from German into English for one of the teams. Otherwise he just sits around and reads paperback books."

"What else have you learned?" Jim asked Candy.

"Well, the chief financial officer's secretary is his mistress and Fritz's secretary is his mistress and the same goes for about half the suits on the top floor," Candy answered.

"What about Watson?" Jim asked.

"No," Candy said. "He's a straight arrow as far as I can tell. Married to the same women for over thirty years. Never any suspicion. The rest of the suits joke about him. They call him the Eagle Scout behind his back, but not where he can hear. That's the worst thing any of them have said about him. I doubt that he would consider it an insult."

"He probably was an Eagle Scout," Jim said.

"They don't even have a document destruction system," Joe added.

"What?" Jim asked.

"No document destruction system," Joe repeated. "Everything just gets dumped into the dumpster. If you wanted to know what was going on in here, all you would have to do is make a trip to the dump once a week. Of course, I haven't seen anything that anyone wouldn't be able to read about in the scientific journals, at least not in the hardware end of the place."

"Nothing earth-shaking?" Jim said.

"Not even a tremor," Joe responded. "They seem to be working on warmed-over ideas that have been rejected by places like MIT and Stanford. The high-speed boys at IBM and Siemens are way ahead of them. Not to mention Hitachi."

"Yeah, don't mention Hitachi," Jim said with a smile. "You never know who might be listening. One strategy of security that I'm sure Watson is familiar with is to make your security so lax that people penetrate it with ease. Then you spy on the people who are spying on you. It's a very old trick, and he knows all the old tricks, or so I'm told."

"The stories the guys down in the basement tell about him would make your hair stand on end," Joe added. "They say he went on his first covert mission to Laos at the age of twenty-one. It was a summer outing while he was still at West Point. They were already installing special listening devices on the main roads from the north to the south. He must have had every special training course for spooks that there is."

They decided to end the meeting and get some rest. They agreed to stay at CCC one more week and then report back to Wordeaters.

The next Monday Donny and Suzie gave a quarterly presentation to the member companies. Representatives came from all over the country. Between visiting people and liaison people and everyone who was interested, over two hundred people crowded into the auditorium to hear the presentation. Donny began with a few jokes about computers learning to think that got no laughs. Then he turned on the overhead projector and began to write strange equations on the screen. Then he threw up diagrams with a lot of arrows and boxes. It didn't mean anything to Jim, and he wondered how much it meant to those in attendance.

That night he went to dinner with a group from California's Silicon Valley. They didn't think Donny had made much progress over the last year, and the discussion turned to what could be causing the slowdown. The consensus was that while Donny had had some great ideas early on, he was running out of steam, and those he had hired did not seem to be making a contribution. Jim wondered why they were not making a contribution. The next day he sat next to Helen at lunch. Helen was a recent graduate from Stanford who had dreamed of coming to work for Donny after she heard him give a guest lecture at Stanford three years before. When she finished her Ph.D., she came straight to CCC.

"So, Helen, how are you liking the Cape?" Jim asked.

"Oh, it's OK, but it isn't the Bay Area," Helen responded. "I guess there's no place like Palo Alto, California."

"Sounds like you're a little homesick," Jim said.

"I guess so," Helen said. "I must say that this place is not what I had expected."

"In what way?" Jim asked.

"Oh, I don't know," Helen said. "I guess I thought there would be more communication between the groups. Why have everyone in the same building if each group is only going to work on its own little project and never take any interest in what other people are doing? Take the translation project. All the other software projects are strictly in English. No one seems to ask what they might do differently to make the programs work better in other languages. That could be very interesting. And then there's Donny's project. He's still on the basics. I must say I thought that after four years he would be much further along."

"Why do you think that isn't the case?" Jim asked.

"Oh, I don't know," Helen said. "I guess these things just take a lot longer than people thought in the beginning. The Japanese think tank hasn't made any more progress than the CCC. Maybe this just wasn't the right approach to the problem. Maybe there really isn't any room between basic research and product design. I don't know."

"Are you going to stay?" Jim asked.

"I don't know," Helen answered. "I'll finish out the year but after that, I just don't know."

Jim, Joe, and Candy spent their last week listening to everyone and reading everything. Then they packed up and went home to Boston. The next Monday Jim went to Walter Jackson's office to give his report. He found a group of a dozen top executives from a dozen major computer companies sitting around a table.

"Jim, these are a few of my friends from around the country," Walter said. "I know this is a surprise, but I wanted them to hear what you had to say."

"Are you sure?" Jim asked. Jim hated surprises.

"Just tell it like it is, Jim boy," Walter said.

"All right, here goes," Jim said. "I believe that the CCC will never provide the member companies with what they want if the organization is not subjected to a drastic change in structure and culture. As for organization, the idea of building each team around one great genius has failed. The other members of the team resent the fact that their ideas get someone else's name on them, and they leave. I believe that new teams must be created around the idea that everyone is equal. There would have to be a leader or manager, but this should not be the great thinker in the field. It should be someone who acts as a coordinator. There is no need to have dozens of executives on the top floor. As far as I can tell, they just take up space and money that should be used to pay researchers."

"That's pretty harsh," Walter said.

"As for culture," Jim continued, "I believe there has to be a complete change. The current culture discourages communication and exchange of ideas. I believe the main purpose of the CCC should be to allow people to see what other people are doing and feed off their discoveries. The member companies could learn a lot from the mistakes and misdirections taken by the people at the CCC, but the current top brass won't allow these kinds of things to be presented."

"What about the CEO?" Walter asked.

"He has to go," Jim said without batting an eye. "I don't know what kind of background would be best, but I don't think the military trains people to run the kind of participatory organization that the CCC must become. There have to be teams of equals, not a strict chain of command. There must be people who dress alike, not the 'suits' and the 'shorts.' There have to be people who feel free enough to say what they actually think about everything. In other words, someone who knows how to create and nurture a participatory environment must become the CEO of the CCC as quickly as possible."

After his little speech there was a long silence. Jim gave Walter the written report and turned to leave.

"Hey, wait just a minute," Walter said. "There might be questions."

"I didn't come here to talk to a committee," Jim said. "After you read my report, if you have any questions, call me."

Jim walked out the door and into the elevator. As he walked back to his office, he couldn't help but think about the time and expense that had gone into building the CCC.

He wondered what Walter and the others would do. He didn't have long to wait. In less than two weeks, Billy Watson resigned as CEO and several of the research projects were canceled. The new CEO came from a computer company that was famous for its participatory style of management. Jim could only hope that the new CEO would be able to get the CCC on the right track.

Questions for Thought and Discussion

1. How can organizations make sure that team leaders are qualified and at the same time allow the team members to decide who should be the team leader?
2. In situations where the "boss" feels that a particular person should be the team leader, how should this be handled?
3. To what extent can a participatory organization deal with special employees who are given special benefits?
4. How can a standard hierarchical organization change over to a team-based organization with employee empowerment?
5. How should team leaders be trained in a participatory organization?
6. To what extent should personality characteristics control the selection of team leaders?
7. How should mistakes and negative results be handled in a participatory organization?
8. What criteria should be used to judge the CEO of a participatory organization?
9. How can a participatory organization encourage internal communication and still keep some things secret from the outside world?
10. If you were the new CEO of the CCC, what would you do next?

Chapter 14

The White House Staff Reorganization

Introduction

The White House chief of staff was given the task of reforming the White House staff so that its members would work together better. He turned to McSam Jackson, an old hand in Washington, D.C. McSam suggested that a more participatory structure might help and that the best way to begin to make the transition would be to hold a staff retreat at Camp David. He suggested that one way to reorganize the White House staff would be to force the staff to reorganize itself.

The White House Staff Reorganization

Frank Bluestone was the fourth White House chief of staff in less than two years. The president had told him to shape the place up. It was not exactly clear what that meant. While the president seemed to be saying that Frank should get tough, Frank knew that many of the members of the staff had the ear of the president or the first lady and that it would be impossible to really get tough with anyone. But something had to be done. Too many people were working at cross-purposes, and too much time was being wasted on insider-bureaucratic politics. It was September, and Congress had just left for the campaign trail. The first two years of the president's term had seen the other party win a lot of special elections, and personal scandals of one kind or another had made it difficult for the president and his staff to concentrate on the job at hand. Something had to change over the second two years or this was going to be just another one-term president. Frank had called McSam Jackson to have lunch at the old Pilgrim Hotel. He knew McSam would have some sage advice for him.

Frank walked into the lobby of the Pilgrim Hotel and saw McSam sitting in one of the large overstuffed chairs that the place is famous for. Frank walked quickly as McSam rose to shake his hand.

"Glad you could talk to me," Frank said.

"Hell, boy," McSam answered, "I'm more than glad to meet you for a little gabfest. At my age, what would I have to do if you young fellows didn't invite me to lunch once in a while?"

McSam had been on FDR's staff during World War II, and at the age of eighty-six he was considered the grand old man of Washington. He was also the one man both political parties trusted for honest advice, and he had a reputation for never repeating anything he saw or heard. That alone made him almost unique in the nation's capital. As they were shown to one of the booths the Pilgrim Hotel restaurant was famous for, booths with high backs and thick curtains that could be drawn to keep out prying eyes and ears, they said nothing. They both ordered the special of the day and iced tea without looking at the menu.

"Now, boy, what can this old war horse do for you?" McSam asked, after taking a long drink from a giant glass.

"Well, I don't have to tell you I'm the new chief of staff at the big house," Frank said. "The president wants the infighting and backstabbing to stop, but of course most of the boys and girls over there have more political connections than I'll ever have, and I can't really fire anyone or even change their job description without expecting a tidal wave to come crashing over my head."

McSam laughed a big laugh and said, "Yeah, boy, that place hasn't really changed much since my day. Of course, Franklin ran the country and fought World War II with a staff of less than two dozen and now you have—what is it, over two hundred at last count, isn't it?"

Frank nodded his head in agreement. McSam continued.

"Look, there are really only two ways to manage people. There is the get tough old-fashioned way, and you say that's not really an option. The other way is to turn the tables on them."

"Turn the tables?" Frank asked. "What do you mean turn the tables?"

"Look, you got big trouble right here in River City," McSam continued. "Everyone on the White House staff thinks they could do a better job as chief of staff than you. OK, let them run things. Turn things over to them and let them tell you how to reorganize the place, who to move where, and so on."

"How can I get away with that?" Frank asked.

"Well, I've been reading a lot about using participatory management," McSam continued. "Why don't you and I and your three or four most trusted assistants prepare a week at Camp David for the whole group?"

"A week?" Frank almost screamed. "I can't take the whole White House staff to Camp David for a week. The media will have a field day. And who will get the work done?"

"What work?" McSam asked. "With Congress gone out to campaign, you and I know that your sacred two hundred will be plotting and leaking stories to the newspapers and everything else that people on a White House staff do when things slow down. It seems to me that if you get them to Camp David for a week, with a few hundred Marines guarding the place, you couldn't ask for a quieter week. And who knows, you might see some good from it."

"You mean you'll help me with this personally?" Frank asked.

"Of course," McSam answered. "I'm the only one who can convince the president to let you do this. I'm also the only one with a security clearance high enough to be in charge of this."

"But is there room for two hundred people at Camp David?" Frank asked.

"Hell, back in 1943 we did something similar with the top brass of the military," McSam answered. "We must have had over three hundred. We put up tents and had the Marines dig a few extra latrines. Man, it was a real show. Of course we can do it. Remember, if there's one place where the president gets what he wants, it's at Camp David. It's his personal little military base. Christ, if he ordered the 82nd Airborne to guard the place there would be paratroopers falling from the sky in a matter of hours."

"OK, we'll do it," Frank said. "Who is going to tell the president, you or me?"

"You'd better let me handle that," McSam answered. "I think I can make him an offer he can't refuse."

"What if he or the first lady wants to come?" Frank asked.

"That's something I have to explain," McSam said. "One of your problems, as I read it in the newspapers, is that the president and first lady are too involved in everything. I think I have to make it clear that this is a retreat for you and the staff, and that if the president or the first lady shows up, things will just degenerate into the usual backstabbing and string pulling."

The waiter arrived with the lunch special, fried catfish and hush puppies. They had given McSam an extra large helping of everything in honor of his three hundred plus pounds. He was well known in the kitchen of the Pilgrim Hotel. The first time he had sat in that booth it was with the then first lady when she convinced him to work at the White House for FDR. Frank Bluestone didn't know it, but he was sitting where Eleanor Roosevelt had sat decades before.

The media didn't notice it when McSam Jackson slipped into the White House after dinner that night. He knew enough to go in after the news media had all filed their stories and left for the day. He walked up the familiar back stairs to the president's personal quarters. The president knew that when McSam Jackson made a suggestion, you took it and he listened and agreed. The whole staff would do a week at Camp David. The president and the first lady had a week on the campaign trail planned, so the timing couldn't have been better. After their brief conversation, the president offered McSam some apple pie with chocolate ice cream. Everyone in Washington knew that this was McSam's favorite dessert, and he accepted the oversized dish with a smile. The president had some himself just to be polite.

The president made a few phone calls the next morning, and everything was set for the big retreat. The commander at Camp David called in two companies of Marines to help with the job of setting up tents and digging extra latrines. There would be a field mess tent to feed the two hundred, plus the Marines, and some special communications equipment was also brought in. Meanwhile McSam and Frank met for several days straight to get things ready. Everyone on the staff was told to pack light for a five-day stay, and it seemed as if the weather was going to cooperate: the forecast was for mild temperatures and no rain. On Monday morning the area around the White House looked like a large group heading off for summer camp. There were two hundred staff members climbing into five military buses for the ride to Camp David. The Secret Service was in charge of security, and their cars led the caravan into the Maryland hills.

When the buses arrived, a group of Marine officers made sure the staff got their quarters as quickly as possible. Then everyone met in the mess tent for an early lunch and a big meeting. After the food, Frank gave a short speech telling them how much he hoped to get out of the week and then turned the show over to McSam. McSam had on bright pink pants and a flowered shirt. He looked like something from a bad commercial for Hawaii.

"Good morning, troops," McSam said with a laugh into the microphone from the small makeshift stage at one end of the mess tent. "You will be here for one week. Why? Because everyone in this room knows that if the White House continues on the path it has been on, you will all be out of a job in two years. Most of you know me, or know of me. I don't lie. Things are serious. Something has to change. I know that each of you worked hard to get this president elected and that each of you wants to do everything you can to help him get reelected. No country is going to reelect someone who can't even control his own staff. It's that simple. None of you are going to be fired or anything like that. Our job during the course of this week is to come up with answers to a lot of questions and then go back to the White House and make changes. If you go back to business as usual, this week will have been a failure, and I'll take the blame. I won't be happy about that. Have any of you ever seen a three-hundred-pound man when he is unhappy? No. Well, you won't like it. Each of you has a pink piece of paper like the one I am holding in my hand. There are five questions on it. You will break up into twenty groups of ten. A Marine officer will lead each group to its work tent. There you will find a blackboard, paper, pencils, and all the rest. Each group must elect a president and a secretary, and before you can get dinner tonight, you must turn in acceptable answers to these questions. By acceptable I mean that you have clearly thought about the questions and tried to answer them. Remember, until Frank Bluestone and I are happy with your answers, no food. After dinner tonight we will meet here again and read some of the responses."

Everyone left to form groups as the Marine officers called out names. The five questions on the list were:

1. What is the purpose of the White House staff?
2. How can the staff be reorganized to better achieve that purpose?

3. What has been the major obstacle to the successful performance of the staff?
4. If I ran the White House staff, I would...
5. If the president is going to be reelected two years from now, the White House staff must...

Several hours later the first group emerged from its tent and headed for dinner. At the door the group members found Frank and McSam sitting at a table. They turned in their answers. Their answer to the first question was "Help the president." McSam sent them back. That was not enough of an answer. The next group had said that the staff was supposed to help the president formulate policy and sell that policy to Congress and the people. That was more like it. One by one the groups made it past Frank and McSam and into dinner. After dinner McSam got up to address the crowd again.

"All right, we will be printing up copies of your answers during the night, and you will pick them up at breakfast. I'll let tomorrow's activities be a surprise. For tonight, I want to ask a few questions, and I just want you to yell out the first thing that comes to your mind. Ready? All right, if the White House is a factory, what does it produce?"

"Bullshit," was the first response yelled from the back of the room.

"Press releases," was the second response from a young woman at the front.

"Leaks to the news media."

"Entertainment for the American people."

"Policy analysis and criticism."

"Stroking for Congress."

"Jobs for staff members."

"Material for the 'Tonight' show monologue."

"Solutions to the nation's most important problems."

"With that last response, ladies and gentlemen, I think we have hit something on the head," McSam said. "Why do presidents get reelected? Because they are perceived as making some headway toward solving some of the nation's most important problems. Whatever you thought of President Reagan, he set out to do three things and he did them: Spend the Russians under the table, provide millions of new jobs, and make the rich much richer. He did just that, and the nation perceived him as doing just that. As the economy got better and the Russians got weaker, people felt that he was doing something. Tonight, before you go to bed, I want you to list on a piece of paper the three things you think this president should do between now and the next presidential election and give it to your Marine officer. Good night."

As the crowd broke up, high-speed copying machines were making copies of the answers to the five questions that the twenty groups had come up with. McSam and Frank sat alone in the cabin next to the president's quarters.

"Well, what do you think?" Frank asked.

"I think we're starting to get through to them," McSam answered. "They came to Washington with hopes and dreams of making America better. Call me crazy, but I really believe that. That's why I came here in 1941. The White House staff wants to do a good job. They have just found themselves in an organizational structure not of their own making that most of them find difficult to deal with. Tomorrow we focus on that."

"How?" Frank asked.

"Oh, you'll see," McSam answered. "And I hope you have a good sense of humor."

Frank left for his quarters. McSam Jackson had the best room at Camp David, and no one questioned that. There was a full moon, and McSam couldn't sleep. As he wandered around the grounds, his mind went back to the old days when President Roosevelt would race around a corner in his wheelchair and challenge you to a game of Ping-Pong or croquet. President Truman liked to get everyone in a circle around a campfire and tell ghost stories. And the Kennedy clan was always good for a practical joke of one kind or another. Eisenhower liked to tell stories about the stupid generals he had been forced to work with coming up in the Army, and Nixon had led a few sing-alongs after dinner. McSam Jackson had seen them all. They all had had trouble of one kind or another with their staffs. It was the same old story. About the time everyone figured out how to get things done, it was time for a new group to learn the same old lessons all over again.

The next morning McSam had new instructions. Each group of ten was to spend the morning preparing a skit. It had to be funny, and it had to illustrate a problem with the way the White House is run. There would be prizes for the best skits and punishment for any group that did not come up with something that was both funny and informative. McSam did not make it clear what the punishment might be, but he held a long bullwhip while he talked and gave it a crack once in a while to punctuate an important point. He had on a cowboy outfit, complete with chaps and a ten-gallon hat. If you don't think the sight of a three-hundred-pound, six-foot four-inch, eighty-six-year-old man cracking a giant bullwhip got people's attention, you have another think coming.

As the groups worked, McSam and Frank moved from tent to tent listening to people's ideas. One group wanted to make fun of the way the president was always interrupting people and screaming at people. That was not a good idea. They could make fun of each other, but not the president or the first lady. Another group wanted to spend its skit on its favorite bad Congressman. That would not help either.

After lunch the skits were performed. One group gave a brilliant presentation of Washington double-talk. It went something like this:

"Hello, White House, how may I help you?" the young woman sitting at the reception desk said.

"I need a really hot story for the evening edition," the man in the hat said, with a pad and pencil in his hand.

"I'll direct you to the hot story department, one moment," she said as she rose and went to the imaginary door. She opened it and screamed, "What's our hot story for tonight?"

The rest of the group sang a chorus of "Our hot story tonight is that the president flunked a spelling test in the fourth grade and changed the grade sheet years later after the teacher was dead in order to get a scholarship. This enabled him to go on to law school and become president of the United States."

Another group had each member of the group hold a mask and say one thing with the mask up, then translate it with the mask down. A tall, thin man who specialized in foreign policy said through his mask, "Oh yes, we really do care about the refugees." With his mask down, he said, "We care that they not look too thin on the evening news."

Another group hit a nerve when they put on a mock policy discussion with everyone contradicting one another and throwing papers around the room. At the end the meeting, each person stood up in turn and said an exit line:

"Well, I know the president will go along with my idea."

"I'm sure the first lady will agree with me."

"The secretary of the department is on my side."

"You know what the news media will say if we really do this."

"My daddy will beat up your daddy if you don't do as I say."

Everyone laughed, but this childish display was too close to the truth. People started asking themselves how things had gotten so messed up. McSam thought it was time to go over some of the answers to the first five questions.

"Everyone, attention," McSam said from the stage. "We have had a little fun, but now back to work. You all read the responses to the five basic questions, and now it's time for us to come up with some answers that mean something. I want to focus now on how you would reorganize the staff if you had the chance. There are basically three suggestions. Some of you think we should have clearer lines of authority, with some people concentrating on working with Congress while others concentrate on gathering information and formulating policy. This group sees the White House as a factory that produces and markets policy and thinks that production and marketing should be more clearly separated. A second group thinks that teams should be formed around particular policy areas and that those teams should both formulate policy and market it. They think that elected team leaders or team leaders that rotate would make a big difference. A third group thinks that there's already too much group interaction. They complain that they spend too much time in meetings that go on forever. They want someone to tell them, as individuals, what to do, and then allow them to do it. I have put you into new groups of twenty to discuss this. Each group has representatives from each of the three camps. I want you to come back after dinner with a choice. We can't reorganize the White House in all three ways. We must make a choice. Do we want production and marketing, subject area teams, or individuals with bosses? You tell me."

Again, as their names were called, people followed a Marine officer to a discussion tent. The discussions became heated in many cases, and Frank and McSam moved around the grounds to break up fights and get people back on track. This was the key discussion. Once all two hundred people had gone over this ground, they would be able to move to the next stage. Until then, there was no hope of making progress. Frank and McSam took a break by the small lake.

"I'll bet this lake could tell some stories," Frank said.

"Hell, boy, you don't need the lake to tell stories when you got me," McSam said. "One time I pushed Bobby Kennedy into that lake. They were all playing football right over there, and I was fishing right here. All of a sudden Bobby Kennedy comes over to me and asks me to throw him the ball. Well, I didn't appreciate being interrupted, so I pretended I couldn't hear him. When he came closer, I just gave him a little push. He was off balance, and he went right in. The whole group jumped in right after him, but I don't think Bobby appreciated it."

"Was President Kennedy part of the game?" Frank asked.

"Sure," McSam answered. "He was the first one in the lake, after Bobby, that is."

As Frank and McSam returned to sit in on the group discussions, it was clear that a consensus was emerging in most of the groups. The major problem, as many staff members saw it, with the current organization, or lack of organization, was that too many people spoke to the same audiences on too many issues. It was decided that the staff should be divided into ten groups, five marketing groups representing the five major regions of the country and five substantive groups. The five substantive groups would cover foreign policy, financial policy, law and judicial policy, industrial policy, and natural resource policy. Each of the ten new teams would have about twenty members. Each of the marketing teams would deal with the politicians and news media in its region. Each of the policy teams would make sure that the president had the best ideas and information from around the country on that policy concern. These teams would interact with the bureaucracy and experts at universities.

The next job was figuring out who would be on which team. Wednesday was spent on this task. Each person wrote on a piece of paper which teams were the first and second choice and why. After dinner Frank and McSam went through these and tried to put everyone on a team. By midnight they had the roster of the new teams. They turned the lists over to the Marines at the copy center and went to bed. The next morning everyone could read what team he or she had been assigned to. The next task was having each team meet and make sure everyone knew everyone else. At lunch McSam conducted a secret ballot election for the leader of each team. Frank had not realized that he would not be the one to pick the leaders. A few groups could not come up with a clear candidate. Frank then made the choice from among the top candidates.

On Thursday, the new teams role-played various problems. Each team had to come up with a role-play exercise in the morning. Then the five marketing teams met in the afternoon. Each of the five teams ran through each of the five role-play exercises. They came up with: (1) dealing with the difficult Congressman who wants a favor, (2) dealing with the difficult newsperson who wants a favor, (3) calling in a favor to get something from a Congressman, (4) leaking to a newsperson, and (5) using the president's time wisely to get a bill passed.

Each of the five policy teams came up with its own role-play exercise. They spent the afternoon in another location (1) telling the president things he doesn't want to hear, (2) getting information out of the agencies, (3) making sure the options have been spelled out, (4) dealing with conflict in a meeting, and (5) keeping the first lady informed without making it seem like she runs the show.

By dinner everyone seemed to accept the new team structure and the new team leaders. Only one team leader seemed really unpopular, and that was from a group that seemed to have a lot of strong personalities. Frank and McSam discussed this problem.

"Hey, you can't expect every one of these new leaders to work out," McSam said. "After a few months you need to evaluate each team's performance with some objective criteria."

"Where will I get objective criteria?" Frank asked.

"Funny you should ask," McSam responded. "Tomorrow is our last day. We're going to explain that you want objective criteria in order to evaluate the ten teams, and they need to come up with some. We won't expect that job to be finished at the end of Friday, but they need to make a start."

"I can't think what you mean in this area," Frank confided.

"Well, let's think about it," McSam said. "Each of these teams will have customers and suppliers that they have to work with. You could survey these people to see how they think the teams are doing. Then there's the success or failure of a policy or the success or failure of a marketing team to get the votes or the right news stories. I think you will have to work with the president to make him be objective concerning how he sees the performance of each team. Part of his job will be to let you know if the teams are accomplishing what he wants accomplished. He is, after all, the ultimate customer of all this stuff."

"But that will be hard," Frank said. "The president doesn't like to say anything bad about anyone."

"Yeah, they all have that trouble," McSam agreed. "Well, in a way it's not your job. It's each team's job to come up with objective criteria for its performance. I think you can count on them to do just that."

"You know, McSam," Frank said. "I can't believe where we are on this project. A week ago I had no idea how I was going to reorganize these people, and now they have done it for me."

"The secret," McSam said, "is to keep this going after this week. You have to work with the team leaders to keep them listening and using participation management. You have to punish people who spread rumors or play too much politics inside the White House. You have to reward people who do their job and get results. Running a group of highly motivated people who know their job and want to do a good job is not easy. You have to get to work before they do and leave after they do. You have to make sure they have the resources they need to do a good job."

"Yeah, I see what you mean," Frank said.

The next day the teams worked hard to come up with a list of objective criteria for their own evaluation. It was difficult going, but things began to emerge. Everyone agreed that the ultimate evaluation would come in two years, on election day. At the end of the last day, Friday, the buses loaded up their special cargo and headed back to the White House. Everyone would be able to spend Friday night at home. That was their reward for working hard and trying to play the game. Frank and McSam reported to the president that night and explained what the group had come up with. They also tried to explain to him how a participation strategy would work at the White House. It would require him to stay out of the process more than had been the case in the past. He would need to work with individual teams and team leaders on problems, rather than wandering around the White House offices talking to everyone about everything. He would have to charge policy teams with particular problems and marketing teams with particular goals. Above all, he would have to set the priorities for each team. The purpose of the White House staff was to help him move the country in a particular direction. He would have to help the teams help him to make that direction clear.

A few weeks later Frank and McSam met again at the Pilgrim Hotel. They sat in the same booth and ordered the special.

"Well, how's it going?" McSam asked.

"Oh, it's coming along," Frank said. "I only wish I could have a retreat at Camp David every few months."

"You can, of course," McSam said. "You can do anything you want. I've often wondered why the president didn't get particular policy teams together with key politicians and bureaucrats for a few days at Camp David. Wouldn't they come up with something unique?"

"I'll mention it to him tonight after the concert," Frank answered.

"Well, what can I do for you now?" McSam asked.

"I need some more help with the team leaders," Frank responded. "Some of them are really getting into this participation style. They like to encourage people to take initiative, and they feel comfortable with group decisions. A couple have reverted to the old way of telling people what to do and how to do it. It's my biggest problem now."

"Easy. Take the team leaders to Camp David for a weekend and have them talk about how to be a participatory team leader," McSam said.

"Do you think that will do it?" Frank asked. "I don't think these guys will ever get it."

"Look, you can't just fire them," McSam said, "without giving them a chance to get with the program. If, after you work with them and the other leaders work with them, they can't do it, then yes, you will have to do something."

"Boy, when you came up with this participation stuff, I thought I would never have to fire anyone," Frank said.

"Oh, you still have to fire people," McSam said. "You just fire them for different reasons. You fire them for not being able to listen and let the group deal with problems. You fire them for giving orders rather than receiving agendas. You fire them for not meeting criteria that they have set up. I never told you that people would not have to go."

"I guess so," Frank said.

The food arrived, fried chicken with mashed potatoes. McSam loved this kind of food, and it showed. As he ate his chicken and watched Frank, he knew that the nation had a lot of hard-working people trying to do the people's business. Fighting a war was really a lot easier than trying to ensure economic growth and the spread of democracy around the world. Peace was always tougher than war. McSam wondered why people couldn't seem to understand that. The nation was always quick to praise the war president and quick to criticize the peace president. Hell, if he were president, but that was a different story.

Questions for Thought and Discussion

1. To what extent can a retreat be useful for a participatory organization?
2. What are the major problems that come up when an organization tries to become more participatory?
3. What is the best approach to team creation in an existing organization?
4. How can the CEO show support for participation without making all the decisions that have to be made when the transition comes?
5. How can bringing in someone from the outside help to make the transition to teams and empowerment easier?
6. How can a basic suggestion plan be used to create change in an organization?
7. How can role-playing be used to teach people what to expect when teams and participation control the organization?
8. What skills do people need to work well in teams?
9. How do you deal with team leaders who just don't get it?
10. How far can a government agency go with teams and empowerment?

Chapter 15
The New College President

Introduction

The new president of Fonderack College was forced, for financial reasons, to cut faculty and staff. She hoped to use teams and empowerment to help make up for the loss, and she turned to the existing staff and faculty for help. This was not as easy as she had thought it would be. She learned a lot about setting up teams to make suggestions for organizational change. She also learned what was possible with the support of the board of directors.

The New College President

Martha Smith had wanted to be a college president ever since she first went to graduate school at Brown University. After receiving her Ph.D. in English, she had taught at several small colleges because she liked being able to get to know her students. She had been chosen dean at her last post, and now she had been hired as the new president of Fonderack College. Fonderack had about 1,200 students and about a hundred professors, which was a great ratio for the students but was too expensive for the college to afford. Martha Smith had been hired to cut costs. The first thing she did was hire a consultant to examine the college and make recommendations. The consultant, Fred Worth, had studied the problem for several weeks, and he was ready to present his findings. Martha decided that she and Fred should meet for the morning at the local hotel to avoid interruptions.

"Well, Fred, what's the good word?" Martha asked.

"I have no good words, I'm afraid," Fred responded. "You have to cut a dozen faculty positions and two dozen support staff positions. You also have to cut the use of paper in half, and you need to make better use of the facilities."

"What do you suggest?" Martha asked.

"I suggest that you reorganize everything, but I think it would be better if you allowed the people who will be directly affected to have an input," Fred said. "Before you get to that stage, you should first announce the layoffs and send away those who will be let go as quickly as possible."

"I can't let the faculty go until the end of the school year," Martha said. "They all have one-year contracts or tenure. Since I have only thirty untenured faculty, I guess I won't have much choice in that area."

"That's true, unless you can get some of the older faculty to retire," Fred said. "I would consider making some kind of golden handshake offer."

"A golden handshake?" Martha asked.

"Yeah," Fred responded. "You tell people, 'if you retire now, we will give you some extra money.' Since the retirement plan is completely separate from your college budget, that will work. I think that if you offer them six or eight thousand a year extra for the next five years if they retire, you will get some takers."

"That's a lot of money to pay for nothing," Martha objected.

"Well, suit yourself," Fred said, "but that's my recommendation. As to the support staff, you have a lot of secretaries around here. Since everyone uses word processors, I think many of them should go. If you put in a voice mail system for the faculty and administrators, the job of taking messages could be taken over by the system. If you introduced an internal electronic mail system, most of the memorandums that are currently typed up and copied and distributed by the secretaries could be sent electronically. While this will cost money in the beginning, I think you could cut a dozen secretaries and pay for the equipment with the money you would save in the first year. I've made a list of other possible positions that could be cut."

Fred handed the list to Martha, who was shocked. "I can't cut some of these positions," Martha said. "These are high-level people."

"Exactly," Fred said. "They take in big salaries, and as far as I can see, they don't really contribute much to the college. Several of these people could be sent back to teach. Others could be sent on to another job.

Frankly, this place is just too small for all of these people. I've examined your current structure. You have two dozen departments for a faculty of less than one hundred. That means that the average department has only four or five faculty members. That makes no sense. I suggest five or six schools, each with a dean and a secretary, to replace this current structure. Since this will eliminate department chairpersons and department secretaries, this will save a lot of time and money."

"I see," Martha said. "Anything else?"

"Yes," Fred said. "I think you should allow the faculty and the staff to come up with the new structure. I think a task force of faculty could come up with the new school structure, and a task force of the white-collar and blue-collar staffs could come up with their own new structure. I suggest putting everyone into teams, and the best way to do that is to fire everyone that's going to lose their job and then help those who are left to come up with the new system."

Martha was almost speechless. She knew that she had to cut, but she had not realized that at a college, most of the money goes for people. To make a significant cut in costs, there had to be a significant cut in people. It was time to put in some automation at Fonderack College, ready or not.

Martha had announced that she would make a speech the next Friday afternoon to explain her cost-cutting ideas. The main auditorium was packed as Martha explained what she was about to do. She made it clear that eliminating positions and putting in automation was something that had to be done. She also announced that she would be setting up groups that would be called change teams to examine everything from courses offered to the use of toilet paper. Every person would be on a team, and some of the teams would have both faculty and staff as members. She also announced the golden handshake for older faculty. Because of the need to plan for change, she asked older faculty who were interested to let her know as soon as possible.

The next week everyone was put on a change team, and the place really got down to business. The automation team, made up of faculty and staff, called in various communications and computer companies to find the best voice mail and electronic mail system for the money. Personal computers that could call up the mainframe computer could handle the electronic mail. Students would be asked to send messages to faculty through the electronic mail system whenever possible. Another team examined the campus mail structure. Currently, one person spent all day taking mail around the campus to the various administrative offices and the departments. It was suggested that the central mailroom be expanded so that every member of the faculty and staff had a mailbox at that central location. That would eliminate one position. The use of electronic mail would eliminate another position and reduce the need for secretaries.

Fred Worth had found that the average faculty member spent a third of his or her time on things other than teaching and research. A change team was given the assignment of cutting that down as much as possible. The students could still be served with fewer faculty if the remaining faculty had more time for them. The president served on that team as just a member.

The first team meeting took place in the faculty lounge at four o'clock. The dozen faculty members who were members came in one at a time, and it wasn't until a quarter past four that everyone was ready. The president began the meeting.

"I am not going to be the captain of this team," Martha announced when everyone was present. "I want you to elect someone today to fill that post. I am here because it's important for me to understand the kinds of things that take up faculty time and that could be handled some other way. Before we pick a captain, perhaps we could just kick some ideas around."

There was silence for several minutes. Finally a young professor spoke up.

"What exactly do you want us to say?" Ted Wilson asked.

"I want you to think about everything you do each day that does not involve teaching or research so that we can find ways to eliminate that drain on your time," Martha responded.

"I don't know if we can just come up with that off the top of our heads," Ted said. "Perhaps for the next week we should all keep some kind of diary and write down how we spend our time every day. Then we get together again and compare notes. I also think that Martha Smith should be the captain of this team and that she should spend a few days following some of us around to see what we do here."

Before Martha could object, this was taken as a motion, seconded, and voted on by everyone. Martha was the captain, and she was to spend several days during the coming week following faculty members around. The first thing she noticed was that the faculty spent a great deal of time listening to the personal problems of the students. She also noticed that when faculty tried to help students understand the various requirements they had to meet in order to graduate, a great deal of time was spent without much to show for it. She brought these and other issues up at her next change team meeting.

"I'm glad you've noticed all these things," Ted Wilson said after Martha had summarized her impressions to the group, "but what are you prepared to do about it?"

"I'm not prepared to do anything, but this group can do whatever it feels it should to increase the amount of time faculty spend on teaching and research," Martha answered.

"Excuse me, Madam President," William Acton said in a very sarcastic tone, "but we've heard this kind of thing before from past presidents and nothing ever came of it. Why should we believe that this will be any different?"

"Because we have to cut costs, and the only way I can cut costs and maintain service is to help faculty to increase the amount of time they spend on important tasks," Martha responded. "I can't do it without your help."

"All right, then we need to greatly simplify the course requirements," William said. "What has happened over the decades is that the departments have added courses to the required course list to the point where I don't understand what the requirements are. What are you going to do about that?"

"I'm not going to do anything," Martha responded, "but this team can change that."

"Oh, sure," William said. "Just like that."

"Yes, just like that," Martha said. "Look, I know you have all been on academic committees before where recommendations were made and nothing ever happened. These change teams are different. I, the president of the college, have given them the power to actually make changes. If you think the required course list is too complicated, then change it. If you think faculty spend too much time listening to students' personal problems, then come up with a way to minimize that time. You have the power, subject only to final approval by the board of directors."

"I suggest that we set up a system where students have four required courses in the first year, three in the second year, two in the third year, and one in the fourth year," Ted Wilson said. "If we could agree on the basic number of general required courses, we could work from there."

There was a long silence. No one on the faculty at Fonderack College had ever made a proposal like that. The required courses would be simple and straightforward. Students would know exactly what they had to take each year. No longer would there be dozens of categories and dozens of choices in each category. There would be ten required courses during the students' four years. The other members were in shock at the very idea. Martha could tell that they were not going to get much further that day.

"I suggest that each of us discuss this idea with other faculty members and come back with a suggestion as to what the required course list would look like based on Ted's proposal," Martha said. "We will each propose what the first-, second-, third-, and fourth-year required courses should be. Now, how do we deal with the problem of students' taking up so much of the faculty's time with their personal problems?"

"Why don't we have a psychologist on staff that we could send people to?" William said. "I know we're cutting back, but I think this would be a useful addition to the staff."

The discussion of that idea took up the rest of the hour. Martha left that meeting and went straight to the group discussing how to organize the college into schools. There were proposals for everything from two to a dozen, but the group came around to five: natural sciences, social sciences, humanities, arts, and business. They voted to eliminate the position of academic vice president. Everyone hated the current academic vice president, and the argument was made that the president would now be meeting and setting policy with the five deans, so there was no need for an academic vice president. The group also decided to eliminate the other vice president positions. The current business affairs vice president was an alcoholic, and the other vice president had announced his retirement. There would be five deans to run the academic side of the college and five directors to run the rest of the college: library, food service, building maintenance, grounds, and finances. The group felt that with a dean of admissions and a dean of students, the president would have twelve people reporting to her, and she should be able to handle that.

Martha Smith was not prepared for the resistance she would find in the staff change teams. She attended several meetings, and there was no discussion and no ideas. Something else would have to be tried. Martha decided to meet with staff members individually to discuss the problem. She began with Wilma Jones, assistant librarian.

"Now, Wilma," Martha began. "The purpose of the change teams is to save money and make everyone's life easier. I attended the team you belong to, and there were no ideas. Can you help me stimulate some ideas from your team?"

"I don't think so," Wilma said. "You see, my team is a combination of professionals, like myself, and people who do manual labor, such as the grounds staff. We simply don't have anything in common."

Martha had not expected that. "OK, then who do you think should be on your change team?" Martha asked.

"I'm sure I don't know," Wilma said, "but you could think in terms of people who have college degrees and people who do not."

"No, Wilma, you aren't going to put this on me," Martha said. "I give you the assignment of forming a change team that makes sense to you. It must have at least ten people on it, and it must come up with at least a dozen suggestions for changes that will save either time or money."

"And what is in it for us besides losing our jobs?" Wilma asked.

Martha realized for the first time that she was asking people to do something without any reward other than the joy of cutting expenses. While that was reward enough for her, it was not for them.

"What would you like me to give you as a reward?" Martha asked.

"I think a staff lounge would be nice," Wilma said. "There's a faculty lounge, but the rest of the staff don't have a place where they can go to have a cup of coffee and take a break. What if you told the staff that if they saved enough money, some of the money would be used to create and furnish a staff lounge?"

"Wilma, that's a wonderful idea," Martha said. "I want you to form three change teams, one professional, one white-collar, and one blue-collar. Tell them they can have a lounge if they can come up with some real money-saving ideas."

When Martha returned to her office, she found the president of the student body, Jane Alexander, waiting for her.

"What can I do for you, Jane?" Martha asked.

"I hear through the grapevine that the faculty is considering making a major change in the required courses here at the college," Jane said.

"That's right," Martha said. "We want to make the requirements easier to understand and administer."

"Fine, but why not let the students have some input into this decision?" Jane asked. "And what about the alumni? Why not ask them which required courses have really helped them in graduate school or later life and which were a waste of their time?"

Martha was shaken. No one had ever suggested asking alumni what they thought about required courses. Doing something like that could cost her the presidency. The faculty would consider her a traitor to their interests, and the alumni would resent it if their opinions were gathered and then ignored. Martha had to think fast.

"Listen, Jane, I don't think we have time for that," Martha said.

"Why not do a random survey?" Jane said. "We could do it as part of my social research class. We could poll 10 percent of the alumni and follow up with phone calls to increase the response rate. I bet the president of the alumni would help by getting some money for postage and printing. Shall I call her?"

Martha was trapped. How could she say no? After all, the idea was to save money and increase the level of education and service to the students. Besides, the alumni might get more interested in the college if they thought their ideas were being listened to.

"All right, Jane," Martha said. "I'll go along with this, but only if you can get some funds out of the alumni president." As Jane left the office, Martha began to wonder if she had created a monster.

The next morning when Martha came to work, there were student demonstrators marching around the administration building. They handed her a list of demands as she walked in the door. The students wanted input into all the change team decisions. They wanted to suggest jobs that could be turned into student part-time jobs, saving the college money and providing work for the students. They wanted the food in the cafeteria to be better (the students put this on every list of demands as a matter of routine). The students wanted to know what courses were being cut, and they wanted to have input into even the smallest changes. As

Martha sat down at her desk, the phone rang. It was Donna Jackson, the alumni president.

"Yes, Donna, what can I do for you?" Martha said into the phone.

"I just want to tell you how excited I am about asking the alumni for their input into the changes you are making at Fonderack College," Donna said. "Imagine, after all these years, someone is finally going to actually ask the alumni their opinion concerning required courses. I would like to expand the survey to include any ideas they might have on changes that might both save money and improve service."

"Why, yes, Donna, that sounds, uh, that sounds like a great idea," Martha said. "Of course, you understand that you will have to come up with the money from alumni gifts for this purpose. I don't have any funds to pay for the survey."

"Oh, that's all right," Donna said. "I've already got pledges from enough people to expand this to a survey of all the alumni, not just a random sample, and I've formed a committee to meet with students to come up with questions. I don't think the faculty should have any input into this. Heaven knows they get their way most of the time. I would like this to be just students and alumni. OK?"

"Why, yes," Martha said. "I wouldn't have it any other way. I just hope you can come up with something as quickly as possible."

"Don't you worry about that," Donna said. "I've got a meeting of the steering committee set for tomorrow night at my house. I think we can get the survey printed and in the mail by the end of next week."

"Great," Martha said. "Well, let me know how things go."

Martha hung up the phone and sat staring out the window. What had she done? How would the faculty react to a survey of alumni opinion about required courses? She knew as well as anyone that there were two motivations when required courses were chosen: the desire to make sure that the students had a real breadth of knowledge, combined with the need to provide courses for tenured faculty who were not popular enough to draw students without a requirement. This was something everyone knew but no one talked about. Just then the chairperson of the foreign language department, Matilda Franks, walked in the door.

"Martha, I have to speak to you," Matilda said, out of breath.

"Of course," Martha said. "Sit down."

"I understand that you are thinking of asking the students and alumni about the required course list," Matilda said.

"Why, yes," Martha said, "I am."

"You can't," Matilda said. "I know what they will say— that there should not be a foreign language requirement. That's what students and alumni have said at other colleges, and I'm sure they will say the same thing here. I have a young and mostly tenured faculty. If there isn't a foreign language requirement, I simply won't have enough courses for them to teach."

"Take it easy, Matilda," Martha said. "Yes, we are going to ask the opinion of students and alumni, but that does not mean we're going to do everything they say. The faculty will still have the final word."

"Yeah, that's what they said in California years ago, and look what happened to their foreign language departments after the language requirements were dropped," Matilda said. "I'm telling you this cannot be allowed to happen."

"Don't worry, Matilda," Martha said. "Everyone knows how important it is that people learn to speak a foreign language. How can America compete with the rest of the world if no one knows how to speak anything but English?"

"Well, it's a relief to hear you say that," Matilda said. "I'll get out of your hair. Oh, I understand you are thinking of doing away with departments and chairs and having only deans and schools."

"That's one proposal," Martha said.

"Well, that's fine, but I assume foreign languages and English will still be independent," Matilda said.

"Why do you assume that?" Martha asked.

"Well, we're the two largest departments on campus and it wouldn't make sense, given the need we have to recruit new faculty every year, to change our structure," Matilda said.

"This will all be open to discussion at the proper time," Martha said, getting up and escorting Matilda to the door. "I'll see you tomorrow at your change team meeting."

As Matilda left, William Acton walked in.

"I have to talk to you," William said. "What is this stuff about asking the alumni about required courses?"

"Yes, we're going to do just that," Martha said.

"You can't," William said. "These people don't have any idea what should and should not be required."

"Come on, William, how can you say that?" Martha said. "We require certain courses because we believe that people need a breadth of knowledge to get along out there in the big bad world. I think it's high time we checked in with that world to see what it thinks."

"Come on," William said. "Those people don't remember any of the content of those courses. The only thing they remember is that they were required to take things they would not have taken on their own, and they resented it. They remember the boring professor droning on at eight in the morning, not the world history that helps them understand what is happening around them on a daily basis."

"Now, William," Martha said, "I'm sure it's not that bad. Why don't you wait until the survey results are in before you go into a panic?"

"Oh, that's easy for you to say," William said. "But I don't want to leave, and I can't see staying if my required courses are no longer required."

"I'm sure it won't be all that bad," Martha said, getting out of her chair and escorting William to the door. "I'll see you at the next change team meeting."

Martha decided to head for the library so she could do some thinking in quiet. When she got to the front door, the student demonstrators were still there. Martha made a short speech.

"Listen to me, all of you," Martha said to the crowd. "I want all of you to know that everyone—faculty, staff, and alumni—has one goal in mind: to make this the best small college in the country. Your ideas and opinions will be solicited at the proper time, and no changes will be made without consulting your student government representatives. Now please, go back to class."

The three dozen students seemed to accept what she had said and left. Martha walked over to the library to find her special place in the top floor corner. She walked into the library and climbed the stairs to the top floor. In the corner, among the old books, she found some peace and quiet for a moment. Then she was spotted by a small group of students, who came over to ask her how the changes would affect them. They wanted to know if they would be able to graduate or if the changes in course requirements would also apply to them. They wanted to know if tuition and fees would be going up again. They wanted to know if their favorite teachers would be fired or urged to retire. Martha tried her best to calm their fears. She had not realized how many people would be upset by the mere possibility of change. She had hoped to bring about both cost saving and rationalization, but things were getting out of hand. How could she slow down the process?

The next day Martha decided to write a long letter for the weekly college newspaper. She outlined the need for change and the kinds of changes that were being considered. She tried to assure everyone that nothing would change until the board of directors had considered the possible consequences of those changes and listened to the opinions of faculty, students, and alumni. She told everyone that the purpose of the changes was to reduce the amount of time and money spent on activities that were not really adding to the educational mission of the college. The college community reacted positively to the letter, and things seemed to quiet down. At least there were no more demonstrations in front of the administration building.

The promise of a new lounge for nonfaculty staff brought out dozens of good cost-cutting suggestions from the staff change teams. The faculty change teams were not able to agree on much that was concrete. They wanted the administration to write fewer memos, and they wanted the students to stop calling them at home. Beyond that, they just wanted to be left alone to teach their courses.

The results of the alumni survey exploded like a bombshell on campus. The results were published in the weekly newspaper at the same time they were released to the faculty and the board. The alumni thought that about half of the current required courses were not necessary. They did not find the foreign language courses helpful because they did not learn enough of a foreign language to really be able to speak it, so they forgot most of what they learned in college. They suggested either dropping the requirement or forcing students to have an intensive language semester during which all they took was the foreign language. They suggested that this could be combined with a summer trip of a few weeks to a country where the language was spoken.

Martha found her phone ringing off the hook. She had expected to hear mainly from secretaries and other staff members who were being laid off. Instead, she heard from faculty who were unhappy about the alumni survey. She assured them that no changes would be made without further study by the faculty and the board of directors.

At the next board of directors meeting, Martha did not know what to expect. The board members surprised her by being very supportive of what had happened so far. They had gotten calls, and contributions, from alumni who were very happy that the college was interested in their ideas. They couldn't praise her enough for having thought of bringing in the alumni. Martha didn't know what to say, so she didn't say much. She asked them what they thought about an intensive semester program for foreign language teaching, and they were all for it. She asked them what they thought about streamlining the required courses and reducing their number, and they were all for it. She asked them what they thought about the idea of electronic voice mail and electronic mail on the computer, and they were all for it. It seemed she could do no wrong in their eyes. She was the woman of the hour, bringing old Fonderack College kicking and screaming into the twenty-first century. They all felt it was high time.

When she returned to campus the next day, she found that the faculty change team concerned with the required courses had actually come to a consensus on the new list. Was that possible? She called William Acton into her office to find out how that had happened.

"Well," he said after sitting down, "we just decided that if we didn't act fast, the momentum of the alumni survey would take the decision away from us. Since we couldn't all have everything we wanted, compromise became the order of the day."

"I see," Martha said. "And I see that your course will no longer be required."

"That's correct," William said. "I've decided to take the golden handshake you talked about. I'd like to travel, and that money plus my retirement will make that possible. Once I decided to retire, all things came easily."

"Oh, so that's the way it was," Martha said. "You're leaving, so you can afford to think of the big picture."

"Well," William said, "I wouldn't have put it that way, but I guess so. I wish you good luck, and sister, you're going to need it."

William left Martha's office. Martha wondered if it might just be possible to change the required course list, eliminate faculty and staff positions, add more computers, and actually have a more efficient college. With the backing of the board of directors, she was now more determined than ever to make that a reality.

Questions for Thought and Discussion

1. How can teams be organized to make suggestions for change?
2. How should a participatory organization handle staff cuts?
3. What should be the role of the board of directors as participatory management is introduced?
4. How should the president of a participatory organization deal with requests for special treatment from some teams?
5. How can a participatory organization solicit and use the ideas of groups such as customers or alumni?
6. How should a participatory organization go about bringing in new technology?
7. How can a participatory organization deal with the fact that some employees are highly educated and some are not?
8. How can an organization such as a college introduce methods of measuring faculty performance?
9. What are the limits of empowerment in an organization like a college?
10. How can efficiency and empowerment go hand in hand?

Chapter 16
Willie Runs the Company

Introduction

When Willie Alden inherited the company from his father, everyone expected him to turn over the running of the business to the same old management team. Instead, Willie decided to turn the company over to the employees. He did this all of a sudden in the space of a few days, and many people were not happy about it. Some people tried to take control of the company away from him, but they did not succeed.

Willie Runs the Company

Willie's father built the Alden Appliance Company into one of the largest makers of appliances in the world. Willie was his only child. Willie was a good kid, but he had an IQ of about 80. Everyone loved Willie, but they wondered what his father would do when it came time for Willie to get a job. When the time did come, Willie was made a vice president in charge of nothing in particular. Willie looked good in a suit and knew how not to say much. When foreign visitors came to the main factory complex in Oklahoma City, Willie would show them around. They felt honored that they were being shown around by the son of the sole owner of such a large company. Willie could also read a prepared speech without making too many mistakes as long as the speech did not have any big words in it. Willie knew right from wrong and was very concerned about other people.

The day after Willie's twenty-fifth birthday, his father died. It was a terrible day for the company. Thousands attended the funeral of one of Oklahoma City's leading citizens. Technically, Willie now owned a company with more than 20,000 employees and with worldwide sales in the hundreds of millions of dollars. Willie's father had elected a board of directors made up of trusted friends and associates. They wondered what Willie would do. The board met in emergency session to pick a new president. Willie walked in and took his father's place at the head of the table.

"I call this meeting to order," Willie said, just the way he had seen his father do hundreds of times before. "The first item on the agenda is the position of president. Is there any discussion?"

The members of the board were struck dumb. Here, running the meeting, was the only stockholder of a giant corporation, who was not smart enough to come in out of the rain. Nothing was said for several minutes.

"There being no discussion, I move that Willie Alden be the next president of Alden Appliance. Is there a second?"

Another long silence. Finally, the oldest member of the board said, "I second."

"Good," Willie said. "Thank you, Uncle Fred." Willie called all the men on the board uncle. "There being no other candidates, the motion is carried. Is there any other business? There being no further business, the meeting is adjourned."

As Willie left the room, eight older gentlemen in dark suits just sat there. Had this really happened, or had they dreamed it? Had they really just elected Willie president of the company? Of course, if they had refused, he could simply have replaced them all at the next stockholders' meeting, so what choice had they really had?

Willie walked straight out of the board of directors meeting to the command center of the main factory complex. From here he could shut down every assembly line and speak to everyone over the loudspeaker system. He did just that. Thousands of workers watched as the assembly lines came to a halt. Then they heard Willie's voice booming through every building.

"Hello, hello, is this working?" Willie said. "This is Willie Alden, the new president of Alden Appliance. As you all know, my father's death leaves me as the only stockholder of Alden Appliance. I intend to make some changes. First of all, from now on, half of all pretax profits will be divided up among you workers, with each worker getting an equal share. Second, no one at Alden will make more than twelve times what the lowest paid worker makes. I intend to raise the pay of the lowest-paid workers immediately. Third, I will be talking to all of you over the next few weeks to see what other changes we should make. That is all. Over and out. Roger dodger. How do you turn this thing off?"

Thousands of workers just stood there. Then, one by one, they began to applaud. Then they began to cheer. Then they began to scream and stomp. Suddenly, with a large noise, the assembly lines began to move again. Everyone was laughing as they went back to the lines to put the dishwashers and washing machines together.

Willie went to the president's office, which was his own office now. It occupied the entire top floor of the ten-story office tower that was the central brain of the company. Sandy Simpson had been Willie's father's secretary. Sandy was the daughter of an old friend of Willie's father, and when she needed a job, Willie's father had given her one. She was in her mid-twenties and had been the president's secretary for two years. Willie entered his giant office and closed the door. Sandy waited a minute and then followed him.

"Mr. Alden," Sandy said.

"Just call me Willie," Willie said. "Take a memo. To all employees: From now on, everyone will call everyone else by their first name only. Everyone, and I mean everyone, will wear a name tag with their first name on it."

Willie always wore a name tag that said "Hi, my name is Willie" because he spent so much of his time meeting foreign visitors. Before foreign visitors came to the factory complex, they would put on similar name tags. Willie had trouble remembering names, so he decided that everyone should have a name tag.

"Sandy, where is your name tag?" he then asked.

Sandy Simpson looked a little confused, but she walked out to her desk, wrote her first name on a name tag, and stuck it on her blouse. Then she walked back into the room.

"Sandy, good," Willie said. "Sandy, take a memo. To every employee: From now on anyone caught wearing a tie will be fired on the spot." Saying that, Willie took off his tie. "There, that's better. They made me wear that thing even though I could hardly breathe. How can people think if they can't breathe?"

Sandy realized that this was a sincere question and tried to answer. "I guess they can't," she said.

"Of course they can't," Willie said.

Just then Mr. Walters burst into the room. Mr. Walters was the chief financial officer. "Willie, what's all this? I hear that you are the new president, that half of all profits will be going to the workers, and that the highest-paid worker will make only twelve times what the lowest-paid worker makes."

"Name tag," Willie screamed at the top of his lungs, "name tag, name tag, name tag."

"What's he screaming about?" Mr. Walters asked Sandy.

"The new president has decreed that from now on everyone will wear a name tag with his or her first name on it," Sandy said. "What is your first name, Mr. Walters?"

"What nonsense," Mr. Walters said.

"Name tag, name tag, name tag, name tag," Willie screamed.

"Oh, all right," Mr. Walters said. He took a blank name tag from Sandy, wrote the word Alfred on it, and stuck it on his suit coat.

"Tie, tie, tie, tie, tie, tie," Willie screamed.

"What is it now, Miss Simpson?" Alfred Walters asked Sandy Simpson.

"The new president has also decreed that no one may wear a necktie any longer," Sandy said.

"Oh, for heaven's sake," Alfred said as he took off his tie and threw it on the floor. "That's just great. I quit. I'll have my secretary type up my resignation and send it up," Alfred Walters said as he stormed out of Willie's office.

Willie smiled. "I never liked that man," he said to no one in particular. "Sandy, take another memo. To all employees: From now on, lunch will be paid for by the company."

"Mr. Alden, I mean Willie, don't you think you should discuss these changes with the other executives before making them?" Sandy asked.

"The other executives," Willie said. "That reminds me. Call the other executives and tell them I want to have a top-level staff meeting in ten minutes."

"But Willie, we can't just call an executive meeting like that," Sandy said.

"Why not?" Willie asked, with a very puzzled look on his face.

"Well, it just isn't done," Sandy said.

"Why not?" Willie asked, with the same puzzled look on his face.

"Well, I—I'll call their secretaries and set up the meeting," Sandy said. She closed the door to his private office and made half a dozen phone calls. A few minutes later the top executives began getting off the elevator. As they did, Sandy told them about the new rules on ties and name tags. Most of them said they would resign instead of taking off their ties and wearing name tags. That left three executives for the meeting. Fred Waters had been with Willie's father from the beginning. He did not have a college education, but he knew a lot about the business. He figured that he was old enough to retire, and he could quit later. Right now his friend's son needed some good advice. George Clauson was a young engineer, thirty-five, in charge of research and development. He had never liked to wear a tie, and he usually didn't except when he came up to the president's office. The new rules didn't bother him. Susan McDonald was in charge of advertising. She wore dresses, not ties, and she had worked too hard to get where she was to quit because the idiot son of the owner had temporarily taken charge of the company. She figured he couldn't last very long and the board of directors would remove him.

"Good, three," Willie said. "Three is a good number. I want you three to divide up the company into three parts. You three discuss it and come to a decision on the best way. I want to be able to meet with Fred, George, and Susan and find out anything. OK?"

In a strange way, they found themselves promoted in an instant.

"Oh, you will be called vice presidents, but you will make exactly twelve times what the lowest-paid worker makes, whatever that is," Willie said. "Do you have a problem with that?"

The three just looked at each other and said no.

"Good," Willie said. "I'm going down to the factory floor to talk to the people and make name tags. You three discuss it among yourselves and then tell the people."

Willie walked out of the office. Fred, George, and Susan sat silently for a minute. Finally Fred, as the oldest, spoke first. "I guess George, as the engineer, should be in charge of both research and production. Maybe you can shorten the time between product development and product production if you are in charge of both."

"OK," George said.

"And Susan," Fred continued, "I guess you can be in charge of everything that has to do with what is outside of the company, from advertising to sales."

"Yes," Susan said, "I think if we put advertising and sales together, we can get better communication."

"I'll pick up on dealing with suppliers and the financial end," Fred continued in a kind of daze. "I don't know what's going to happen now that Willie is in charge, but we might as well make the best of it."

Meanwhile Willie was down on the floor of the dishwasher assembly line passing out name tags and talking to people. When the bell rang to stop the line for a break, everyone gathered around Willie to thank him for the new profit-sharing system. Willie just said that he had decided that it would be easier to figure that out than to have so many different wage and pay systems. After the break, Willie headed back to his office. He found the head of the union local waiting in the outer office.

"Mr. Alden," the union boss said, "I have to see you right away."

"Willie," Willie said pointing to his name tag. "Where's your name tag?"

Sandy jumped up and put a name tag on him that said "Francis."

"Now, Francis, come into my office," Willie said with a slight laugh at the idea of a man with the name Francis.

"I don't know how to tell you this, but you can't raise wages and introduce profit-sharing without negotiating with the union," Francis said.

"Why not?" Willie asked.

"Well, you see, we have a contract and it has a year to run," Francis said. "You can't make a change in the contract without consulting the union."

"Are you unhappy about it?" Willie asked.

"No, not at all," Francis said. "We love the idea. In fact, we've been trying to get your father to agree to raise the basic wage and introduce some kind of profit sharing for years. It's just that these things have to be done in a proper way. Why don't we call a meeting of the negotiating committee and sit down and figure this out?"

"Oh, I see," Willie said. "You want some of the credit for this. Why didn't you say so? I'll tell everyone that you convinced me to do this. How's that?"

"Well, no. You see," Francis said, "There is a procedure for everything, and we have to sit down and bargain over things like this."

"OK, let's bargain," Willie said. "I agree to raise the basic wage and introduce profit sharing. What do you agree to do?"

"What?" Francis said.

"I said, what are you going to give me in return for my changes?" Willie said.

"Well, what do you want?" Francis said.

"I don't know, what should I want?" Willie said.

"Well, how about a commitment that we will work to improve quality and cut down on defects?" Francis said.

"OK, that sounds good to me," Willie said. "What else?"

"How about, we agree to let you introduce new computerized systems on the line," Francis said, "as long as you agree not to lay off anyone."

"That sounds good to me," Willie said. "What else?"

"You drive a hard bargain Mr. Alden," Francis said.

"Willie," Willie said pointing to the name tag on his chest.

"How about, we agree to increase production by 5 percent over the next two years," Francis said.

"OK," Willie said, "but that's enough. I don't want to play this game anymore."

"I'll have a new contract drawn up," Francis said.

"Drawn?" Willie said with a puzzled look on his face. "How do you draw a contract?"

Francis thought about explaining, but decided to just leave the office.

Sandy walked in. "You have George on line one and Susan on line two."

"All right," Willie said, pushing a button on the phone. "Hello, this is Willie, who is this?"

"This is George," George said. "I want to knock down the wall between the design engineers and the production engineers and buy a new computer system that will link everyone to the same set of design programs."

"All right," Willie said, pushing the next blinking button on his phone. "This is Willie; who is this?"

"This is Susan," Susan said. "I want to have a contest to decide on the next advertising campaign. I want to let the employees suggest what the theme of the new campaign should be."

"You mean we'll have a contest with prizes?" Willie asked.

"Yes, exactly," Susan answered.

"Great," Willie said. "I can give away the prizes at the end of the contest." Willie hung up the phone.

Sandy came in with Mr. Ferndock, the attorney. "Mr. Ferndock, the attorney, is here to see you."

"Tie, tie, tie, tie," Willie screamed.

Rather than explain, Sandy just took off Mr. Ferndock's tie, folded it, and placed it in his suit pocket. She then ran and got a name tag and put it on his lapel. It said "Franklin."

"Great, Franklin, come in," Willie said, grabbing Franklin by the arm and pushing him into a chair. "What can I do for you?"

"I just want you to know that now that you are president, my law firm is ready to continue to serve the Alden company the same way it has done for the last four decades," the attorney said.

"I don't want the same, I want different, I want better," Willie said. "I think I just negotiated a new contract with the union. Would you please look at it when the union boss gets a picture made of it?"

"What?" the attorney said.

"Just call the union office, I'm sure they can explain it to you," Willie said, showing him to the door. "Oh, and from now on, when you come over here, be sure to have your name tag on."

"Yes," Franklin Ferndock said as he was all but pushed out of the office.

"What's next on my schedule?" Willie asked Sandy.

"Well, the president of some new company wants to demonstrate a new small engine he hopes we will use in our washing machines," Sandy said.

"Great," Willie said, "I love demonstrations. Have him set it up in the cafeteria."

Willie left the office and headed for the washing machine assembly line. He pulled the switch and shut down the line.

"Hey, everyone," Willie screamed. "I want you all to come with me."

Willie then walked out the main door and toward the cafeteria. For a long moment hundreds of workers just stood there, then, one by one, they followed Willie out the door. When they arrived at the cafeteria Willie jumped up on stage, grabbed a microphone, and blew into it several times.

"Testing, one, two, three, testing, one, two, three," Willie said into the microphone. "Can you hear me?" Willie asked the crowd.

"Yes," a man in the back of the room yelled.

"Good. Today, we have—what is your name?" Willie asked the small man in glasses standing on the stage with him.

"My name is Jack Winters," the man said.

"This is Jack Winters," Willie said into the microphone, "and he wants us to put his motors into our washing machines. Go ahead, Jack, oh wait, you don't have a name tag." Willie produced a name tag and stuck it on Jack Winters. He took out a large felt-tip pen and wrote "Jack" in big letters. "OK, go ahead."

"Go ahead?" Jack said. "All right, well, this is a new motor I have invented. It will use one-third the electricity and be much quieter. Let me demonstrate." With that he pushed a button and the little motor began to whir and whine. People in the audience began to call out questions.

"How much does it weigh?" a woman in the front called out.

"Less than four pounds," Jack answered.

"What kind of casing does it have?" a man in the middle of the cafeteria called out.

"I am using a stainless steel casing now, but I think I could also come up with an aluminum one," Jack said.

"Stainless steel is fine," the man called back.

The crowd continued to call out questions, and Jack answered them. When there were no more questions, Willie said, "All right, all those who think we should send this man to the production department to talk this over with George, raise your hand." Almost everyone raised a hand. "OK," Willie said. "You can go back to work now." The hundreds of workers got up and walked out of the cafeteria. Willie took Jack by the arm, ushered him over to the engineering section, and left him with George.

Meanwhile, the foreman on the washing machine line had called several of the members of the board of directors to complain about Willie's shutting down his line twice in one day. He said it was bad for the production quotas and it was bad on the system. The members of the board of directors listened and began calling one another. Something had to be done about Willie.

Meanwhile, as Willie walked back to his office, a young man on the dishwasher line stopped him.

"Willie, my name is Tom," Tom said. Willie got out a name tag and put it on him as he spoke. "I've been working here for a year, and I think we could save a lot of time and money if we bought three electronic components already assembled from one manufacturer instead of buying them from three manufacturers and putting them together ourselves. The manufacturer could test them to make sure they work together, and we wouldn't have to do that. I think we could get all three components for less if we got them assembled from one source."

"Great," Willie said. "Come with me." Willie took him by the arm and escorted him to Vice President Fred's office. "Vice President Fred, who is in charge of ordering supplies?"

"I am," Fred said.

"Good. Listen to this guy, and if it makes sense, do what he says," Willie said, putting Tom down in a chair next to Fred's desk. "Oh, and Fred."

"Yes, Willie?" Fred said.

"I think we need some kind of better system for employee suggestions than grabbing me as I walk by, don't you?" Willie asked.

"I'll get right on that," Fred said, "as soon as I hear Tom's idea."

Willie walked out of the office toward the cafeteria. He walked up to big Bertha, the woman who had been in charge of the cafeteria for decades, and fired her. Willie hated Bertha because she would never let him have seconds as a child. He then gathered the cafeteria workers together. "I just fired Bertha," Willie said. "Who should I promote to be the head of the cafeteria?"

There was a long silence, then one name was called out, then another. Willie could only remember three names, so he stopped and held an election. The cafeteria workers elected Sally Smith to be the head of the cafeteria.

"OK," Willie said. "I've done something for you; now you have to do something for me. I'm willing to spend more money and I'm willing to buy new machines or whatever it takes, but I want to be able to eat lunch with both shifts and not have to throw up afterwards. I expect Sally and you folks to come up with new selections, and I expect you to buy some new cookbooks. I don't see why we can't have real food around here."

"But Willie," Sally said, "we would love to cook and serve real food. We would love to be proud of what we serve. The folks in accounting wouldn't let us spend the money."

"I don't care about money," Willie said. "I want people to look forward to eating at this place. I want them to want to bring their friends and families to eat here. I want this cafeteria to be the best in the whole wide world. I'll give you the extra money, but I'm also going to ask the people every month how they rate the food and service. You'd better get good grades from now on. OK?"

The cafeteria workers all said OK. Willie headed out to the warehouse. There he found a lot of people standing around doing nothing. Willie grabbed a big young man by the arm and pulled him aside.

"Why are you guys standing around doing nothing?" Willie asked.

"Because the shipment from the Walden parts company is late again," Harry answered. "We can't unload em if they ain't here."

"Hey, you don't have a name tag," Willie said, pulling a name tag out of his pocket. "What is your first name?"

"Harry," Harry said.

"OK, Harry," Willie said. "You say this Walden bunch does not get their parts here on time. I'll tell you what I want you to do. I want you to call that company and ask to speak to the president of the company. Tell him you are calling for the president of Alden Appliance Company."

"Yes, sir," Harry said.

"Not sir," Willie said, "Willie. Remember, It's like William only you take off the *am* and add *e*. Got it?"

"Yes," Harry said, walking over to a phone. "What's the number of the president of Walden?"

"Just tell the main operator to get you the president of Walden parts," Willie said. A few minutes later Harry handed the phone to Willie. "Hello, this is Willie, president of Alden Appliances, who is this?" Willie yelled into the phone. "John, good; listen, John, I've got a problem. Everyone here in my warehouse is standing around waiting for your trucks to arrive.

Now I'm going to put you on with Harry. What Harry says goes around here. If Harry says we should drop you as a parts supplier, then you get dropped. Am I coming through loud and clear?" Willie loved to say that phrase. He said it some more. "I want to make sure you are receiving me loud and clear. The people here in my warehouse get profit-sharing money only if we make a profit, and we can't make a profit if they have to stand around all day waiting for your trucks. Now you and Harry work this out. Where are those trucks anyway? You don't know? You mean they are lost? Well, for heavens sake, find them. Here, I'm giving you over to Harry."

Willie gave the phone to Harry and smiled. Harry began to discuss the missing trucks with the president of Walden Parts Company. Willie went around to the other people standing on the loading dock and made a name tag for each one. As he wrote each person's name down and stuck the name tag on, he told that person how much he appreciated the person's working for him. If any more suppliers gave them any more trouble, they should come and get him down from his office. His dad had always said that sometimes you just have to kick some butt. Willie liked to say that phrase as well, so he said it several times. He told them to kick some butt and get the parts in on time. They all laughed as they pictured Willie kicking someone in the butt.

As Willie left the warehouse, the supervisor of the warehouse called several members of the board of directors. They had to do something about Willie. He was getting everything all messed up.

Willie then went over to shipping and noticed that a lot of boxes were piled over to one side.

"Why are those boxes piled up over there?" Willie asked the first person he came upon, who happened to be Jane.

"Those are machines that are missing something," Jane said.

"You mean like a part?" Willie asked.

"Well, usually they just need a knob or an owner's manual or something like that," Jane said.

"Why don't you or someone here go get what they need when you have some spare time?" Willie asked.

"Well, we can't do that," Jane answered. "We are not allowed to go to the assembly line and take a part off the shelf. An assembly-line worker has to come out here when the line is down and take care of it. The line hasn't been down much recently, so these have stacked up."

"That makes no sense," Willie said. "Who made up that rule?"

"I don't know," Jane answered. "It has just always been like that. Assembly-line workers are the only ones who can put things on the machines. I think it has to do with the union rules or something."

"Oh, the union rules," Willie said. "I see. I'll have a talk with Francis about that."

As Willie left the shipping area, the union steward called Francis to complain about Willie's not liking the union rules on who could handle parts. They both agreed that Willie had to go.

Willie walked into the washing machine assembly area, and the people told him how much they appreciated being asked to look at the possible new motor. No one had ever asked their opinion on anything before, and if they were asked, they had a lot of ideas. Willie explained that Fred was setting up a suggestion plan and that it would have prizes; there would be a big party soon to celebrate it.

Willie went back to his office and put his feet up on his desk. He had seen his father do that a thousand times, but it didn't feel comfortable. Willie moved over to the couch and took a nap. Later that afternoon he was awakened from a deep sleep by Sandy's shaking him.

"Willie, wake up," Sandy was saying. "There is an emergency board of directors meeting going on in the board room."

"Why wasn't I told?" Willie asked as he came out of his deep sleep.

"I don't know, but you'd better get in there," Sandy said. As Willie got up and went across the hall to the board room, he found the members of the board coming out. The one who had seconded his becoming president that morning, the man Willie called Uncle Fred, stopped to talk to Willie.

"I'm sorry, Willie, but we had to do something," Uncle Fred said. "It was for the good of the company."

"What did you do?" Willie asked.

"I'm sorry, but you are no longer president," Uncle Fred said.

"We'll see about that," Willie said. Willie walked to the central control room and shut down everything. His voice was again heard around the complex. "This is Willie calling, this is Willie calling. The board of directors has just removed me as president and is leaving the complex. What do you think about that?"

The workers began to chant, "We want Willie, we want Willie" at the top of their voices. The whole complex seemed to vibrate with the sound of "We want Willie." The members of the board of directors rushed out of the complex and into their waiting cars. Meanwhile, Sandy had called the attorney and found out that under the company bylaws, if a third of the stockholders agreed, they could call an emergency meeting of the stockholders with twenty-four hours notice. Sandy prepared the proper notice and called the local newspaper to place an advertisement telling the world about the stockholders' meeting that would be held in the cafeteria in exactly twenty-four hours. When Willie returned to his office, she explained it all to him.

"You mean in twenty-four hours I can vote in a new set of board of directors?" Willie asked.

"That's right," Sandy said. "You can vote for anyone you want, since you own all the stock in the company."

"Who shall I vote for?" Willie asked.

"Well, let's see. I guess yourself for one," Sandy said.

"Of course I'll vote for myself, but there have to be seven more," Willie said. "Who else?"

"I guess you could vote for your three top executives," Sandy said.

"Yes, of course," Willie said. "Who else?"

"I don't know," Sandy said. "Vote for four more people that you really trust."

"But I don't know who to trust," Willie said. "I might as well be drawing names out of a hat."

"Why don't you do just that?" Sandy said. "Why don't you put the names of all the employees in a hat and draw out four names? They can sit on the board of directors."

"Of course," Willie said. "Who knows the company better than the people who work in it?"

Willie went around the complex telling everyone that the next day he would hold a big drawing and pick four employees to sit on the board of directors. Some employees were excited about the idea, and others thought that this was crazy. Willie went around to the second shift and told them the same thing. The next day, at the change of shift, he would pick four names out of a barrel, and they would sit on the board of directors. Everyone thought he was a little carried away with the idea.

The next day Willie and Sandy spent most of the day printing out names from the computer and cutting them up. The names were then put into boxes and carried over to the cafeteria stage. At the appointed time, attorney Ferndock showed up to declare that the emergency meeting of the stockholders had come to order. The only agenda item was electing a new slate of directors. Attorney Ferndock asked Willie who he wanted to vote for. Willie named himself, Fred, George, and Susan. Then Willie pulled out four names one at a time from the big barrel. As he read off each name, the crowd in the cafeteria cheered. The four new employee members of the board were found and sent up to the stage. Then Willie took the microphone.

"I want you all to know that my dad would have been very proud of you today," Willie said. "My dad was tough, but he loved everyone who worked here. He thought of you as part of his family. I want you to know that I've made some changes and I'll make some more changes. But mainly I will be relying on your experience to make the right choices. I'm not smart enough to run a company by myself, and I'm not stupid enough to think that anyone can run a big company single-handed. It takes a team of people—no, it takes a family. That's what I hope we can still be, a big happy family of people who just happen to make the best darn appliances in the whole wide world."

Everyone cheered as Willie finished. Then he continued, "Now get back to work or I'll have to kick some butt around here."

Everyone laughed and headed for the assembly lines. Sandy gave Willie a big kiss on the check. "Willie, you were wonderful," Sandy said.

"You aren't so bad yourself," Willie said.

Questions for Thought and Discussion

1. One obstacle to the introduction of participation and empowerment is the old-style middle managers who do not think they will fit into the new organization. How should this potential problem be handled?

2. How can employees and managers be prepared for the introduction of participation and empowerment?
3. What should a CEO in Willie's position have done to bring participation and teams to the company?
4. How would a company trying to move toward participation introduce a profit-sharing plan?
5. How can participation and teams be combined with a new emphasis on quality?
6. How should new ideas about what executives should wear to work be introduced in a participatory company?
7. How can the top executives of a company be treated more like a team and less like individuals?
8. How might unions be brought into the change process when participation and empowerment are introduced?
9. How can the desire to force the organization to change be reconciled with the desire to allow people to have input into that change?
10. Where are the teams in Willie's new organization?

Chapter 17
The Music Store

Introduction

Danny Mason inherited a small business and built it into a larger business, but at the end of that process, he wasn't making a profit. He took the retirement of several key people as a chance to cut costs and introduce participation and teams. His idea was to break up the store into three small units and treat each unit as an independent small business. His goal was to make a profit again, as he had when the whole business had been small.

The Music Store

Danny Mason's father was a well-known country and western singer in the 1940s and 1950s. In order to be able to spend more time with his son and wife, he started Mason's Music on Main Street of the small city in the south that he called home. Many professional musicians lived in that city, and they gave Mason's their business because they were friends of Danny's dad. When Danny's dad died in 1975, Danny took over the business. He had three good salespeople and a small store. During the next two decades, the store grew as competing stores went out of business.

By the mid 1990s, Mason's Music had over twenty employees and filled almost a whole block along Main Street. Danny Mason should have been happy, but he was not. He was losing money. When three of his oldest employees chose to retire, Danny decided not to replace them. He also decided to fire the two delivery men and sell the delivery truck. From then on he would hire a local moving company to deliver pianos and organs when the need arose and save the overhead. The next question was how he could reorganize the business so that he actually made money again, as he had when he first took over the business.

Many of the salespeople were afraid that they would not make much now that the three sales stars were gone. These salespeople had drawn a lot of business to the store. Danny decided to take this as an opportunity to make some changes. From now on there would be three units to Mason's Music. Unit One would handle the pianos, organs, band instruments, and sheet music. Unit Two would sell guitars, drums, and electronic equipment. Unit Three would repair instruments. There would be five people in each unit, at least to start. He, the office manager, and the bookkeeper would make up the office staff. To announce the changes and get everyone involved, he called a Sunday afternoon meeting at the big hotel downtown. Danny paid for a really nice after-church dinner for everyone and then laid out the new system.

"I'm glad you could all be here," Danny began. "As you know, we have lost our three top salespeople during the last six months, and I have decided not to replace them. Instead, I want to reorganize the whole store. There will be three teams, one for pianos, organs, and band instruments; one for guitars, drums, and amplifiers; and the repair shop. Each team will have five members, and I want each team to select a team leader. I have been talking to my accountant, and he tells me that I can figure out the overhead costs for each team. From now on, each team will operate like an independent business. There will be no specific individual commission rates. Instead, the money you make every quarter beyond your base salaries will be split, half to me and half to you. The members of each team can divide up the team's share the way they see fit. If you want to keep track of individual sales or repairs and divide it up that way, fine. If you want to put everything into a kitty and divide it up every quarter, that will also be fine. As you know, the second half of the year provides three-fourths of our business, what with new school bands forming and Christmas. I hope we can all come up with ways to make money during the first half of the year. Any questions?"

Fred Conner had expected to become the head salesperson in guitars, drums, and amplifiers. He didn't like the new setup at all since he expected to bring in a lot of the business from now on.

"Listen, I can tell you right now that I'm not happy about this," Fred said.

"Why not?" Danny asked.

"You know why not," Fred said. "I'm due to be the top salesman in my section. I'm due to get the biggest commissions under the old plan. How do I know what I'll get now?"

"That will be up to you and the other members of your team," Danny answered. "I realize that some of you may quit, but I think I have to make some changes in order to guarantee that I make some money. Fred, do you think it's right that my old man started the business and I don't make any money from it?"

"No, of course not," Fred answered, "but I don't see why we have to change things."

"I think we have to change things," Danny said, "but I'm willing to allow each team to decide how to divide up the money. If your team wants to stay with the old individual commission system, then fine. You can keep track and divide up the money based on individual sales. I have to get everyone to realize the overhead costs that affect the business. From now on, advertising will be charged to the team that wants it. I have to get everyone to begin to realize what costs what."

"I'd like to say that I like the idea," said Susan. "I think my team will work well together to sell pianos, and I think everything will be great."

Susan was known as Little Miss Sunshine because she always had a smile. She was small and blond and very nice to everyone. She loved to talk to people on the phone, so she liked being the receptionist for the store as well as the person in charge of selling sheet music. Of course, she never sold much except a little sheet music, so she would make more money under a system that divided up commissions. Since she was the best piano player, in the past the piano salespeople had often asked her to demonstrate a piano and then kept the commission for themselves. Everyone felt that this was not exactly right. It was clear from what Susan said that she expected to get a bigger piece of the action in the future.

Scatman (everyone called him Scatman from his days with a big jazz band) was the next to speak. He sold mainly band instruments. "I think I'm willing to try dividing up the commissions as a team," he said. "I know that Susan helps me and doesn't get anything for it, and I think the three piano and organ folks will agree. I think it would be better for them—since they make so few individual sales, their incomes might even out a bit if they got some money from sheet music and band instruments."

Mary was large, about three hundred pounds, and always wore black, but she was now the best salesperson in the piano and organ area. "You all know that I stand to make the most from the old system, and I'd like to say that I'm all for this new system. Of course, I expect the other members of my team to help me send out reminder cards to old customers and all the rest."

While they were talking, the repair shop people had been huddling in the corner. These were all men. Two of them had been in the business a long time and brought in most of the repair business because of their reputations. They had a higher base salary because of this, and everyone agreed that this was the way things should stay. In the past the money taken in for repair time on an hourly basis had been divided up between the person doing the work and the store. The team members decided that from now on they would divide up the money the team made after deductions for the overhead, with 25 percent to each of the two older professionals and the rest divided equally among the other three. That seemed fair to everyone involved, and their new team leader, Jackson, told their plan to the group.

"Listen, everyone," Jackson said slowly. He was not accustomed to public speaking. "We've talked it over, and we like the idea. I assume we won't be charged for overhead that is none of our doing, like interest on instruments and advertising that doesn't help us. With that as a, how do you call it, stipulation—hey, pretty good, just like Perry Mason—with that as a stipulation, we are for the new system. We've agreed to a divide-up method, and all's set with us."

That left the guitar, drum, and amplifier department. Fred had made it clear how he felt about keeping some kind of individual commission. The guy who sold most of the drums, Bob, and the guy who sold most of the guitars, Steve, felt the same way. The other two members of the team generally sold small things like guitar strings and had never made much commission over their base salary under the old system. But they didn't work very hard either, and they liked it like that. Bob and Steve agreed with Fred, so that was that. This team would divide up the quarterly profits based on individual sales.

"Listen, what you decide today is not written in stone," Danny said. "You can change your minds. I want it clear what the teams will do in the future. Each team will decide on advertising for its area and be charged for it. Each team will decide how much stock to keep in the store and be charged the interest the store has to pay to keep those items on the shelves. Each team will pay one-third of the general overhead, which means the rent and utilities and the salaries for the bookkeeper and the office manager. From now on I will take only my half share of each team's profits. I won't take any kind of fixed salary. Each team will be responsible for deciding what to keep in stock and placing the orders. Each team will deal directly with suppliers. Each team will be responsible for making sure that salespeople are always on the floor throughout the day. If someone is sick, the team has to fill in. If someone needs to visit a supplier, the team will make up for it. Is that clear? Any more questions? I'm sure things will come up. See you all on Tuesday."

Mason's Music was open Tuesday through Saturday from ten in the morning until seven at night. Everyone took a half hour for lunch and two fifteen-minute breaks and worked an eight-hour day. Most business was done between three and seven: The professional musicians didn't get up until after noon, and the working public usually came during lunch hour or after work. That meant that between ten and eleven was a good time for the teams to hold team meetings if they were needed.

On Tuesday, each team elected a team leader. The piano and organ team elected Mary, the guitar and amplifier team elected Fred, and the repair team elected one of the old professionals, called Slim by everyone. He was known throughout the South as the greatest guitar fix-it man around. The repair group got team spirit without much trouble. The repair shop had always seemed like anarchy to an outsider, but instruments came out like new and on time, so no one ever objected to the fact that there didn't seem to be any system. If Slim and the other famous expert, Pete, felt like it, they would work very hard. If they didn't, things piled up while Slim smoked pot and Pete drank whiskey. Under the new system, the other team members spent more time doing what they could do while Slim or Pete was out of commission. When Slim or Pete sobered up, he would look over the work and make some adjustments. No one knew that Slim and Pete had not made every correction, and no one cared as long as the instrument sounded right. Slim and Pete were perfectionists from way back. The instruments always sounded right before they left the store.

Under Mary's guidance, the piano team also got along well. Susan no longer resented demonstrating pianos so that someone else could make a commission. Now that she was getting a piece of the action, she played better and had a big smile every day. She also began to learn about the band instruments from Scatman. Scatman would need help from the others during August, when the band instrument business boomed.

The problem was the guitar, drum, and amplifier team. Early on, old Willy decided to retire and the team decided not to replace him. This meant that old Sam, the other guy on the strings and parts counter, would actually bring in enough commission to amount to something. When he was dividing it with old Willy, there was not much to it. Danny explained that hiring new team members was up to the team. The team members had to be able to cover the counter and serve the customers, even during the rush periods. As long as they did that, Danny was glad not to have to pay another base salary. This lowered the overhead for this team by reducing the base salary costs.

Soon after the new arrangement went into effect, a conflict arose between the repair team and the guitar team. When a beautiful woman entered their part of the store, the guitar team had always picked up the intercom and announced it. The loudspeaker system would boom out, "Code nine" or Code ten" depending on the degree of female beauty that was present. (All women were rated on a scale of one to ten, with ten being Bo Derek on her best day.) The men in the repair shop would then wander through that section of the store to take a look. It gave them a break from the routine. Danny held a meeting between the two teams, and they discovered that this had been old Willy's duty. Old Sam agreed to make the intercom call, and everything was fine. Danny realized that solving these kinds of disputes between teams and helping teams work together for the good of the whole store was now a big part of his job. He no longer spent his time making decisions and worrying about the receipts. That was the job of the teams. He was now a coordinator and peacemaker, and he slept better at night.

The end of the first quarter brought a shock to every team. None of the teams had any idea how much money went to overhead. And the piano and organ team had no idea how much money went to pay the interest on the money that was borrowed to keep three dozen pianos and organs in stock. The piano and organ team decided to spend some money on a big spring sale to cut down on the stock. This would save interest and make room on what everyone agreed was a too crowded floor. The guitar and drum team agreed to hold a sale at the same time and split the cost of the advertisements.

Everyone complained about the high overhead. As the team leaders did more of the office manager's job, from setting up sales to dealing with suppliers, there was less and less for the office manager to do. As her salary was the largest in the store, it accounted for a big part of the overhead. The bookkeeper had learned the ropes, and Danny now had time to do some of the things the office manager had done when Danny was making up advertisements and deciding on sales. Now that the teams were doing that, Danny had to face facts. The office manager was just extra baggage. She was his old friend from high school, but as the second quarterly statement rolled around with very little real profit for the piano and organ team to divide, Danny knew that their morale was more important than his friendship with her. He talked it over with the office manager, and she understood. She had been thinking of retiring, and this was a good time for her to go. As summer was starting and her husband had just retired, she could spend the summer traveling.

As fall rolled around, everyone was still concerned about overhead. Danny held several giant meetings on Tuesday mornings, and everyone discussed what the teams could do to get the overhead down. The rent was fixed by a long-term lease, and water and garbage were constant. The bookkeeper was doing a good job, and everyone agreed they needed one. The main variable cost was electricity. Did they need to use so much electricity? One major use of electricity was the large neon sign on top of the store. Danny called around and found that he could get a much more efficient sign, but it would cost a large amount up front. He held an election, and a majority of each team voted to spend the money now to save money in the future. Danny agreed to finance the new sign over three years so that the cost would not all come in one quarter. Everyone agreed to have a "new sign" sale. The teams loved any excuse to have a sale and get people into the store.

Susan had been the receptionist for the whole store under the old system. Now she resented answering the phone for everyone else. Danny called another big meeting, and everyone agreed to have four different numbers printed in the phone book. That way each team could answer its own phone and the bookkeeper could get calls from credit accounts directly. The other members of Susan's team agreed to answer the phone in the piano and organ section from time to time, so she was happy again.

As fall moved along, the only one who was not happy was Fred. He spent most of his time selling big electronic sound systems to professional bands. His business was big in the summer and fell off in the fall. For everyone else on his team, particularly guitars, business picked up as Christmas approached. Fred, as the elected team leader, called a meeting for Tuesday morning at ten. He started to lie and tell the team that he had had a change of heart, but when it came time for the meeting he told the truth. He felt that since they now had four team members instead of five and the Christmas season was coming up, he would like to change the way they divided up their share of team profits. Old Sam thought that was pretty funny, given what Fred had said in the beginning.

"Let me get this straight," old Sam said. "Now that our big Christmas season is coming up, you want to change the system."

"Yes," Fred said. "Look, I don't mean for this quarter but for the future as well. I think we can work more as a team if we do this. I can show you guys how to sell sound systems, and I can help with guitars and drums when things get busy over the next two months, November and December."

"I have to admit, things do get busy this time of year, and with only four of us, we are all going to have to work hard," Bob, the drum expert, said. "But if we make this change for this quarter, it has to stay this way."

"I agree," Steve, the guitar man, said. "And I think we should all work together to push all these guitars out the door this Christmas."

"Even me?" old Sam said. Old Sam had been a great guitar player in his day, but booze and drugs had ended his professional career.

"Yes," Fred said, "even you. I know, why don't we have Sam get some of his old buddies together for a jam session to kick off the Christmas season? We could make it an all-day thing the day after Thanksgiving. What do you think, Sam?"

"Well, we'd have to pay them, of course," Sam said. "But Bob can play drums, so we only need one or two more guys. I'll make some phone calls."

Fred went to the organ and piano team with the idea of a big day after Thanksgiving event. They liked the idea. Mary, who taught piano in her home, agreed to play and to have a couple of professional piano players on hand for the day. The event would be from noon to six the day after Thanksgiving. Fred and Mary went to Danny with the idea.

"I don't know," Danny said. "You'll have to have a big sale at the same time or it will be a waste of money."

"Right, let's have a big sale," Mary said. "If we sell the stuff in November instead of December, we save on interest payments on the instrument financing charges. We could even give something away in a drawing at the end of the day."

"Great idea," Fred said. "You give away a piano, and I'll give away a guitar."

"Hold it," Mary said. "My team can't afford to give away a real piano. But we could give away one of the little portable electric pianos. They sound great, and that might go over big."

"Do you want to have hot dogs and Coke and stuff like that?" Danny asked.

"Sure," Fred said. "Let's make it like a music fair. I bet if we made some phone calls we could get some big names to drop by to play a little and sign autographs."

"Yeah, that might work," Danny said. "But you two realize that the cost of the advertisements and food and all the rest are going to be on your tab. The repair shop people aren't going to get anything out of this."

"Yeah, we know," Fred said. "That's all right. Who knows, if this works it could become an annual event. The Mason's Music on Main Street After Thanksgiving Madness."

"I like it," Danny said. "That's the kind of thing my dad used to do when we didn't have any money in the bank. I wonder if I could get any of his old band members to come."

"That would be great," Mary said. "People would come from as far away as Missouri to see old Salty Jones lick the guitar one more time. And I can remember the keyboard action from Wild Bill Simpson. Are they still alive?"

"I think so," Danny said. "My dad was the oldest of that group by quite a bit. Of course, there's no guarantee that they can still play."

Danny took the idea to the repair shop guys, and they agreed to spend the day handing out hot dogs and stuff like that. It would give them a chance to look at the women that they expected to show up for the festival. Even the bookkeeper agreed to let her hair down and serve drinks. Danny had promised her a Christmas bonus if he managed to make some real money in the fourth quarter. He agreed to give her 10 percent of whatever he got as his share. That made her much more interested in the business of the store. The bookkeeper was not bad looking when you took off the glasses and put a dress on her.

The weeks leading up to the big Thanksgiving Sale were exciting times at Mason's Music on Main. Salty Jones and Wild Bill Simpson agreed to come and play in exchange for some cash under the table. Several professionals agreed to drop by, and Mary lined up a couple of real hot piano players. They decided to blow the budget and take out a full-page ad in the newspaper and do some spots on the big rock radio station. The radio station agreed to be a cosponsor of the event, publicize it for free, and have some disc jockeys at the event. It would lead to increased goodwill for the station if a big crowd showed up. Besides, the station owner owed Danny a favor.

The Friday morning after Thanksgiving was quite a sight. The repair guys all bathed and shaved and put on clean clothes without holes. The rest of the store personnel had never seen them looking like that before. The bookkeeper—Sally was her name—let her hair down and wore her new contact lenses. With her long southern belle dress and big hat she looked like Scarlett O'Hara. Salty Jones and Wild Bill Simpson sat down and started to play, just like old times. People started coming to hear them as soon as the doors opened. Several older ladies looked as if they might faint just from hearing those two play their big hits one more time. Everything in the store was a third off the regular price, which was a good deal, and the merchandise started moving right away. The banker's wife had to have the baby grand piano after Mary, her teacher, got through playing Mozart for half an hour. It seemed as if every teenage boy in town had brought his parents so he could sign up to win the electric piano or the electric guitar. The moving service that delivered pianos and organs agreed to deliver anything sold that day for free in exchange for a large sign advertising the company at the event. The stores across Main

Street had a sale the same day that drew people to downtown like never before.

At the end of the day, everyone was happy. The bookkeeper had been asked for a date by a handsome accountant. The repair staff had gotten an eyeful of female beauty, and half the pianos and guitars in the store had been sold in one day. It was the biggest day in the history of Mason's Music on Main. The teams decided to continue the sale for a week and almost emptied the store of merchandise.

As Christmas got closer and closer, the store got emptier and emptier. Everyone decided that it would be fun to empty the place and close for a couple of weeks for badly needed painting and repairs. A new floor had been needed for a long time, and Danny agreed to borrow the money with a three-year loan and spread the cost out, just as he had done with the sign. Each team got to pick the color scheme for its section of the store. The repair guys couldn't agree, but finally an artist friend agreed to paint the repair shop to look like a giant marijuana forest, and that was acceptable to everyone on the repair team. Even Danny's office was to get new paint.

As Christmas Eve came closer and closer, the store got emptier and emptier. Danny decided to have a half-price sale on Christmas Eve. Everything in the store would be half off. By six o'clock on Christmas Eve the last guitar and drum set was moved off the floor. A few pianos and organs were all that were left. It had been an amazing season. Danny opened champagne bottles, and everyone celebrated. Danny and the bookkeeper prepared a rough estimate of everyone's share of the profits from their team, and everyone had a nice check coming the day after Christmas. The store closed for a few weeks for remodeling, and when it opened again it looked like a million dollars.

Danny couldn't believe what had happened. A year before he had been losing money with no hope of ever seeing a profit. Now he was running the store more efficiently with fewer people, and everyone was making more money. Everyone had gotten into the spirit of cutting overhead once they knew how much that came to every month. Even toilet paper use had gone down. Fewer paper towels were used in the bathroom, and less furniture polish was needed for some mysterious reason. Interest costs were down, and merchandise turnover time was less than ever before. Danny couldn't believe that even Fred had come around to the idea of sharing team profits equally among the team members. Danny also couldn't believe that the teams were able to do almost everything themselves. Even without an office manager, Danny still had less to do on a daily basis than before he put in teams. He viewed himself as more an adviser to the teams than their boss. Ideas came from them, and he approved or disapproved. He found himself bending over backwards to approve in order to keep the team spirit going. Now that he had a substantial profit from the store and time on his hands, he began to wonder if opening up a second store on the other side of town might not be such a bad idea. Now that he had employees who knew so much about the business, he could send some to the new store and keep some at the old location. He would discuss this with the employees after the new year got going. But they would have to agree. He couldn't make a move like that on his own.

QUESTIONS FOR THOUGHT AND DISCUSSION

1. What are the options when putting teams into a small business?
2. What are the options when introducing profit sharing into a small business?
3. In what other ways could the question of commissions have been handled? Can we have both team and individual commissions?
4. If quarterly profits are going to be shared, what should we do with quarterly losses?
5. On what kinds of issues should the owner in a situation like this have the right to veto team decisions? How should this be handled?
6. How should an owner deal with teams that want to cut costs too much for the good of the company?
7. As this business grew, how could people such as the bookkeeper be made part of a team?
8. Who should decide how, when, and where the company should expand in the future?
9. Should new employees be treated any differently from old employees when a new store is created?
10. What are the limits of empowerment in a business this size?

Chapter 18

The New Bus Company

Introduction

The city of WaHoo wanted to have an efficient and well-run bus system, so it called in Donald Farmer. Donald thought that teams and employee empowerment could bring about positive change, even in a public agency like a mass transit district. Of course, a public agency has special problems, and Donald had to find ways to solve them.

The New Bus Company

WaHoo was a typical growing city in the southwestern United States. What had been a nice little city of 100,000 in the 1960s was fast becoming a metropolitan area of almost a million in the 1990s. One of the major problems was mass transit. There was no real way to put in a subway, so more buses were the only answer. A metropolitan bus district was formed, supported by tax revenue and grants from the city, county, state, and federal governments. The big problem was that not enough people wanted to ride the bus. In desperation, the board of directors called in Donald Farmer. After doing a random survey of riders and employees and looking at the finances of the situation, Donald Farmer suggested trying to set up the system more like a private company with a twist. Donald figured out that the cost of new equipment, repairs, and fuel was covered by the tax revenue. Bus fares paid by the riders came close to covering the salaries of the drivers and maintenance workers. Donald proposed that the system write a ten-year contract with the employees. For the next ten years, the board agreed that taxes and grants would pay for all equipment and fuel. All money taken in from the riders would go to the employees. Donald then divided the company into four parts based on the four basic regions of the city, northwest, northeast, southwest, and southeast. Each would operate as an independent company for the most part, with the buses of each region painted a different color: red, white, blue, and green, respectively. All money made by a regional team beyond what was needed to pay salaries and benefits would be divided up in December as a December bonus. The goal of each regional team, to increase revenue, was clear, and the only way a team could increase revenue was to increase riders. Donald also suggested that riders be encouraged to buy bus passes good for anywhere from one day to three months. Each bus would be equipped with a machine, and the holder of a bus pass would simply put the plastic pass in the machine, which would record that the pass had been used to ride in a particular region. The money made from the passes could then be divided up among the regional teams. All bus routes in the system passed through the central terminal at some point, so that anyone getting on any bus could easily transfer to any other bus at this point.

When the day finally came to explain all this to the employees, they were less than enthusiastic. Donald Farmer met with them in large groups at the new downtown convention center. The first meeting was typical. Donald was introduced to the group by the president of the transit system, Fred Waller.

"Good morning, everyone," Fred Waller began. "I know you have all been hearing that we are going to make some changes around here. Let me introduce to you Donald Farmer, the consultant who is going to guide us in our efforts to increase ridership and make this the best transit system in the country. Donald."

"Thank you," Donald said as he stood at the podium. "I know you have all heard a lot of rumors. I am here to explain the new system. First of all, let me assure you that none of you are going to lose your jobs and none of you are going to take a cut in pay. As you leave here, you can each pick up a brochure that explains how we intend to operate this system over the next ten years. You have a firm commitment from the board that this is how things are going to be.

"Second, let me assure you that it is my goal, and everyone's goal, to make working for this system as enjoyable as possible. What we have done is divided the system into four regions. The buses will now be color-coded by region, red, white, blue, and green. Each region will operate as a separate company, except that every route will at some point make a stop at the central terminal. Each region will have ten routes, so that people can see that they take the red three route from their home to the terminal and the blue one route to the airport."

"Third, and most important, if ridership and revenue in your region increase, you will get to keep the money in the form of a December bonus. We believe that there is great potential for increased ridership, but we have to listen to two groups more: you the drivers and the riders. Each new regional group will spend the next month passing out ridership forms door to door. We want to know how we would have to change the routes and route schedules in order to attract people to the bus. We also want to get as many people as possible to buy monthly or quarterly bus passes. That is the easiest way for us to operate. As part of the change, there will no longer be any such thing as paying for a single ride. From now on, people will have four choices. They can buy a day pass for three dollars, a weekly pass for fifteen dollars, a monthly pass for fifty dollars, or a quarterly pass for one hundred and twenty dollars. If riders want to buy a day or week pass, they can buy it from you with cash dollars. If they want to buy a monthly or quarterly pass, they can do so at the central terminal or at dozens of businesses located around the city. They can buy these passes with credit cards or with a personal check. Each pass, except a day pass, will be plastic and encoded so that all the rider has to do is stick it in the machine. The machine will tell the driver that the pass is still good and record that the pass was used on a particular route. The driver will have to look at each day pass and punch into the machine that it was used. The best part of the new system is that if your regional group can increase ridership, you get to keep the extra money as a bonus. Are there any questions?"

"Yeah, I got a question," a large man in the front row said, standing up. "I work in the repair shop. Where do we fit into all this bonus stuff?"

"Good question," Donald said. "You will get a bonus based on the extent to which you can decrease the length of time buses are off the road. The less time buses have to spend in the shop, the bigger your year-end bonus will be. Each year a certain percentage of old buses will be retired and replaced by new buses. Your old goal was—well, I don't know what your old goal was. Your new goal is to do whatever it takes to make sure the buses don't break down, and if they do, to fix them as quickly as possible. The fewer buses we have out of service, the more money we can make. Next question? Yes, you with the blue hat."

"I drive a route through a new part of town," said a fat lady wearing a large blue hat, "and there are very few riders. Will I have a chance for a bonus?"

"Yes," Donald said. "First of all, you are now part of a team. Even if your particular route is not doing so well, your fellow team members may make up for that. Second, it will be your job to increase ridership on that route. If you do, then your team will have a larger December bonus. You can do that in any one of a number of ways that we will be discussing. This may mean taking time to go from door to door to find out why people aren't riding the bus in your area. Each team will have extra drivers every day, and they can be used for that or for any of a number of other activities. It will be up to you and your fellow team members. Next question."

"Who is going to be in charge?" a young man in the back called out.

"I'm glad you asked that," Donald said. "Each team will have one team leader elected by the team. We figure that each team will have a total of about fifty drivers on it. You will have to meet as a group and elect one person to be the team leader. It will be my job and the job of the central office to help you and your new team leaders come up with ways to provide better service and increase ridership. Yes, you in the green shirt."

"Will we be able to wear something other than these silly uniforms?" a young woman asked.

"You will have to have some kind of uniform so that people know who the driver is, but each team can design a different uniform or set of uniforms. What you wear will to a large extent be under your control. That is a good point. What we want to do is put control of what you wear and how you act in your hands. People will ride your buses more only if they enjoy the experience. What can you do to make the ride more fun? That will be the biggest test. Yes, you, sir, on the right."

"What if one team comes up with a great idea and the other teams steal it?" a man asked without standing up.

"Well, there's nothing to prevent that," Donald said. "In fact, we hope that when some teams are successful, the other teams will copy them. Remember, while this is a competition of sorts, every team can win in that every team can increase ridership and revenue. It can be a win-win game. However, each year the team that increases ridership and revenue the most will also win a prize. We haven't decided what it will be yet because we want all of you to have some input into the decision. The goal is to get more people riding the bus, which cuts down on air pollution now that the buses are all powered by natural gas and cuts down on the congestion on the roads. If you win, everyone in this city will win. You will be the heroes of WaHoo. I see that my time is up. Please pick up a brochure as you leave. I will be at the meetings we will be setting up for each team. The meetings will generally be on Saturday morning, and, yes, you will be paid overtime to attend them. It is hoped that each team will break up into smaller teams and task forces to deal with particular problems. Good luck."

There was a lot of grumbling as this group of about a hundred drivers left the meeting hall. Over the course of the next few weeks, Donald Farmer appeared in television and radio commercials explaining the new system to the people. Everyone could see that the buses were now color-coded and painted with a big number from one to ten that could be seen a long distance away. At each bus stop, the sign now had from one to four colored flags with numbers to tell people quickly which buses stopped there. The central terminal was now painted with the four colors so that anyone who wanted to get from red route one to blue route three could simply follow the colors and numbers painted on the floor. The central terminal was a square building with ten bus stalls on each side, and so it was easy to move from the red to the blue section and get the right bus. The new fare system was fairly popular also. Although some people objected that they just wanted to ride the bus once and that three dollars was a lot to pay for one ride, most people found that they used the bus enough to make buying a monthly or quarterly pass worthwhile. Students attending the big state university in the middle of the town could buy a monthly pass in September and quarterly passes in October, January, and April and get to class on time. The new metro system thus replaced a system of special shuttle buses provided by the university. This increased ridership for all four regions, but especially for the region that contained the university. The ease of getting to the airport from the central terminal and the express airport buses that went from the airport to the central terminal and back cut down on the traffic and parking congestion at the airport. The airport was in the blue team's area, and the blue team decided to put on more buses to carry the load. This made it possible for the other teams to almost guarantee that people could get to the airport within thirty minutes of getting on a bus anywhere in the city, which made the buses more popular. The three-dollar day pass was a lot cheaper than paying for parking or taking a cab.

The elected leader of the blue team was Max Washington, a fortysomething black man who had worked in a lot of jobs and knew the difference between jive talk and straight talk. He came to meet with Donald soon after being elected. As he walked in and sat down, Donald could feel the animosity.

"I don't think this new system is going to work," Max began.

"What's the problem?" Donald asked.

"Well, I've already got a large increase in riders because of the new express buses to the airport," Max said. "I need more buses and more drivers. But if I put on more drivers, that will cut into our December bonus."

"Not necessarily," Donald said. "Look, we can calculate what you need to take in from riders to make a profit with a new driver. If you know the monthly cost of a new driver, you can see that if the revenue exceeds that cost, you make more bonus money for everyone."

"But the bonus also gets divided up with another person," Max said.

"Well, yes, that's true," Donald had to admit. "But if the bonus is bigger, everyone might still get more money, or at least as much. And the more service you provide to people in your region, the more they will want to ride the bus. Adding buses and drivers could be a big winner for you. I am allowed to allocate ten more buses this year. I will be asking the team leaders to justify the number of additional buses they each want. You might get all ten if you make a good case."

"Yeah, we'll see about that," Max said. "I've got another problem. These meetings are cutting into everyone's social schedule."

"Then make them social events," Donald said.

"Say what?" Max asked.

"Look, you can pay yourselves overtime to attend meetings, and you can have the team meetings any time you want. You can have them on

Saturday afternoon and include a picnic or on Saturday night and have a band and dancing after the meeting. I'll bet there are a number of dance places in town that would let you have your meeting before the regular crowd shows up in exchange for the business your people will provide."

"Hey, man, let me get you straight now," Max said. "You mean I can call a team meeting for Saturday night at the Blue's Palace down on Sixth Street and then have a dance party after the meeting?"

"Exactly," Donald said. "And you can have special task force meetings over lunch or dinner, and the company will pick up the cost of the food. Every team has a food and entertainment budget that will come from me, so it won't cost you a thing out of your salary and benefits budget."

"Man you are shittin' me," Max said. "Oh, excuse me, I guess I should say you are telling me an untruth."

Donald Farmer was white, but he had talked to a lot of different people over the years. He knew exactly where Max was coming from.

"Listen, Max, the whole point of all this is to get your people to have fun and to make the riders feel that they are having fun," Donald said. "I know there's a limit to how much fun people can have on a bus, but if they have a little fun, and are greeted in a friendly way, they just might start riding the bus. Your region is a key for us. You have the airport run, and you also have a lot of poor people who live around the airport and depend on the bus. If you can make those people feel comfortable about riding the bus, the sky's the limit in terms of your year-end bonus."

Max was still skeptical, but he left mumbling about the Blue's Palace. The next team meeting of the blue team was held at the Blue's Palace at seven o'clock on a Saturday night. Max got a great turnout, and the discussion was very lively. The team voted to have a mass neighborhood walk that would start by passing out brochures at every church on Sunday and then go from door to door. Every team member agreed to donate the time because there was not enough overtime in the budget to pay them. They hoped, of course, to get the money back through the December bonus.

The red team covered the northwest part of town and had the most trouble getting people onto the bus. Its routes went through upper-middle-class neighborhoods. Everyone knew that poor people and apartment dwellers ride the bus much more than upper-middle-class people who live in single-family houses. Donald's next visit was from Ruth O'Grady, leader of the red team.

"Look, Donald, I'll come right to the point," Ruth began. "I can't motivate my people to beat the bushes for riders. Our buses are full at rush hour and empty the rest of the day, and there's nothing we can do about that."

"Sure there is," Donald said. "You can appeal to the things that appeal to your potential riders. Hit them with the environment thing. Our buses run on clean-burning natural gas and are much better for the environment than gasoline burners. I've been thinking that we could introduce some electric buses on your routes. They would be even cleaner, of course. Also, try snob appeal. Why not get one of the fancy restaurants in town to donate some free dinners and have a monthly drawing that riders can sign up for every time they ride a red bus? I'll use some of the advertising budget to get the message out in your area. But you're going to have to go door to door and find out what it will take to get people in the bus. Perhaps they need some kind of shopper's special that hits the main shopping areas or something like that. You and your people have control over this now; come up with something."

"You know, Donald," Ruth said, "you've got plenty of blarney in you. There must be some Irish blood in your veins." Ruth left the office with a smile on her face.

The next appointment was with the green team leader, Bill Baxter. Bill's team had no airport and no big shopping centers. People either rode the bus to the central terminal to transfer or rode it downtown to work.

"Look, I don't see how we can increase ridership," Bill began. "You know our situation: no airport, no shopping centers, no nothing. People want to get to downtown or to the central terminal, and that's it."

"Well, talk to your people about how you can turn that to your advantage," Donald said.

"But how?" Bill asked.

"How about making a big deal about how fast you can get people to the central terminal?" Donald suggested. "Talk to the drivers about setting up the stops and routes so that 80 percent of the riders will get to the central terminal in less than thirty minutes. That should get their attention."

"You mean we can change the routes?" Bill asked.

"Of course," Donald answered. "All we care about is increased ridership. If a stop isn't producing any riders, cut it out. If a route is too long, make it shorter. You have ten routes, and they all end up at the central terminal. Beyond that, you can rearrange things any way you want to. Just do it with the advice and consent of the team members. Remember, they elected you to be the team leader, not a god. You should ride the routes and have a task force do the same thing. Send out surveys and go door to door to find out who wants to ride the bus and who couldn't care less. This is like a political campaign. You don't want to spend time and money on people who will never ride the bus. Your job is to identify the ones who might ride the bus if you changed something and then find out what you have to change. Of course you can't please everyone, but you can get more people on the bus. I know you can."

"Well, I'll try," Bill said as he walked out of Donald's office.

The next few months saw a lot of activity as each of the four teams worked to get more bottoms on the seats. Everyone heard about the blue team's Saturday night meetings and tried to copy that. Everyone heard about the free dinner contest of the red team and tried to copy that. The city raised the price of the major downtown parking garages, and Donald put on a series of commercials to let everyone know that the bus made more sense than ever. He took out full-page adds comparing the cost of a second car, including car payments, insurance payments, and parking fees, with the cost of four quarterly bus passes. The passes added up to $480 a year. The second car added up to over $3,000 a year if you bought the cheapest car. That was certainly quite a bargain. The four teams agreed that every route would go until midnight and begin at six in the morning. That made it possible for people to count on the bus to get to work, to school, to shopping, and to entertainment. Ridership began to go up for every team.

The blue team designed a set of new uniforms. Which uniform they would wear would depend on the weather. The buses were heated and air conditioned, but the drivers still wanted to wear shorts in the summer and heavy pants in the winter. They also thought that dark blue, the color of the old uniforms, was boring. They came up with bright pink and yellow. Some of the men refused to wear pink, but in the blue team, the women outnumbered the men, so pink and yellow became an option. The uniforms had to look like bus drivers' uniforms, and Donald had to work with the blue team's uniform task force to get things within acceptable limits. The drivers had been used to having the radio on for themselves and their passengers. Some drivers liked classical music, and some liked classic rock. Some liked to listen to the all-news channel, and some liked to hear talk radio. Donald suggested that they try asking the passengers from time to time what they wanted to hear. Some drivers did and found out that the passengers were mainly interested in the news and weather. One driver came up with the idea of having a special radio station just for the buses. Donald got a special license from the FCC, and RadioMetro was born. By selling advertising on the station, Donald was able to make a fast profit with RadioMetro, and the passengers and drivers got what they wanted: news and weather in the morning and late afternoon, classic rock during the middle of the day, and strictly classical after eight P.M. Surveys of passengers confirmed that this combination met the average rider's desires at those times.

The bus employees were beginning to get used to the idea that the riders were important to them. This was a whole new attitude for some drivers. A few couldn't stand being nice and quit. Others became too nice, bringing cookies for the passengers and getting crumbs all over the bus. Rules had to be written to keep that from happening. Everyone liked the cookies, but no one liked the ants they seemed to attract. Being stung by a fire ant while sitting in a bus was not a pleasant experience.

One team decided to have a contest for the most popular bus driver on the team. They advertised it on their buses for a month and then held an election one Friday. Everyone who got on a bus in the red zone was given a ballot. Riders could circle any driver's name. The winner was Maude Jenkins. The prize was a new color television, which Donald agreed to fund out of his employee participation funds.

Everyone soon realized that the key to increased ridership was more buses hitting more stops on time. The blue team got seven extra buses because they could demonstrate a real need for them. They also got fifteen extra drivers. The blue team knew that this would make sense only if enough people rode the bus, but they could now guarantee a fifteen-minute ride from the central terminal to the airport and a bus leaving every ten minutes from six in the morning until midnight seven days a week. Given the difficulty in parking at the airport, this was a big hit with everyone. Ridership went up on the blue team airport buses and on the other teams' buses as people decided to skip the hassle and take the bus to the airport. Many people who had to fly on business would take their bags with them to work and then catch the bus to the airport when the time came.

The white team couldn't seem to get its act together. The team leader, Arnold Wilson, had no ideas, and he couldn't seem to get any out of his people. They didn't change the routes, they didn't survey their potential riders, and they didn't do much of anything. Donald had several meetings with Arnold to try to get him to copy some of the good ideas the other teams had come up with, but nothing seemed to get through. Donald decided to focus on the other teams and let the white team fend for itself. Its ridership had gone up a little simply because the activities of the other three teams generated more riders and some of that activity spilled over into the white team's area.

Donald developed a system that would show every team how many riders a particular route generated in the course of a day. The new electronic machines and plastic fare cards made this possible. Each month a printout was given to every driver showing the number of riders who got on the bus hour by hour and day by day. Donald also kept track of the number of people changing buses at the central terminal. As this number climbed, everyone could see that the new plan was working. Of course, the white team's numbers were the lowest, but ridership was still up on most routes.

With the coming of fall, more and more people realized that the bus was going to be their best transportation bargain. The sale of quarterly passes for the last quarter of the year exceeded everyone's expectations. A high-visibility advertising campaign in September also helped sales. Putting a more powerful air conditioner and heater in the central terminal also helped. The new colored buses with big numbers made it easier for people to take the bus. Every bus had a little box with note cards showing the route. A passenger who wasn't sure could take a card. The cards would fit in a man's shirt pocket, and the central office would send a set of forty to anyone who called.

Donald provided prizes for each team having a suggestion contest. He also let everyone know what the winning suggestions were for each team. There was also a contest for ideas that might not increase ridership but were still good ideas. The winner in that category suggested that the system sell advertising on the back of each seat. That raised another million in revenue a year for the system and made it possible to convert the last buses to natural gas a year ahead of schedule. The winner for the blue team suggested that each bus have a large digital clock that everyone could see. That would stop people asking the driver for the time and would also make everyone time-conscious. The winner for the red team suggested that an electronic machine be set up to say and flash the name of each stop. That way the bus driver would not have to shout it out, and everyone would know exactly what stop was coming up. The technology for this had been on line for some time. The metrosystem agreed to equip each bus with the new machines.

As the end of November approached, everyone knew that all the teams had increased ridership enough that there would be a bonus for everyone. Donald set up a big Saturday night dance at the biggest hotel in town to announce the size of the bonuses. Every team member was given two tickets. It was a formal affair, with the best food and a real live 1940s-style big band. Most of the drivers showed up with a spouse or a date. The tuxedos and formals made you think that a class of very old seniors was having a senior prom. At ten o'clock, Donald stepped up to the microphone.

"And now, the moment you have all been waiting for," Donald said. "The December bonus for every member of the white team is $650. The December bonus for every member of the green team is $1,400. The December bonus for every member of the red team is $2,300, and the December bonus for every member of the blue team is $2,800. Congratulations."

Everyone cheered with each announcement, and the biggest cheer came from the blue team. They had known that they were probably the winners, but they hadn't known how much the bonus would be. The party continued as the band played on.

The next morning Donald Farmer got ready to leave the city of Wa-Hoo. His mission was accomplished. The metro-transit system was now on its way to actually performing its function. The system had tried everything to increase ridership, and nothing had worked. During the year Donald Farmer was in charge, ridership increased 42 percent. Most of the members of the board of directors had been very skeptical of his ideas, but they had tried everything else, so they gave him the OK. Now he could point to the numbers. The employees were happier, the riders were happier, and the system was generating a lot more revenue, between increased fares and increased advertising revenue. The air was a little cleaner, and the traffic congestion was a little less, particularly downtown and at the airport. People who had to ride the bus found the drivers to be nicer and more helpful. They liked the colored buses and the big numbers. Most of all, they liked the convenience of using monthly and quarterly passes. These made bus riding easier for everyone. Tourists liked the weekly bus pass. At fifteen dollars, it was a real bargain, given the speed and convenience of the bus system. College students found that they really didn't need a car. With quarterly passes, they could budget forty dollars a month for transportation. It was a real bargain. With express service between the airport and the central terminal, they could get home and back easily.

Donald Farmer wondered if he could take the same ideas and transfer them to a giant city. He would get his chance. The mayor of Gotham City back east was hoping that Donald Farmer could make enough of a difference in his city's transit system that everyone would want him to serve another term. This would be harder, but Donald believed in participatory management, and he believed that any organization could benefit from its principles. We'll never know. Donald Farmer died in a plane crash on the way to Gotham City.

Questions for Thought and Discussion

1. What are the special problems public agencies have when they try to introduce participatory management?
2. How can most routine government work be made fun?
3. How big can a team be before it is no longer effective?
4. What are the problems with sharing profits in a government entity?
5. How can internal competition be handled in a participatory organization?

6. To what extent does competition inside an organization hinder co-operation between units of the organization?
7. What do you think the general public would think about a public agency's sharing profits with employees?
8. Would the general public be willing to allow public employees to work fewer hours as long as they met a particular production target every week?
9. What are the limits to the use of teams in government?
10. How could questions of financial accountability be dealt with in a public agency that instituted participatory management?

Index